SELF-ALTERATION

How People Change Themselves across Cultures

EDITED BY

JEAN-PAUL BALDACCHINO
AND CHRISTOPHER HOUSTON

RUTGERS UNIVERSITY PRESS
New Brunswick, Camden, and Newark, New Jersey
London and Oxford

Rutgers University Press is a department of Rutgers, The State University of New Jersey, one of the leading public research universities in the nation. By publishing worldwide, it furthers the University's mission of dedication to excellence in teaching, scholarship, research, and clinical care.

Library of Congress Cataloging-in-Publication Data

Names: Baldacchino, Jean-Paul, editor. | Houston, Christopher, editor.
Title: Self-alteration : how people change themselves across cultures / Edited by Jean-Paul Baldacchino and Christopher Houston.
Description: New Brunswick : Rutgers University Press, [2024] | Includes bibliographical references and index.
Identifiers: LCCN 2023011121 | ISBN 9781978837232 (hardback) | ISBN 9781978837225 (paperback) | ISBN 9781978837249 (epub) | ISBN 9781978837256 (pdf)
Subjects: LCSH: Identity (Psychology)—Cross-cultural studies. | Self-presentation—Cross-cultural studies. | Change (Psychology)—Cross-cultural studies. | Ethnopsychology.
Classification: LCC GN512 .S45 2024 | DDC 155.2—dc23/eng/20230620
LC record available at https://lccn.loc.gov/2023011121

A British Cataloging-in-Publication record for this book is available from the British Library.

This collection copyright © 2024 by Rutgers, The State University of New Jersey
Individual chapters copyright © 2024 in the names of their authors
All rights reserved
No part of this book may be reproduced or utilized in any form or by any means, electronic or mechanical, or by any information storage and retrieval system, without written permission from the publisher. Please contact Rutgers University Press, 106 Somerset Street, New Brunswick, NJ 08901. The only exception to this prohibition is "fair use" as defined by U.S. copyright law.

Scripture quotations are taken from the New Revised Standard Version Updated Edition. Copyright © 2021 National Council of Churches of Christ in the United States of America. Used by permission. All rights reserved worldwide.

References to internet websites (URLs) were accurate at the time of writing. Neither the author nor Rutgers University Press is responsible for URLs that may have expired or changed since the manuscript was prepared.

rutgersuniversitypress.org

SELF-ALTERATION

We dedicate this book to James Hughan Houston (1932–2022), beloved father, close friend, loving man. Vale Dad.

CONTENTS

Introduction
A Time for Change—Modes of Self-Alteration 1
JEAN-PAUL BALDACCHINO AND
CHRISTOPHER HOUSTON

PART I: RELIGIOUS CULTURES, SPIRITUAL PRACTICES,
AND SELF-ALTERATION

1 Exemplary Masters, Exemplary Reeds:
   Pedagogies of Self-Alteration in Sufi Music 25
   BANU ŞENAY

2 Reimagining Self and Self-Alteration in Contemporary
   New Age, Pagan, and Neoshamanic Spiritualities 41
   KATHRYN ROUNTREE

3 Wounded by Grace: Becoming a Prophet
   in an Evangelical Revival in Solomon Islands 56
   JAAP TIMMER

PART II: SELF-ALTERATION AND POLITICAL ACTIVISM

4 Fabricating the New Man and Woman:
   Self-Alteration through Revolutionary Socialism 73
   CHRISTOPHER HOUSTON

5 Transcendental Terror: Zen Self-Transformation
   through White Supremacist Atrocity, from Nazi Germany
   to Utøya and Christchurch 90
   MAX HARWOOD

PART III: GENDERED BODIES
AND THERAPEUTIC INTERVENTIONS

6 Beautiful, Moral, Functional: Bodily Self-Alteration
   in an Italian Center for Eating Disorders 111
   GISELLA ORSINI

7	Porous Individuality as Self-Alteration: Commercial Self-Improvement in Urban China GIL HIZI	128
8	How Is Psychoanalysis a Mode of Self-Alteration? Anthropological Interrogations JEAN-PAUL BALDACCHINO	145

PART IV: SELF-ALTERATION, THE HUMAN, AND THE MORE-THAN-HUMAN

9	Mutualistic Self-Alteration: Human-Pigeon Assemblages in Rural Pakistan MUHAMMAD A. KAVESH	163
10	Self-Alteration as Human Capacity and as Cosmopolitan Right NIGEL RAPPORT	178

Afterword
Making Oneself Otherwise—Reflections on Natality 194
MICHAEL JACKSON

Acknowledgments 209
Notes on Contributors 211
Index 213

SELF-ALTERATION

INTRODUCTION
A TIME FOR CHANGE
Modes of Self-Alteration

JEAN-PAUL BALDACCHINO AND
CHRISTOPHER HOUSTON

A MOMENT THAT CHANGED ME

For years now, the *Guardian* newspaper has been running an occasional column titled "A Moment That Changed Me." Written by readers who send in their accounts of their experiences, the articles have recounted a huge number of life-altering events. The death of a loved one, of course, but also the inexplicable visitation of sadness; a violent beating, but also the day a man first dressed as a woman; illness; joining a choir; the realization that one was Black—all were events that set a new course in people's lives. In these short, sometimes profound stories of shock and transformation, nearly all authors narrate the moment of change as simultaneously the end of a long process of self-formation and the beginning of a new journey of self-alteration. Change happens in an instant, but it also takes a lifetime to actively embrace or reverse.

Most of these stories of becoming involve those living in Britain. And Britain, like many places around the world, has been subjected by its political class to decades of neoliberal public policy. Do the narratives reflect neoliberal discursive formations, affects, and values, say, in their appreciation of the uptake of virtues such as entrepreneurship, self-responsibility, self-promotion, or competitive self-care? Certain scholars (e.g., Illouz 2008) claim that it is primarily neoliberal capitalism that produces the current global demand for self-optimization, coercing employees and employers alike into altering themselves by propagating the claim that success depends on enhancing oneself.

Questions of another kind arise from the column as well. Newspapers' online columns are routine features of national and regional societies nearly everywhere. Would an equivalent people's column in Malta or Istanbul, Honiara or

Christchurch, Jinan or Aberdeen give rise to similar stories, testifying to comparative experiences? Would they, too, reveal that to alter is human (and to stay the same is divine)? Or could it be that in some places, the invitation of the newspaper would be spurned, its archive empty because, as Pierre Bourdieu once claimed for precolonial Algeria, members of that society feel the sentiment of existing "only as a member of a group and not as an individual in [their] own right" (1962, 20)?

Self-alteration, the subject of this volume, is more widespread and complex than either of these questions assumes. The essays collected here show that both minor and major modes of self-alteration have existed in many places and times and across very different modern societies. Describing processes of self-alteration in China, Italy, Pakistan, Norway, New Zealand, Turkey, Malta, Britain, and Solomon Islands, the chapters identify a huge variety of projects, methods, and practices through which people seek to alter themselves. In doing so, they relativize neoliberal trends and programs, rejecting the argument that contemporary projects and motivations of self-alteration are generated solely by global capitalism. Each essay affirms that the study of the self is best initiated with the revealing of its new structures caused by the dynamic processes and modes of alteration themselves.

How and why do people alter themselves? To organize this investigation, the volume has been divided into four parts. The essays of part one examine self-alteration via people's engagement with spiritual practices and religious cultures, where divine actors sometimes help shape persons and events. The essays in part two trace out self-change fostered in individuals' varied participation in political activism. The chapters in part three analyze *ethical* self-modification through subjects' practices of bodily discipline, as well as through their involvement, willing or otherwise, in therapeutic programs and gendered care services. Part four's essays discuss mutualistic self-alteration through intersubjective relationships with self and others, in particular with more-than-human beings. Together, the chapters illuminate a number of profound anthropological, psychological, and philosophical issues concerning self-alteration: the question of its (im)possibility and (un)limited scope; the complexities of its partial enabling by beyond-the-individual beings, historical traditions, institutions, and cultural affordances; and the significance of people's experiences of and testimonies to self-transformation.

We structure our introduction into three sections. *Part one* investigates certain manifest "puzzles" about the embodied and conscious self that appears with its alteration. Privileging selves in motion, we identify insights and consequences that emerge in foregrounding self-change rather than the ontology of the self. *Part two* broadens this discussion to engage with the sociopolitical contexts of self-alteration, sometimes said to be "provoked" by global forces and discourses but equally significantly understood as conditioned by national and regional practices. Here we complexify these social processes by delineating more carefully relations between individuals' events, journeys, and narratives of self-alteration and the historical contexts and (cross-)cultural *affordances* that part enable them. *Part three* identifies various cross-cultural *modes* and domains of self-alteration as described and investigated in the case studies and chapters of the volume. We assert that self-alteration is best understood as a set of practices that seek to bring about a different self, even as we note that the content and conditions of the formation of those selves vary from one ethnographic situation to another.

But first, below we briefly identify and summarize what we call the "conceptual instrumentarium" of self-alteration: six vital dimensions critical to its eventful happenings and processes. In different ways, each essay in this volume variously wrestles with these elements.

The first crucial question concerns the *temporality* of self-alteration, both of its duration and of its tempo. Ecclesiastes says there is a season for everything, including presumably a time for change. This change is itself, however, subject to different temporalities. In some projects, self-alteration is a continuous action that depends on constant renewal, as shown by Susan Friend Harding (2001) in her study of Pentecostalism. In others, it is a moment of irreversible change. Further, the temporality of self-alteration also includes people's making of a new "time" for themselves through their eclectic recombining of events and institutions from varied histories, texts, and periods. These temporalities of self-alteration are also oriented toward future worlds whose realization is brought nearer to the present through the actions of the altered self.

A second issue involves the *causality* of self-alteration. People embark upon or undergo a season of self-alteration for many personal or collective reasons. As some of the contributors to this volume show, self-alteration can be experienced as a deliberative act, a "decision-event." Indeed, for Nigel Rapport, it is precisely this capacity for self-alteration that defines agency. In other contexts, self-transformation is experienced as a process of mutualistic co-constitution with others, including with nonhuman agents.

A third aspect concerns the riddle of the broader *contexts* of the self's alteration, including enabling histories, social affordances, cultural ideas, and institutions that are entailed in its various processes. To what extent is self-alteration a constitutive act of the subject in making his or her worlds, and to what extent are its possibilities delimited, if not dictated, by the historical circumstances that inhabit people?

A fourth dimension involves the actual *methods* through which individuals alter themselves. Self-alteration can be achieved through deliberate regimens and disciplined techniques that modify our very embodied engagement with the world. As phenomenology has long asserted, alterations in individuals' embodied intentions toward things and people change the constitution of those things at the same time. Self-alteration can also be the result of intimate encounters with exemplary others who show us alternate ways of being in the world, goading individuals into becoming different. In a contemporary world that may be variously interpreted as incomplete or, in more extreme versions, as even intolerable, people reformulate the self through playing with the past.

A fifth feature involves the *ethics* of self-alteration. Self-alteration may be understood as a reworking of people's moral worlds. Self-change may be oriented toward a new truth claim, whether revealed or discovered. In turn, such truth claims have profound consequences in the ethical practices of everyday life and for the way we relate to others.

All these issues lead us to a sixth concern, the question of the *nature of the self itself*—its fixity and its malleability. Do we posit a universal self-reflexivity and plasticity of the "me"? The self is oftentimes best recognized through experiences and accounts of its alteration, as the column in the *Guardian* shows us. The role that such narratives play in constituting the very experience of the altering self becomes a crucial matter in the study of self-alteration.

Declarations concerning any one of these issues may provisionally determine answers to others. For example, if it is claimed that it is "merely" neoliberal capitalism that is responsible for people's contemporary desires and facilities for self-alteration, then the possibility of non-, counter-, or postcapitalist practices, projects, moralities, and histories of self-change is null and void. Or if it is asserted that the self is fully conditioned by the historical social formation that socializes it, then individuals from certain non-Western cultures that (supposedly) do not foster critical attitudes toward their own society's imaginary significations are unable to alter themselves.

The essays in this book tell us a different, more comprehensive story. They show us that self-alteration is a universal practice. They reveal its political and (cross-)culturally enabled affordances and experiences. They illuminate its ethics, freedoms, and limitations. And they delve into self-alteration's dual character and meaning, as confirmed by its hyphen. *Self-alteration* describes the "activist" altering of ourselves by our self. But it acknowledges, too, its accompanying more "passive" intersubjective altering of the self by the not-self—by events, other people, environments, institutions, discourses, education, and so on. These processes are always frictionally combined. As Christopher Houston claims, studying self-alteration means analyzing the "alteration of the self by both the 'world' and the 'self'—the work of the self and the work of the world in the self's re-formation over time" (2022, 483).

But projects of self-alteration can be welcome or unwelcome as well, especially in situations in which subjects are forced to perform a dominant narrative or called upon to testify to self-change. For example, Kate Rossmanith (2022) shows how in the Australian legal system, where the perception of the sincerity of an offender's expressions of remorse significantly affects the decisions of judges, criminals are expected "to produce a certain form of narration to demonstrate self-insight." Coercive self-alteration may take more extreme forms as well, as the striking metaphor "brainwashing" or "indoctrination" suggests. Indeed, forms of therapeutic interventions may be experienced in a similar light, as the chapter by Gisella Orsini on the treatment of anorexia nervosa demonstrates.

In the main, the forms of self-alteration under discussion in this volume are not of that order. Nor are they alterations experienced by people as random and inexplicable—the sort of transformation experienced by Gregor Samsa in Franz Kafka's (2009) *Metamorphosis*, for example, in waking up as a giant insect. Instead, the essays reveal multiple causalities engaged in altering the self, tracing out its ambiguities and compound experiences of agency, passivity, and reflection.

In the pages below, we set out the broad parameters of what we think is a new field of emerging scholarship. Anthropologists have long been interested in the self, but few have focused on a comparative anthropology of self-alteration as opposed to the cultural relativity of the concept of the self. Here we argue that some form of self-alteration is a cross-cultural universal and that, accordingly, attention should shift from an understanding of the self toward a focus on "modes of self-alteration." Methodologically, attention to self-alteration allows insights and knowledge into the self's prior formations. Existentially, it is in the very alteration of our sense of self that light is thrown on what it means for us to have a sense of self in the first place.

CHANGING CONCEPTIONS OF THE SELF AND ITS ETHICAL FORMATIONS

For decades, the self has been of intense interest in the disciplines of anthropology, psychology, social theory, history, and philosophy. Psychoanalysis has long argued for the influence of unconscious drives in the formation of selfhood and its associated psychopathologies. Differently, psychology and cognitive science posit a universal structure of mind that underlies our selfhood, although with the development of so-called second-person psychology and interpersonal neuroscience, the study of the self as extended, intersubjective, and even intercorporeal is also widespread. By contrast, with its sensitivity to cross-cultural differences, anthropology has been committed to explorations of selfhood in and across different societies, structured according to their own cultural principles.

Despite these divisions, in his last essay in 1938, Marcel Mauss addressed the question of the universality and historical specificity of the "category of the self" (Mauss 1985, 20), although it was only in the eighties that his work on the subject was given due attention (see Carrithers, Collins, and Lukes 1985). In it, he distinguished between the "sense of the self," which he relegated to the domain of psychology, and the ideas that people from different societies have about the nature and constitution of the person—the proper subject of "social history." Regarding the former, he noted this: "Let me merely say that it is plain, particularly to us, that there has never existed a human being who has not been aware, not only of his body, but also at the same time of his individuality, both spiritual and physical" (Mauss 1985, 3).

Today, this fragmented situation continues. Even within disciplines, it is difficult to find a unifying theory of the "self," particularly since apparently equivalent terms—*subject, person, individual, mind, brain*, even *psyche*—rarely converge in their usage. New theories have proliferated, and distinctions seem provisional and contingent. Whereas Mauss used the word *person* to denote the Western idea of the self, others such as Louis Dumont and Alan Macfarlane have employed the term *individualism* (La Fontaine 1985, 124). Mauss's student Louis Dumont famously contrasted two civilizational ideas or complexes of the self, those based on hierarchy and holism and those based on equality and individualism. Historically, individualism was reflected in the development of socio-legal institutions such as private property, the political and legal liberty of the individual, and the idea of the individual's direct communication with God (Macfarlane 1978, 5).

Mauss's work left an important imprint on the development of ethnopsychology. The distinction between a universal awareness of a sense of self and cultural ideas of the person, often including self-aggrandizing claims concerning qualities of the Western "individual," continued to be utilized even as scholars sought to redefine the terms (see, for example, Fajans 1985, 370). Clifford Geertz would go on to argue that what begs explanation is the Western notion of the person as "bounded, unique, more or less an integrated motivational and cognitive universe, a dynamic centre of awareness, emotion, judgement and action organized into a distinctive whole" (2000, 59). In Bali, by contrast, "it is dramatis personae, not actors, that in the proper sense really exist" (62). The anthropology of Oceania has similarly stressed the difference between the Western "individual" and Melanesian "dividual" selves, where "persons are frequently constructed as the plural and composite site of the relationships that produce them" (Strathern 1988, 13). Scholars of Melanesia are still conflicted over the impact of charismatic Christianity on Melanesian "personhood" (see Timmer in this volume). As critics have noted, however, such dichotomies "fetishize difference" and take the ideology of Western individualism as an ethnographic fact in the lives of so-called Westerners themselves.[1]

Nevertheless, within anthropology, there are those who claim that the "actuality and universality of the individual self" (Rapport 1997, 8) eclipses the significance of any surface variation in cross-cultural concepts of the person. As Rapport notes in this volume, such concepts are "rhetorical constructs and political claims that do not necessarily correspond with phenomenological reality." Instead, individuals everywhere must be conceived within a "liberal-humanist" mindset as the "seat of consciousness" and the "guarantor of meaning" (Rapport 1997, 7).

In many ways, the discipline has entered an impasse both in its long-standing critique of the purported universality of the Western self and in its more recent doubts about whether the occidental idea of a specific Western self is applicable to "Western" lives anyway. As Caroline Humphrey notes, "While anthropologists continue with the long-running onslaught on the sovereign individual, in philosophy there have emerged from amidst the deconstructed ruins of the old subject several complex post-deconstructive formulations" (2008, 359).

Within philosophy, the decolonizing movement has also led to a reevaluation of certain underlying Western assumptions of personhood. Writing about African ideas of personhood, Kwazi Wiredu (1996) notes how Akan conceptions denote a state that is achieved in degrees rather than given at birth (160), referring in important ways to an individual's moral status. Wiredu draws upon linguistic/cultural differences to provide a critique of some fundamental philosophical positions. Descartes's cogito, one quintessential articulation of the Western person, is singled out for its assumed individualism. In the Akan language, existence is always locative: "to be" is always to be someplace or something, which would make "Cogito, ergo sum" appear nonsensical (141). Here reading philosophy becomes almost indistinguishable from reading an anthropological critique of the projected universality of the Western self.

Clearly, there is scope to develop a politics and theory of the self and of its dynamic self-alterations more suitable for the varied worlds we live in, even if we remain wary of Humphrey's use of the work of Alain Badiou in her suggestive account of subjects' self-alteration through what she terms *decision-events*.[2] Similarly to Humphrey, however, the essays in this volume come at the subject of the self in a particular way through their presentation of case studies of its *alteration*. In doing so, they begin with people's projects, practices, and personal perceptions of self-innovation, which reveal that the subject acquires a significant and fresh new meaning in and through its very process of change. Indeed, perceiving that we are altering exposes the self in a way that other experiences do not, becoming a privileged "site" for an anthropological exploration of self-awareness and personhood.

At the same time, these personal projects of self-alteration as discussed in this volume highlight the *cross-cultural* composition of the self—*cross-cultural* here referring to people's synthetic mixing of elements and cultural affordances from various places and times to fabricate social-self change. To give two examples, in Kathryn Rountree's chapter on self-alteration among modern shamans in Malta, she discusses a group of women who have lived and worked in many parts of the world, experiencing a range of Pagan and polytheistic spiritual practices upon which they draw. By contrast, Max Harwood investigates how mass murderers Anton Breivik and Brenton Tarrant altered themselves through reconstituting a common (intersubjective) political time with imagined generations of "White" and/or Christian warriors, a world they tie together through racist-nationalist-fascist imaginary significations and practices.

But how revolutionary are projects of self-alteration?

The essays in this volume show us that these practices and perceptions do not have to lead to a radical self-alteration—that is, *self-transformation*—or literally to a change of *form*. Metamorphosis is too high a bar. There are indeed various examples of projects that *aim* to produce a radically different self—a new man and new woman—as discussed in Christopher Houston's comparative analysis of revolutionary socialism in this volume. However, even in such events, it is often the case that the alteration is more aspective: partial and incomplete.

Instead, as this volume illustrates, processes of self-alteration may also involve more minor modes and methods that entail modest changes to established or taken-for-granted aspects of people's perceptions, relations to others, embodied capacities, ethical valuations, and encounters with the more-than-human. The chapters trace out and explore people's practical experiments in altering aspects of themselves, experiments that through narrated testimony to their efficacy also reveal how people constitute themselves. Experiences of alteration may also be enabled by activities oriented more explicitly toward other ends and goals. For example, in this volume, Muhammad A. Kavesh explores how through their love of pigeons, his interlocutors undergo an alteration in their masculine selves. As he describes, "On the rooftop with his pigeons, where a flyer spends much of his time during the day, he forms a type of 'gentle masculinity' . . . , [which] can be conceived as almost the opposite of the values of 'hegemonic' or 'hyper'-masculinity."

For these reasons, we have chosen to use the more neutral term *self-alteration* to illuminate and describe the ways people change aspects of themselves, as it does not presume the perception—or privilege the language—of transformations in the way that other terms (e.g., *self-creation*, *self-making*, or *self-rupture*) might. But our focus is different, too, from that of Joao Biehl and Peter Locke (2017) in their edited book *Unfinished: The Anthropology of Becoming*, which emphasizes what it calls the plastic power of people, presuming unfinishedness as a general feature of social life. By contrast, the concerns of our volume are more specific, exploring explicit social practices of self-change and their connections, obstructive or useful, to individuals' efforts to alter themselves.

Nevertheless, in embarking upon new affective and embodied projects of self-alteration, people often experience an ethical revisioning of the world. In doing so, they may assert truth claims that are, from the perspective of an outsider, radically selective. Becoming a modern shaman, a revolutionary, a White nationalist, a prophet, a *ney* (reed flute) artist, an anorexic, a pigeon flyer, a psychoanalyst, and so on is also, for better or worse, an act of ethical self-constitution or *autonomy* (as Castoriadis 1997 reminds us, literally, a giving of the law to oneself). As the chapters in this volume disclose, in projects of self-alteration, new ethical practices and convictions are invariably reformulated in tension with existing moral ways of dwelling in the world. Under certain conditions, these self-altering truth claims become conflictual and antagonistic toward other specific ways of living against which they are asserted. In Banu Şenay's chapter on Sufi music, she traces changes in the practical ethics of ney students that develop in increasing tension with legal-supremacist conceptions of Islam. In many cases, self-alteration is informed by a utopian hope for a different world (see, for example, the essays of Houston, Timmer, and Harwood in this volume), thus becoming much more than an exercise oriented toward self-evolution, self-improvement, or conventional moral superiority.

Perhaps most importantly, the chapters reveal the crucial role that experiences of *intersubjectivity* play in engendering self-alteration. Individuals' active becomings are vitally enabled (or obstructed) through the affordances of relations with the Other. The Other in this sense is not limited only to encounters between human subjects, as in the master-student dyad described by Şenay in Islamic music pedagogy. Rather, as anthropologists have increasingly come to recognize, self-Other relations may expand to include a range of agencies. These include more-than-human beings (such as the pigeons in Kavesh), metapersons (such as inspirited nature in Rountree or the Holy Spirit in Timmer), imagined communities (such as the "White nation" in Harwood), and epistemic orders (such as the mechanical models of the body that emerge in Orsini's discussion of scientific therapeutic interventions). Orsini's essay explores the embodied self-alteration pursued by some young women in Italy through their initiating of specific eating *orders*, understood by them as aiding in their moral endeavor to exert control over the body. By contrast, treatment in the clinic involves a veritable reeducation, the staging of an encounter with the mechanical/biological discourse of "science" to show them that they suffer from a medical condition and an eating *disorder*. In these oftentimes conflictual self-Other relationships, discerning where the altering self ends and the "Other" begins is often hard to do.

Intersubjective self-alteration can be conceived of in different ways too, as shown in Michael Jackson's chapter, which makes a case for thinking of it equally as an *internal* experience of "shape-shifting," whereby an inconstant self changes or is changed by its situation. Alteration here could be said to incorporate our own alterity, the "multiple subjectivities harboured in any one subjectivity as we navigate the landscapes of the other" (Kusserow 2017, 84). Alternatively, self-alteration may be understood as *generating* new versions of oneself or *alter* egos, translatable as "other me(s)." Humphrey's work synthesizes these two ideas. She argues that people construct themselves as new *singular* selves through action-oriented "decision-events." But they do so by foregrounding or "plumping for" a specific way of being a person, a decision that keeps an array of other (inter)subjectivities at bay (2008, 363).

In sum, focusing on self-alteration tells us something crucial about the ontology of the self. Self-alteration reveals the intimate and dynamic relations among the self, the other, the world of the other, and the modes of connectivity—for example, intersubjectivity or temporality—that tie them together. Exposure to projects of self-alteration changes participants' intentions and attentiveness toward the world, causing the world to alter in turn. Just as previous ways of relating to the world were accompanied by ingrained ethical judgments and understandings, so too does the new attentiveness of altered selves bring with it new ethical entailments. In short, perceiving the same world differently, altered selves simultaneously constitute different worlds.

BEYOND THE SELF: SOCIAL AND POLITICAL AFFORDANCES OF SELF-ALTERATION

How are worlds and selves brought together in experiences of self-alteration? To alter themselves, people and groups braid different histories and fields of social practice, drawing together in an improvisational manner a range of resources from their own and other societies and times. In doing so, they create new modes of self-alteration that have mixed and multiple genealogies. Emerging from immanent economic realities, political contexts, religious imaginaries, and social processes, individuals and communities constitute and take up ready-to-hand "tools" as *affordances* to help them change.[3]

As originally used in environmental psychology by James Gibson, the term *affordances* denotes the possibilities provided to the organism by virtue of the properties of the environment. Those same features of the environment furnish different opportunities to different beings: "This is because affordances are relational in nature, [being] both a fact of the environment and a fact of the organism" (De Carvalho 2020). As Tim Ingold (2000, 20) says, the environment is relative to the being who constitutes its objects of experience.

In the same way, social and political environments provide a range of possibilities for the perceptive self. These *social affordances* are themselves historically produced by the actions of predecessors and are therefore also simultaneously regenerated, appropriated, and transformed by subjects' actions in the present. Cultural traditions of self-alteration—for example, Sufism—are reworked in this process. Contributors to this volume identify a variety of affordances in their respective case studies. Here we briefly investigate three of the most important: the "messy" affordances offered by gender dynamics, colonial legacies, and neoliberal policies, respectively. Individuals (and movements) reckon with these affordances in their projects of self-alteration. Affordances may equally be constituted as "negative," inciting creative opposition and resistance.

One key affordance is the ways in which *gender* is understood and practiced within specific ethnographic environments. Rountree, for example, describes a community of women (or "sistren") who are modern shamans, based mostly in Malta. As she notes, New Age discourses as they emerged in the 1960s countercultural movements were described by practitioners themselves as alternative: "a response to their alienation from and a critique of powerful religious and other cultural institutions that denied their right to a self-determined religiosity and failed to reflect their beliefs, values, concerns, or frequently—given that women predominated in many of the movements—gender." While the group that Rountree studies comprises only women, their self-alteration involves the formation of a collective Self that not only includes all individual selves but also encompasses all beings in a larger intersubjective Self, "irrespective of . . . gender identities or lack of them."

Similarly, Orsini examines a highly gendered field, the self-alteration of women diagnosed with anorexia nervosa in a residential treatment facility in Italy. Her work demonstrates how broader cultural ideals of womanhood may inform women's noneating as well as become a basis to challenge normative expressions of those ideals. In devoting their lives to becoming thin, these women also sculpt emaciated female bodies that are beyond the standard norms of beauty, becoming as a result subject to the intervention of medical and therapeutic orders. Thinness becomes an index of the *moral* triumph of an idealized mind-self that gains mastery over its bodily needs and desires, even as not eating overlaps with gendered ideas of self-sacrifice, the negation of bodily needs, and devotion to the family. Paradoxically, one could argue that in so doing, these women challenge normative expectations of their gendered selves, leading to their medicalized reconstitution as disordered. Harwood's chapter on mass murderers Brevik and Tarrant identifies the disciplined processes that led to their production of a hypermasculine identity. This virile masculinity is constituted in the service of a militaristic ideal mobilized against a perceived dominant multicultural and feminist social order.

By contrast, in Şenay's chapter, the making of alternate masculinities and femininities is more the inadvertent result of processes of self-alteration that are not directed toward challenging gendered ideals as such. Learning the ney had historically been a male practice associated with Turkish Sufism right up until the twenty-first century. It is only in the ney revival in recent decades that women have been afforded this privilege. At the same time, in the studio that Şenay attended, learning the ney also involved learning to cook, which was a novel experience for many of the male students in a cultural context in which cooking is a predominantly female task and skill.

Anthropologists have paid increasing attention to a second cluster of affordances, identifying ways in which *colonialism* has not only transformed the social and political structures of colonized societies but altered in fundamental ways people's understandings of themselves as persons. John L. Comaroff and Jean Comaroff note, for example, how colonialism and the introduction of Christianity in southern Africa set in motion a series of questions about selfhood among the southern Tswana themselves. The result was that while some "found the liberal individualism of *sekgoa* ('European ways') highly appealing and took on its terms, others repudiated it entirely, even while being affected by it. Yet others forged hybridity out of the antinomy" (2001, 278). These responses brought to light various social affordances born out of the colonial encounter.

In our volume, Kavesh's study of pigeon flyers in rural Pakistan draws attention to the ways in which colonialism transformed relationships between humans and more-than-humans. At the same time, his chapter also highlights decolonizing efforts to reimagine and reevaluate precolonial human-animal relations. *The Myna from Peacock Garden*, a children's story by celebrated author Naiyer Masud, effectively represents the sultan of Oudh as someone with a serious regard for life, both human and more-than-human, in contrast to contemporary accounts in the colonial archive that represent him as indolent and sunk in enfeebling debauchery. In this context, both literary and ethnographic accounts of humans' intimate relations with the more-than-human become postcolonial affordances that highlight and seek to reclaim precolonial mutualistic understandings of this human-Other intersubjectivity.

Equally interestingly, the history of the emergence of the postcolonial state in Solomon Islands has been majorly informed by the development of Christianity and debates over the nature of a Christian polity. The chapter by Timmer on the self-alteration of Michael Maeliau, a key figure in the Christian revival and separatist movement on the island of Malaita (the most populous island in Solomon Islands), draws attention to Maeliau's prophetic revisioning of a new theocratic Christian state that cannot be simply seen as a legacy of colonial-Christian theology. As Timmer notes, "Maeliau has used this evangelical revival to redefine both himself and Malaita as a Christian nation." Christianity and colonialism have a complex and conflicted history in Solomon Islands, providing an important source of social affordances at both the individual and the collective levels. In becoming Christian and independent, Malaitans have "reorganised their society, their spiritual as well as their human relationships . . . but within their Christian society some serious contradictions remain unresolved, representing the contradictions of their own colonial history" (Burt 1994, 1).

A third vital issue concerns the vexed role of *neoliberalization* in encouraging people to employ and enhance their own selves in their making of livelihoods (Dunn 2014, 2017). Anthropologists since 2005 have increasingly used the term *neoliberalism* to describe key global trends in capitalism and its associated ideology and forms of governmentality—even though the concept is not without its detractors, as debate over its explanatory efficacy shows (e.g., Eriksen et al. 2015). Under its theoretical rubric, in different places, analysis has examined neoliberalism's reorganization of welfare rights and responsibilities, its restructuring of state institutions, its shrinking of taxation and social spending in some areas and expansion in others, its deepening of market relations and inequalities, and its undermining of public health coverage (Harvey 2005; Muehlebach 2012; Wilson and Spies-Butcher 2016).

Simultaneously, the term has also been used to denote the fabrication of a new kind of ethical subjectivity, a "responsible, bounded, autonomous, maximising individual, who is simultaneously a moral agent and a rational person but fully accountable for his or her actions" (Eriksen et al. 2015, 917). The concept connects the broader contextual affordances of neoliberalism with a reconceptualization of the self. For many scholars of contemporary capitalism, it is global neoliberalism itself that seduces individuals into seeking to improve themselves, propagating the claim that success depends on developing an "entrepreneurial subjectivity" (Scharff 2016). The argument is, then, that varieties of neoliberal capitalism provide affordances for many contemporary projects, narratives, and motivations of self-alteration, ensuring its policy reproduction by inculcating subjects with dispositions and desires to change themselves in ways that enable them to prosper in its brave new world.

For Eva Illouz (2008), neoliberalism's generation of subjectivity builds upon much earlier social affordances—in *Saving the Modern Soul*, she traces back the rise of "self-help culture," a key feature of neoliberalism, to the take up of Freud's ideas in America in the early twentieth century. She credits Freud with developing "the meritocratic and voluntarist narrative of self-help" (50). Contradicting such claims, in Jean-Paul Baldacchino's clinically informed accounts of his own psychoanalysis as well as of his encounters with patients in Malta, he shows how motivations and outcomes in the therapeutic encounter are neither predetermined nor reducible to simplistic notions of "self-help." Indeed, for Baldacchino, psychoanalytic therapy fosters self-alteration by putting the neoliberal self itself into question through analysis of the person's constitutive experiences of suffering and lack.

Baldacchino's chapter is not the only one in this volume to question the influence, universality, or ubiquity of neoliberal affordances of self-alteration. Other essays do so less by denying neoliberalism's "psychopolitics" (Han 2017) and more by empirically examining and revealing contemporary countermodels and modes of self-alteration alternative to it, modes that contradict and sometimes directly resist global capitalism's manipulation of "souls." Rountree, for example, asserts that both she and her own interlocutors alter themselves in a manner that cannot be understood by tropes of "self-empowerment" that have been used to characterize New Age religion in the more recent present. Instead, the women shaman of whom she is a part produce a radically *alternative* collective Self. Similarly, while neoliberalism has been used as a catchall framework to explain the educational policies of the AKP (Adalet ve Kalkınma Partisi; Justice and Development Party) government in Turkey (e.g., İnal and Akkaymak 2012), Şenay's essay shows how the slow process of cultivating skills in ney musicianship involves a different experience of ethical development for students. She relates it to centuries-old Sufi practices that enable an alteration of the self from its "lowly instinctual nature to the ultimate state of subsistence in God" (Sviri 2002, 196).

Even the essay that deals explicitly with the question of neoliberal self-alteration—Gil Hizi's analysis of extracurricular programs of "self-improvement" in the Chinese city of Jinan—argues that there are multiple histories and ideologies at work in self-development courses there. He concludes that rather than producing a subjectivity that accommodates the market economy, such training mainly reinforces social contradictions, such as the individual versus the relational self.

In short, the essays in this volume demonstrate that minor and major modes of self-alteration exist across very different modern societies today, alongside and in tense relationship to global neoliberal affordances. These diverse projects and processes of self-alteration are facilitated by a huge number of different social and political affordances.

Lastly, affordances should not be thought of as only objective and external. Rather, they are more properly understood *phenomenologically*, relative to the person who in dialogue with other beings, both human and nonhuman, constitutes them. Rapport phrases it even more individually, noting that affordances may (also) be understood as particular and personal, private to the individual rather than publicly generated or arising out of any interactional setting (Nigel Rapport, pers. comm., 2021). Individuals are not delimited by contextual affordances, neoliberal or otherwise, but can only ever be self-made. For that reason, in his essay, he contends that self-alteration is a human right.

However, regardless of the processes by which social and political affordances are interpreted and taken up by individuals and groups to change themselves, many of the essays wrestle with the affordances' most important features. Individuals' utilization of affordances is often adversarial. Coeval projects of self-alteration may be mutually incompatible, while in other cases, as Harwood's essay on White nationalists shows, the altering self constitutes itself by fixing upon others as hostile, which can lead to acts of terrible atrocity. In some situations, access to techniques of self-alteration can be restricted. Finally, certain affordances—for example, the spatial affordances of urban space—may be fought over, as Houston's chapter on activism in Istanbul illustrates.

METHODS AND TECHNIQUES OF SELF-ALTERATION: HOW EASY IS IT TO ALTER ONESELF?

For some intellectual traditions and practices that explicitly foster alteration through slow-won self-knowledge—for example, psychoanalysis—the self-protecting obduracy of the self means that true self-alteration is profoundly difficult. As a psychoanalyst friend once said to the editors of this work, "You can never drain the swamp." Its presumption is that the self's historical and developmental growth is built up like a pearl from prebirth "nothing" through the intense friction of family and *extra*family intersubjective relationships—for example, with Kemal Atatürk throughout the entire schooling system in Turkey. Given its assumption of below-conscious psychic density, for psychoanalysis, many of the methods and practices of self-change extant in the world do not warrant the term (see Baldacchino's chapter).

Whether the goal is some form of "enlightenment" as in the case of psychoanalysis as discussed by Baldacchino or indeed an equally difficult political transformation of the world as pursued by the socialist revolutionaries described by Houston, the theocrats envisaged in Timmer's case study, or White nationalists as discussed by Harwood, we can identify certain crosscutting modes of alteration that are deployed in such projects. Many of these means can be usefully analyzed as *techniques*, referring to what Foucault describes as "technologies of the self": practices that "permit individuals to effect by their own means or with the help of others a certain number of operations on their own bodies and souls, thoughts, conduct, and way of being, so as to transform themselves in order to attain a certain state of happiness, purity, wisdom, perfection, or immortality"

(1988, 18). These technologies require varying degrees of skill and mastery built upon a specific kind of knowledge. *Techne*, or "craft," defines a practical knowledge. In the Aristotelian schema, *techne* is distinct from *episteme*. *Episteme*—"to know" in Greek—refers to knowledge of universal, context-independent principles, whereas *techne* is a form of skill whose aim is practical, a making or doing, rather than knowledge as an end in and of itself. Self-alteration, we argue, develops through certain practical techniques that take the self (individual or collective) as their intentional object.

Perhaps one of the first and most readily accessible techniques of self-alteration involves *bodily practices*. The role that the body plays in self-alteration has long been a puzzle in Christian philosophy and is also a topic of interest in anthropological studies of ritual. Why should prayer require ritualized bodily expressions? For Augustine, bodily performance acts to "enhance and intensify the proper religious attitudes" (Matthews 1980, 339). As Gareth Matthews observes, however, Augustine is unhappy with his answer: "And he should be puzzled. For, as Augustine conceives it, the intensification of a religious attitude or feeling by the performance of a ritualistic act is a case of movements of the body having the effect of moving the soul" (340). For Augustine, this is a problem because the body is inferior to the soul.

Leaving aside Augustine's puzzlement, we can draw out the relevance of his intuition for our own study of self-alteration. In what ways does acting on the body—whether in religious ritual, in practices of sexual and gendered transgression (Heyes 2007), or indeed in the gym—alter the self? As Orsini points out in her chapter, her own informants also have a radically Cartesian vision of their self where the body and the mind are split and experienced as *two* kinds of self—a body-self and a mind-self. The disciplining of appetites and the highly ritualistic practices that govern their relationship to food retrain and transform their bodies through deliberate actions of the mind. In turn, the therapeutic regimen of the clinic involves a reeducation—enforcing a new set of bodily practices, forms of eating, exercise, and indeed bodily revision.

This abnegation of bodily appetites and desires is not unique to the Western Christian world. James Laidlaw's (2005) exploration of self-alteration through Jain fasting is a good example. In Jainism, practiced by high-caste and mostly affluent individuals, nonpossession and nonviolence form cardinal moral virtues. The telos of a good life comes in a good death—in this case, achieved through the practice of meditation and fasting to death (Sallekhana). Through disciplined practices of austerity, devout Jains aim to achieve a state of "ultimate indifference to worldly pleasure or pain" (186). Although the transformation of the self is frequently associated with ideas of human flourishing, here what flourishing means and entails is radically contrary to neoliberal visions of a good life and death. Perversely, in Harwood's discussion, Tarrant and Breivik make themselves indifferent to the worldly pain of others through a hermit-like regimen of isolation from their social environment, as well as gendered bodily discipline focused on increasing physical strength and stamina (including through pharmaceutically enhanced bodily alteration). Making themselves killers for the White nation, they present their violence as a form of *self*-defense in a hidden war, motivated by a confrontational ethics built on a mixture of far-right-wing political theory and a cross-temporal imagined West.

In Houston's discussion of the alterations of the self in Stalinist Russia, we get a much harsher and more violent account of bodily techniques. Soviet penal philosophy sought to transform criminals into dedicated communists through work camps. Through the "redemptive path of *physical labor* and duress in a work collective" motivated by the rewards of extra food rations and early release for "heroic" labor performance, the work-camp system aimed to "reforge" a new man/woman. Houston also provides an intimate account of the ways in which the value of work in transforming oneself was an important "rite of passage" in the 1970s among revolutionary socialists in Istanbul. For revolutionary students in the 1970s, "working in informal settlements [*gecekondu*]—perceived as sites of unfolding revolution—was a process of character formation." Since these were also highly dangerous places prone to attacks by the *ülkücü* "commandos" (anti-communist nationalists), part of the discipline involved crafting a different relation to the city itself: "the assembling of a microgeographical knowledge of places and the developing of a political-spatial intuition to minimize risk."

Bodily techniques, however, are not necessarily predicated on the *austere regimentation* of the body (as in labor camps and in forms of ascetic secular and spiritual practices). They can also act in a more gradual and subtle manner through a *retraining of our sensorium* (as shown in changing relations to the city among revolutionary Turkish socialists). Şenay explores how a spiritual discipline is communicated in Sufism through the metaphorical identification between the ney and the individual human. In playing the ney itself, students are also encouraged to reimagine themselves as alterable beings "played" by the breath of God. Participation in the ney pedagogy alters learners' own embodied capacities. The modification of aural sensibilities is also intimately linked to an alteration of the moral self. Through the slow and continuous process of transformation that emerges from the master-student dyad, the self is fundamentally altered by the reattunement of its embodied capacities—learning how to breathe, how to listen, and ultimately how to relate to others and to God.

Another important experiential technique of self-alteration involves exposure to and practical adaptation of a new *language* (and indeed grammar) of intersubjective relations. Baldacchino's account of training to become a psychoanalyst draws attention to the ways in which learning a different language also leads to a radical revision of the ways in which the self *and* the other are perceived and relatively constituted. Outside analytical training per se, the very act of psychoanalysis as a "talking cure" is premised on a fundamentally linguistic operation. "Free association"—that is, speaking without censorship in front of a stranger without looking at them—is a speech-act that destabilizes ordinary communication conventions. Through long-term and frequent sessions, the self becomes altered in subtle yet significant ways.

Rountree's study draws attention to the important role that new *communication technologies* have played in enabling self-alteration. During the COVID-19 pandemic, the WhatsApp group of shamans became "a dynamic sacred space." In the case of Breivik and Tarrant, online platforms such as 4chan played a pivotal role in developing a new sense of collective identity. They also provided them with witnesses to their passage to an altered self. In his chapter, Timmer writes how he observed firsthand the way in which God communicated with the Malaitan prophet Michael Maeliau. In front of a gathering of people on a "pilgrimage" in Israel, Maeliau pulled out his laptop and closed his eyes, "connecting with God through the internet for some important 'download'" concerning guidance on the new constitution of the state of Malaita. In this case, the communication was enabled through a particular articulation of "the internet." Maeliau's prophetic self-alteration was forged through repeated acts of divine inspiration, his various books and sermons in turn relaying this vision of a new world.

Finally, the chapters in this volume also draw attention to the efficacious function that *narratives* of self-alteration fulfill in not only testifying to but also ultimately constituting the altered self. In the autobiographical narrating of selves and contexts, we hear individuals' attempts to take power back from social forces, critical events, or malignant individuals who have staked dominion over self-awareness. As Michael Jackson puts it (1998, 24), narrative "mediates a reinvention of identity," its scenarios "expedient lies" (or liberating half-truths).

Further, in studying self-alteration in its various forms, anthropologists often have to rely on narrative accounts of the self in motion in order to encounter the experiences of change. It is only once they are described and recounted by our informants that we can understand and make sense of these experiences, and as in the chapters of Harwood and Houston, sometimes retrospective narratives are all that we can go on. Harwood's essay is largely based on Breivik's and Tarrant's prolific manifestos posted online before their atrocities. When seen in tandem with the self-alterations that they represent, these narratives themselves become dangerous templates for future others to emulate.

Narratives can be said to create the experience of coherence, assigning meaning to an experience by establishing a temporal and oftentimes causal order complete with its own distinct chronotope.[4] Such self-narrations can be considered as literary genres and have an important role in shaping the experience of self-alteration. In the context of medical anthropology, the notion of "illness narratives" has become increasingly significant. Arthur Kleinman (1988) proposes that the dialogue generated between physician and patient in the account of the experience of illness is an important retrospective tool that can improve and assist the healing process itself. Others, however, have pointed out that the search to produce such coherent narratives/selves cannot encapsulate the incomplete and partial experience of human bodies (Kokanović and Flore 2017). Kenny et al. (2017) note that the narratives of individuals living with advanced cancer often resist unificatory integration, exposing, by contrast, disorder and incoherence and as such falling "outside of coherent normativity" (2). Seen in this light, coherence comes to be seen as a *normative* requirement.

Şenay contrasts illness narratives with the accounts of the self-alteration of the *neyzens* (ney artists) she studied with. Unlike in illness narratives that present a self radically and definitively changed, the self-transformation of the neyzen is continuous and, more importantly, always unfinished: "Even the greatest master never ceases to be a talebe [pupil]." Similarly, even though Orsini is working with subjects who have undergone a radical bodily transformation, she also makes the point that the way in which her informants narratively constitute their selves does not follow the chronotope of conventional illness narratives. "Disease" among her informants is not attributed a causal role. Instead, their self-alteration is narrated as an act of agency born out of a deliberate choice that leads to a medical condition. In other words, we should not assume that all narratives of self-alteration follow conventionalized tropes too closely.

In essence, narratives of self-alteration are first narratives "for" the self, in that they provide templates and dispositional frameworks through which the self becomes lived in the world. Coherence is only one of the features that make narrative a technique of self-alteration. Nevertheless, even given the fact of a good story, projects of self-alteration, self-given or communal, may also result in uncertainty and failure. Participation in modes of self-alteration is a gamble, not a promise; and self-alteration may sometimes lead to self-falteration. Only the individual can say whether it is better to have altered and lost (oneself) than to have never altered at all. But that would be another story.

CONCLUSION: A PROJECT THAT CHANGED ME

For anthropologists, there is one other central dimension to narratives of self-alteration. When we ourselves *participate* in the practices of self-alteration of our interlocutors, it is only in narrative presentations of our own change that readers can gain access to them. Bonnie Glass-Coffin tells how she spent years working with shamans in northern Peru seeking to encounter the "unseen world," a key theme of her research being "the change that transpires through engagement" (2010, 207). But she writes that for more than eighteen years, she remained "blind to their world." It was only during an unexpected moment in Florida that she had a sudden "awakening," able to experience firsthand the "cognitive and spiritual maps of relatedness and of human-spirit connection" (207). In this book, the essays of Şenay, Rountree, and Baldacchino can be read, at least in part, as "experiential ethnography," the result of attempts to undergo self-alteration and subsequently to produce accounts of changes encountered through that experience.

Nevertheless, even when not experimenting with processes of self-change per se, we contend that the very praxis of anthropological *fieldwork* engenders self-alteration. Wherever and however pursued, fieldwork is a technique of self-alteration, a method of becoming an anthropologist through the slow learning of other ways of being. This requires the development of myriad skills, including body techniques. In an unfortunate analogy, this learning is sometimes said to involve the anthropologist in becoming like a child. Perhaps this is why, too, some anthropologists have developed an interest in studying the developmental lives of children—because, as Christina Toren claims, "the problem with adults is that they are, by and large, the finished product" (Duraõ 2012, 460).

The studies in this book show that Toren could not be more wrong. Subjects of their own self-alteration, adults are, as Biehl and Locke assert, *unfinished* beings. The same is true of the anthropologist, who in fieldwork acquires a new language *for* the self. To be sure, it is a form of self-alteration that is also the result of specific affordances taken up by us through our passage through the academy and our embodied participation in its associated rites (Bourdieu 1988, 2007). But just as significantly, anthropological self-alteration is also the result of an encounter with the other, however conceived, whether human, divine, or more-than-human.

NOTES

1. "To assume that there exists an opposition between societies based on substance and those based on relations, cultures of the fully dividual persons versus a Western world of individuals, is not only to accept Western ideological notions of the person (which sees the person as un-dividedly individual), but to use that ideology to construct the Other as its opposite image" (LiPuma 1998, 57).

2. Caroline Humphrey sketches out how an individual "might put him or herself together as a distinctive subject by adding to, or subtracting from, the possibilities given by culture as it has been up to that point, through the very process of taking action" (2008, 358). For a critical application of her argument, see Christopher Houston and Banu Şenay's (2017) analysis of protesters' self-alteration through their making of the Gezi Park event in Istanbul in 2013.

3. David Shulman and Guy G. Stroumsa's (2002) collection *Self and Self-Transformation in the History of Religions* explores the way that major religions "insist" on the need for the person to radically change, as well as how this self-transformation is patterned and culturally determined. Its focus is textual rather than ethnographic. By contrast, here we consider a greater variety of domains and projects of self-alteration and argue that self-alteration is at once more diffuse and often more personal.

4. *Chronotope*, as coined by Mikhail Bahktin, means the ways in which time and place are interwoven in literature (Lipset 2004, 209).

REFERENCES

Biehl, Joao, and Peter Locke. 2017. "Introduction: Ethnographic Sensorium." In *Unfinished: The Anthropology of Becoming*, edited by Joao Biehl and Peter Locke, 1–41. Durham, N.C.: Duke University Press.

Bourdieu, Pierre. 1962. *The Algerians*. Boston: Beacon.

———. 1988. *Homo Academicus*. Stanford, Calif.: Stanford University Press.
———. 2007. *Sketch for a Self-Analysis*. Chicago: University of Chicago Press.
Burt, Ben. 1994. *Tradition and Christianity: The Colonial Transformation of a Solomon Islands Society*. Chur, Switzerland: Harwood Academic.
Carrithers, Michael S., Steven Collins, and Steven Lukes, eds. 1985. *The Category of the Person: Anthropology, Philosophy, History*. Cambridge: Cambridge University Press.
Castoriadis, Cornelius. 1997. "The Imaginary: Creation in the Social-Historical Domain." In *World in Fragments: Writings on Politics, Society, Psychoanalysis, and the Imagination*, 3–18. Stanford, Calif.: Stanford University Press.
Comaroff, John L., and Jean Comaroff. 2001. "On Personhood: An Anthropological Perspective from Africa." *Social Identities* 7 (2): 267–283.
De Carvalho, Eros Moreira. 2020. "Social Affordance." In *Encyclopedia of Animal Cognition and Behavior*, edited by Jennifer Vonk and Todd Shackelford. Cham, Switzerland: Springer. https://doi.org/10.1007/978-3-319-47829-6_1870-1.
Dunn, Cynthia Dickel. 2014. "'Then I Learned about Positive Thinking': The Genre Structuring of Narratives of Self-Transformation." *Journal of Linguistic Anthropology* 24 (2): 133–150.
———. 2017. "Personal Narratives and Self-Transformation in Post-industrial Societies." *Annual Review of Anthropology* 46:65–80. https://www.annualreviews.org/doi/10.1146/annurev-anthro-102116-041702.
Durão, Susana. 2012. "Interview with Christian Toren: How to Make Categories Work Analytically." *Análise Social* 47 (2): 452–469.
Eriksen, Thomas Hylland, James Laidlaw, Jonathan Mair, Keir Martin, and Soumhya Venkatesan. 2015. "The Concept of Neoliberalism Has Become an Obstacle to the Anthropological Understanding of the Twenty-First Century." *Journal of the Royal Anthropological Institute* 21 (4): 911–923. https://doi.org/10.1111/1467-9655.12294.
Fajans, Jane. 1985. "The Person in Social Context: The Social Character of 'Psychology.'" In *Person, Self, and Experience: Exploring Pacific Ethnopsychologies*, edited by Geoffrey M. White and John Kirkpatrick, 367–397. Berkeley: University of California Press.
Foucault, Michel. 1988. *Technologies of the Self: A Seminar with Michel Foucault*. Edited by Patrick H. Hutton, Luther H. Martin, and Huck Gutman. Amherst: University of Massachusetts Press.
Geertz, Clifford. 2000. "'From the Native's Point of View': On the Nature of Anthropological Understanding." In *Local Knowledge: Further Essays in Interpretive Anthropology*, 55–73. New York: Basic Books.
Glass-Coffin, Bonnie. 2010. "Anthropology, Shamanism, and Alternate Ways of Knowing-Being in the World: One Anthropologist's Journey of Discovery and Transformation." *Anthropology & Humanism* 35 (2): 204–217.
Han, Byung-Chul. 2017. *Psychopolitics: Neo-Liberalism and New Technologies of Power*. London: Verso.
Harding, Susan Friend. 2001. *The Book of Jerry Falwell: Fundamentalist Language and Politics*. Princeton, N.J.: Princeton University Press.
Harvey, David. 2005. *A Brief History of Neoliberalism*. Oxford: Oxford University Press.
Heyes, Cressida Jay. 2007. *Self-Transformations: Foucault, Ethics, and Normalized Bodies*. Oxford: Oxford University Press.
Houston, Christopher. 2022. "Alternative Me? Anthropology and Self-Alteration." *HAU: Journal of Ethnographic Theory* 12 (2). https://www.journals.uchicago.edu/doi/10.1086/720356.
Houston, Christopher, and Banu Şenay. 2017. "Humour, Amnesia and Making Place: Constitutive Acts of the Subject in Gezi Park." *Social Analysis* 61 (3): 19–40.

Humphrey, Caroline. 2008. "Reassembling Individual Subjects: Events and Decisions in Troubled Times." *Anthropological Theory* 8 (4): 357–380. https://doi.org/10.1177/1463499608096644.

Illouz, Eva. 2008. *Saving the Modern Soul: Therapy, Emotions, and the Culture of Self-Help*. Berkeley: University of California Press.

İnal, Kemal, and Güliz Akkaymak, eds. 2012. *Neoliberal Transformation of Education in Turkey: Political and Ideological Analysis of Educational Reforms in the Age of the AKP*. New York: Palgrave.

Ingold, Tim. 2000. *The Perception of the Environment*. London: Routledge.

Jackson, Michael. 1998. *Minima Ethnographica: Intersubjectivity and the Anthropological Project*. Chicago: University of Chicago Press.

Kafka, Franz. 2009. *The Metamorphosis and Other Stories*. Oxford: Oxford University Press.

Kenny, Katherine, Alex Broom, Emma Kirby, David Wyld, and Zarnie Lwin. 2017. "Terminal Anticipation: Entanglements of Affect and Temporality in Living with Advanced Cancer." *Subjectivity* 10:374–392. http://dx.doi.org/10.1057/s41286-017-0034-x.

Kleinman, Arthur. 1988. *The Illness Narratives: Suffering, Healing, and the Human Condition*. New York: Basic Books.

Kokanović, Renata, and Jacinthe Flore. 2017. "Subjectivity and Illness Narratives." *Subjectivity* 10:329–339. https://doi.org/10.1057/s41286-017-0038-6.

Kusserow, Adrie. 2017. "Anthropoetry." In *Crumpled Paper Boat: Experiments in Ethnographic Writing*, edited by Anand Pandian and Stuart McLean, 71–90. Durham, N.C.: Duke University Press.

La Fontaine, Jean Sybil. 1985. "Person and Individual." In Carrithers, Collins, and Lukes, *Category of the Person*, 123–141.

Laidlaw, James. 2005. "A Life Worth Leaving: Fasting to Death as Telos of a Jain Religious Life." *Economy and Society* 34 (2): 178–199.

Lipset, David. 2004. "Modernity without Romance? Masculinity and Desire in Courtship Stories Told by Young Papua New Guinean Men." *American Ethnologist* 31 (2): 205–224.

LiPuma, Edward. 1998. "Modernity and Forms of Personhood in Melanesia." In *Bodies and Persons*, edited by Michael Lambek and Andrew Strathern, 53–79. Cambridge: Cambridge University Press.

Macfarlane, Alan. 1978. *The Origins of English Individualism: The Family Property and Social Transition*. Oxford: Wiley-Blackwell.

Matthews, Gareth. 1980. "Ritual and the Religious Feelings." In *Explaining Emotions*, edited by Amelie O. Rorty, 339–355. Berkeley: University of California Press.

Mauss, Marcel. 1985. "A Category of the Human Mind." In Carrithers, Collins, and Lukes, *Category of the Person*, 1–25.

Muehlebach, Andrea. 2012. *The Moral Neoliberal: Welfare and Citizenship in Italy*. Chicago: University of Chicago Press.

Rapport, Nigel. 1997. *Transcendent Individual: Towards a Literary and Liberal Anthropology*. London: Routledge.

Rossmanith, Kate. 2022. "Ditching the New Yorker Voice." Public Books, May 26, 2022. https://www.publicbooks.org/ditching-the-new-yorker.

Scharff, Christina. 2016. "The Psychic Life of Neoliberalism: Mapping the Contours of Entrepreneurial Subjectivity." *Theory, Culture & Society* 33 (6): 107–122. https://doi.org/10.1177/0263276415590164.

Shulman, David, and Guy G. Stroumsa, eds. 2002. *Self and Self-Transformation in the History of Religions*. Oxford: Oxford University Press.

Strathern, Marilyn. 1988. *The Gender of the Gift: Problems with Women and Problems with Society in Melanesia*. Berkeley: University of California Press.

Sviri, Sara. 2002. "The Self and Its Transformation in Sufism." In Shulman and Stroumsa, *Self and Self-Transformation*, 195–215.

Wilson, Shaun, and Ben Spies-Butcher. 2016. "After New Labour: Political and Policy Consequences of Welfare State Reforms in the United Kingdom and Australia." *Policy Studies* 37 (5): 408–425. https://doi.org/10.1080/01442872.2016.1188911.

Wiredu, Kwasi. 1996. *Cultural Universals and Particulars: An African Perspective*. Bloomington: Indiana University Press.

PART I RELIGIOUS CULTURES, SPIRITUAL PRACTICES, AND SELF-ALTERATION

1 · EXEMPLARY MASTERS, EXEMPLARY REEDS
Pedagogies of Self-Alteration in Sufi Music

BANU ŞENAY

BECOME A HUMAN

During my field research among *ney* (reed flute) musicians in Istanbul, I heard a striking story about musical apprenticeship from my teacher's teacher, Neyzen (ney artist) Niyazi Sayın (1927–). Sayın began lessons with his own teacher, Halil Dikmen, in 1949, when he was twenty-two. Dikmen was also a professional painter and, at the time, the director of Istanbul's Academy of Fine Arts. Sayın said, "One day, on the way to my lesson, I ran into a fellow *talebe* [pupil] in the courtyard of the academy building. 'Did you have your lesson?' I asked my friend. 'I did, but I'm giving up,' the man replied. 'I will never get a sound from the ney like the sound of our teacher. But I will continue to come to him to learn morals [*ahlâk*],' he pronounced." Sayın went on to say that he had never forgotten this remark, telling me that he similarly had never yet managed to accomplish the sound of his teacher on his own ney. This from the musician renowned as the greatest ney virtuoso ever. Sayın learned from Dikmen for fifteen years up until his teacher's death. "Ney and ahlâk lessons," he called them.

My own teacher, Neyzen Salih Bilgin (1960–), told me about *his* first lesson with Sayın. He became the master's student at the Istanbul State Conservatorium in 1980. Bilgin stated, "Sayın asked me why I wanted to learn the ney. 'To become a neyzen,' I answered him. 'Forget becoming a neyzen,' Sayın remarked, unsatisfied with this answer. 'Let the aim of learning the ney be to become a human,' he asserted."

SELF-ALTERATION AS PERCEPTUAL MODIFICATION

These biographical snapshots speak to the core issues I address in this chapter. I begin with the premise that the process of becoming a neyzen entails an altering of the person in ways far beyond technical adeptness.[1] For the dedicated group of practitioners with whom I did fieldwork, long-term embodied engagement with the ney pedagogy generates vital transformative effects on the self. Given that this pedagogy makes little distinction between "music" and "life," or "neyzen" and *insan* (human being), apprenticeship under the guidance of a master (*hoca*) socializes learners into new ways of being and relating to other selves. This slow process of musical cultivation is simultaneously a process of ethical development.

Drawing on extensive field research carried out in Istanbul irregularly between 2012 and 2018, in this essay, I trace out a concatenation of enabling forces that make apprenticeship in this artistic practice to be experienced and retrospectively singled out as a self-altering "event" in the lives of individual musicians. The approach I take here explores the relationship between self-alteration and mastery of a new skill and builds on insights from the anthropological literature that credits the self-making potential of learning practices (Marchand 2008; Yen 2005; Kondo 1990). Mastering a musical instrument, a visual art, or a dance form not only involves acquiring skills but also entails the crafting of a particular kind of embodied subject. A fuller understanding of learning requires, then, consideration of the "historical production, transformation and change of persons" (Lave and Wenger 1991, 51).

Edmund Husserl's (1970) concept of "modification" is instructive in explicating what such an experience of change might entail in the case of ney musicians' creative becoming. As Alessandro Duranti tells us, modification helps account for the ways in which "the phenomenal world changes for the perceiving, thinking, acting, and interacting subject" (2009, 206). For instance, acquiring musical competence requires an intentional modification of aural perceptions fit for that practice. The outcome is a new form of attentiveness toward the sonic phenomenon.

In capturing the micro changes that apprentice practitioners of the ney go through in the pedagogical process, a modification-oriented approach provides a more modest take on the experience of self-alteration. This avoids imputing an overly totalizing reconstruction of selfhood to that pedagogy, one that might claim its facility to generate a radically new subject. Selves are rarely formed by single causes. In the globalized yet nationalistic city of Istanbul, the intentions of individual neyzens toward the world are conditioned by a range of social forces that simultaneously seek to deposit in them ethical sensibilities, affectual sentiments, and modes of perception. One might consider, among other things, Turkey's nationalist education system, state-sanctioned historiography, compulsory male military service, patriarchy, controlled media, and urban practices, all of which seek to mobilize actors' spatial experiences, affective loyalties, and everyday practices. Any account, thus, of self-modification must recognize the premise that selves are partly constituted within multiple and even contradictory moral horizons.

In addressing musical apprenticeship as a slow process of guided modifications—sensory, somatic, affective, and ethical—in this chapter, I call attention to the *relational* aspects of altering the self. This relationality concerns both embodied and material engagement with things (i.e., the ney) as well as intersubjective relationships with other selves (i.e., one's master and fellow students). Central to this argument is the claim that both the ney and the master provide a model of self-change for the apprentice: the former in a poetic-metaphorical and material way, the latter through their person and work.

I start with a discussion of why the sound of the ney is perceived by many prospective students as a spiritual force charged with certain transforming powers. I then examine how the apprenticeship practice fosters new perceptual modifications in players through its varied methods and pedagogical mechanisms. Third, I elaborate how emulating esteemed figures or models is central to self-alteration, as exemplary masters incite in their talebes a desire to change, to become more like them.

My analysis of these issues draws upon autobiographical interviews with the generation of master musicians directly taught by Niyazi Sayın. Today they are themselves expert musicians and respected teachers in their own right. Their insights are complemented by my reflections on my own apprenticeship with Salih Bilgin, an experience that involved extensive participation in the daily life of his art studio in Istanbul and long listening sessions in the company of others.

THE REED AND POETIC IMAGINATION

An end-blown reed flute, the ney is the beloved breath instrument of what is today known as Ottoman-Turkish classical music, an urban art tradition that developed as an independent genre from the late sixteenth century on. In Istanbul, the ney's public life thrived in the devotional sites of Sufi orders, one of the key patrons of this music. Indeed, the majority of neyzens in the Ottoman capital city were either dervishes or sympathizers of various Sufi orders (most commonly of the Mevlevi order), and their lodges (*tekkes*) offered primary sites for ney teaching. Although this spatial connection was broken in 1925, when the Turkish Republic closed down the tekkes, the ney's intimate bond with Sufism has been influential in shaping both the communal meanings attributed to it (the "sacred" ney) and its methods of teaching, grounded in the learning relationship between hoca and talebe.

Although the ney was gradually rehabilitated by the late 1970s (Şenay 2020), the revitalization of Sufi music in both the Turkish and the global music industries in the early 2000s and the popularization of selective images of Sufism (including the ney) in the hands of state and private actors in Turkey have enabled the ney to reach ever larger groups of audiences and learners. Today, ney lessons are offered at private workshops, conservatories, religious associations, and council-sponsored adult education centers scattered around the Istanbul metropolitan area. The learners attending these pedagogical sites are heterogenous, their profiles crossing gender and class lines. While no single narrative captures the motivations of novices in taking up ney learning, those who pursue this practice for devotional purposes especially stand out. This is not surprising, given the ney's sonic identity as the Sufi sound par excellence, a reference that makes it heard by many as an "Islamically appropriate" instrument. Many devout learners told me that the ney's voice helps "draw oneself closer to God." Others likened the reed's thin, vertical shape to *alif*, the first letter of the Arabic alphabet and a visual symbol of the oneness of God. If for some learners this musical practice carries overtly religious meaning, such a perception is not necessarily shared by more "secular" Muslims who pursue this artistic training for their own purposes. In a nutshell, this broadly Muslim practice may be simultaneously meaningful as a pursuit of piety for some players and an act of aesthetic enskillment for others.

At studio Hezarfen—where I took group lessons between 2012 and 2015 and less regularly in 2016, 2017, and 2018—each week more than eighty people came from different parts of the city to learn the ney. Roughly half of them had been learning from Salih Hoca for many years, among them university students and people with various professional jobs. Women made up one-third of the students. When new pupils were asked by Salih Hoca why they wanted to learn the ney, many intuited that the ney itself has "transformative" (*dönüştürücü*) powers, promising to enable them to live a more spiritual life however understood.

Where did such preknowledge about the reed flute's transformative powers come from? What caused novices to hear and comprehend the ney as a sonic entity conducive to an alteration of oneself?

Let me answer these questions by way of a story:

> Ascending to the presence of Allah, the Prophet Muhammed was emotionally overcome by a single drop from the ocean of secrets entrusted to him. Despite God's instruction to discretion, he had to speak to someone. He told them to the saintly Ali, his son-in-law, warning him in turn not to reveal this secret to anyone. But Ali, too, felt crushed by the weight of the secret. In desperation, he traveled out into the desert, and coming upon a well, he revealed to it the beauty of what he had been told. The very same excitement came upon the well. Struggling to contain the secret, it overflowed, and in the water that it poured upon the earth, a reedbed began to grow.
>
> One day, the Prophet Muhammed was passing by the well and heard the divine secret that he had shared with saintly Ali. When he looked up, he saw the reeds swaying in the wind, whispering the Word of God.[2]

This tale, narrated in the literary sources of Sufism, is both typical of Sufi narratives and rather extraordinary. It is typical because, like most Sufi tales, it constructs and communicates nonnormative meaning about Islam through metaphor and paradox. In it, we hear of a great secret, which is never revealed. All we have is the sound of the reed. It is precisely the narrative's subterfuge in deferring the exposure of the secret that allows the story to perform its extraordinary work. The story tells us that there is a Divine secret, even as it refuses to authorize or reveal it. The Unseen and the Unheard (the secret of God) remains unnarratable and apparently unknowable, undermining illusions that God's mystery can be "comprehended" or, worse, possessed and confined. It is only in listening to the sound of the reed that we might sense the mystery of the divine truth for ourselves.

For those with (en)skilled ears to listen, the secret sounded out by the reed can be discerned in other examples of Sufi prose and poetry. The reed flute's message is most forcefully sealed and revealed in Sufi mystic Celaleddin Rumi's *Mesnevi-ya Ma'navi* (Doublets of meaning), famously described as the "Qur'an in the Persian tongue." In Rumi's opening couplets in this twenty-six-thousand-verse work, just as the reed is now parted from its reedbed, so the human soul is separated from the Divine: each yearns for reunification. Rumi continues his sly analogy between the reed-ney and the human-ney in different ways too. "To become empty inside like the ney," he says, "is the only way to become complete" (Çetinkaya 2019, 1982). At other times, he foregrounds the divine neyzen, whose breath gives life to the ney/human: "Without the influx of the *nafas ar-rahman*, the 'Breath of the Merciful,' human beings cannot act, speak, or think, just as the flute cannot reveal its secrets unless the musician breathes into it" (Schimmel 2005, 13).

In the most striking of his poetic images, Rumi immortalizes the reed flute as *insan-ı kâmil*, literally the "complete human" or "perfect human," who has attained divine self-knowledge—or in the words of Seyyed Hossein Nasr, "reflects [God's] Names and Qualities" (2007, 21). Concerned with the transformative potential of the human self, Sufi mystic Ibn Arabi's concept of the "perfect human" suggests that "all human beings are potentially perfectable or complete-able" (Ahmed 2016, 79). The perfect human is really the perfected human. But only by proceeding through a dedicated spiritual discipline can a person attain perfection. In the end, the reed becomes a "perfect human" only by way of alteration. First, it is plucked out of its reedbed. Then it is hollowed out and made straight through fire. Finally, its body is pierced with holes. In the same way, then, alteration is the only way for the human being to *become a ney*.

This deep reservoir of metaphorical meanings with which Sufi poetry constitutes the ney does not create mere symbolic discourse about the instrument. What interests me about these images are the impulses they charge. I suggest that this ensemble of poetic meanings incites people to imagine the ney as filled with "transformative" powers, predisposing learners to become candidates for the ney's work. According to Gaston Bachelard (1983), the efficacy of these metaphors lies in the way they activate the imagination by offering a tangible or "concrete" model of change for many ney enthusiasts so that one may "become a ney."

In the same way, by changing one's way of experiencing the material world, Sufi poetry can act as a powerful force in the prompting of the imagination, a means for "launch[ing] out toward a new life" (Bachelard 1983, 3). Indeed, even though Bachelard's main concern is understanding how our position in the world occurs through our relationship with nature's core elements (fire, water, air, earth), he is also interested in "poetic revery." He focuses attention on poets, describing their making of poetic images as "microscopic phenomenology." Bachelard warns against studying poetic images as "things," insisting that images are "lived" and "experienced" and inviting us to seize their "specific reality" (xix). When Rumi says "Listen to the reed and the tale it tells / How it sings of separation" (trans. Helminski 1981, 19–20), he gives us a powerful poetic image to dwell within as he makes us hear the reed in a new way.

Equally efficaciously, the *material* features of the reed also feed into many novices' perceptions about the ney's transformative powers and the sensual relationship they develop with it. My informants often described the ney as a conduit that provides access to one's interiority, an "image" that arises from the somatic union between breath and the neyzen's body in its playing. As the key technology of its sound making, the breath joins the reed with the neyzen's lips, making the ney feel like an "extension of the player's body," as one friend put it. Working on one's breath carries a dual meaning, entailing the act of both "disciplining the *nefes*" (breath) and "disciplining the *nefs*" (self)—a connection that already semantically exists in the Arabic language. The breath/reed allows the neyzen to refine them both. "The ney is like water," said one of my neyzen informants. "It is pure and purifies you" (Temizdir ve temizler). For ney musicians, the sound one obtains from the ney is not separate from the "sound" one attains in life: the ney-sound is a revelation of both a musical and an ethical self. What more powerful expression of this meaning than in my teacher's spoken words? "We should aim to get a good sound from this ney [pointing at his own body] so that this ney [the instrument-ney] also sounds good. Achieving a beautiful sound is a precious thing. This is because there is a real neyzen who blows into this ney [human], a neyzen who plays us. 'I breathed life into you, and now you breathe life into the things I said,' says that neyzen to us." These words invite us to think about sound as a developable means, as the master's analogy entangles the skilled actions of refining one's ney-sound and one's self-sound, making this task the target of conscious transformation. Nevertheless, questions remain: How does one get a good sound from the ney/life? And how does musical apprenticeship prepare one for this goal? It is to these questions that I turn next.

NEW CAPACITIES OF HEARING, LISTENING, AND BEING

Embodied participation in the ney pedagogy generates vital transformative effects on the self on a number of levels. Skilled learning demands, in the first place, a reworking of existing bodily habits and aural capacities already acquired in living. A key perceptual modification apprentices must go through is the cultivation of a new kind of hearing fit for the sonic aesthetics of Ottoman-Turkish music.

Because this music system follows the melodic principle of *makam* (musical mode), it requires the development of a profound aural acuity to discern the makam in which the melody is set as well as to know the affective atmosphere and feeling of each makam. Around sixty to seventy makams are played today, each with its own compositional rules, scales, accidental notes, and melodic features. Skillful hearing also involves mastery in hearing the microtones that make up the tonal spectrum of this musical art, as well as the task of bringing forth the sonic "place" of a note effectively while satisfying the tonal demands of the larger form, the makam. This is no straightforward undertaking, as many microtonal pitch inflections are not captured by the notation system. As I have discussed elsewhere (Şenay 2022), this ambiguity in knowing the "right" note is a valued feature of ney artistry. It also means that the only way to learn the pitch of a note is to hear it directly from one's master, a condition that assigns a pedagogical authority to learning through the hoca-talebe dyad. Over time, by way of altering learners' pre-hearing and presentiments, musical apprenticeship guides novices into perceiving sonic entities in a new light, simultaneously sponsoring a new capacity to be affected by them.

Another perceptual modification that the pedagogy demands from learners is an attentiveness to the ney sound itself as opposed to its playing of a melody. The quality of the sound one obtains from the ney, a breath instrument, is a core element of its mastery. Not only should one develop a full sound from the reed, but a certain texture with just the right amount of breath in it is to be produced. To achieve this, learners must resist the urge to play a melody and practice a single note only. Not everyone can endure this arduous task, and dropping out is not uncommon among novices. One must attend to sound articulation as something to be perfected rather than a means for melodic execution. In other words, one must value the means over the ends and grasp that a good action has itself as its own end.

Alongside these new aural capacities, the accretions of change enabled by musical training also involve what we might call ethical modifications. Insofar as ethics is deeply embedded in our ordinary lives (Lambek 2010)—including in our speech acts, modes of perception, ways of living, and relations with other selves—it is the most fulsome term to capture the "aspect" of the self being altered here. My informants acknowledged unanimously that it is in the reshaping of their moral selves that the transformative efficacy of the learning process was most powerfully felt by them.

What are the pedagogical mechanisms that create the conditions of such a transformative experience? While sitting side by side with one's hoca and watching and copying their skilled actions form the primary mechanism of learning, the actual time spent with one's teacher does not consist in playing only. More learning takes place through talebes' immersion in long hours of companionable speech, an event known as *sohbet* (in the first instance, conversation). An essentially Sufi disciplinary practice with a long trajectory in Islam (Silverstein 2008), sohbet has a vital pedagogical, affective, and ethical force in ney learning, so much so that "the ney cannot be learned without sohbet," as one ney master tells me. Why this particular stress on listening? The firsthand accounts of those masters who had been exposed to sohbet give us the best clues. Below, Neyzen Sadrettin Özçimi (1955–), taught by Sayın, recounts how his lessons happened in sohbet:

> We used to gather once a week on Wednesdays around eight o'clock, and we would continue way into 4 or 5 a.m. of the following day. We were there to play the ney with our hoca, right? But believe me, the time spent playing the ney in that six- to seven-hour lesson would hardly make half an hour. Apart from that, there was always sohbet. There was sohbet about Sufism, about music. Hoca passed on many things to us about his own teacher, about the great musicians of his time, and about the Sufi elders whom he knew from his own years of growing up in Üsküdar. We obtained a lot of criteria from those sohbets, humanistic criteria.... Learning was not just about playing. A talebe should try to learn not only the actual art from their hoca but the spiritual and ethical dimensions of that art as well.

Similarly, Neyzen Bülent Özbek (1959–), who worked with Sayın in the 1970s at his Istanbul home, reports that lessons involved a wide range of activities, including photography, cooking, repairing old objects, working on the lathe machine, and doing craftwork. "I can't remember taking my ney out of its bag in the first six months of lessons," Özbek says, reflecting on "nonplaying" as a core feature of the pedagogy he was exposed to: "And we always had sohbet. Much later I understood that I was learning the ney all that time.... I learned it by listening to Hoca, not by playing. This is what I tell my own students now, that the ney is not like other instruments. You teach it through words." It is correct to say that in my group lessons I, too, learned the ney by listening to my teacher's sohbets. Salih Hoca had been exposed to this Sufi pedagogy not only through his own sohbet lessons with Sayın but also through his long attendance at the sohbet gatherings of the Cerrahi and Şabani orders. The discipleship relationship that he had formed with a Sufi guide in the earlier years of his life had also been formative in his own self-formation. Well versed in sohbet himself, he skillfully fused his musical instructions with poetic speech, fostering a way of learning/knowing music by bringing it into a mutually affecting relationship with Sufi theology and everyday life. The discursive tools that allowed such interlocking relationships were his metaphors. Like poetry, his spoken language reawakened and created poetic images, constantly expanding learners' way of seeing and hearing the world.

Salih Hoca's speech act quoted earlier illustrates the metaphoricity and analogous reasoning characterizing his language of pedagogy. Metaphors and analogies do not just transfer meaning but are devices of meaning making. His analogous language facilitated a way of sensing one thing (i.e., the human-ney) in the image of another (i.e., the instrument-ney), enabling new perceptions of both (the body is an empty flute in the hands of the Divine). The perceptual modification that the language affords occurs not only in what we see but in *how* we see.

Yet there is much more to sohbet than receiving its referential content. Poetic speech can also generate certain emotions in listening selves, something significant in its own right. William Kirkwood draws attention to this: "If a narrative succeeds in evoking a certain mood or state of awareness, sometimes it is the resulting feeling, not a conceptual message, which is to be valued and cultivated" (1983, 66). In this light, certain affective states (e.g., equanimity, awe, devotion) "are not just the means, but the ends of spiritual discipline" (66). Charles Hirschkind's exploration of sermon listening in Cairo illustrates this point, too, that the "ethical affect" invoked by listening is an action in and of itself (2006, 90). The same applies to sohbet audition. The affective responses (patience, humility, discernment, surrender) it generates for those who possess ears to hear are the conditions for the neyzens' ethical modifications.

In all this, receiving knowledge through listening carries prime importance. This is in keeping with the great authority that the oral (and aural) transmission of knowledge occupies in methods of Islamic instruction, which, as Brinkley Messick (1993, 92) points out, "finds a model both in the initial transmission of the Qur'an and in its subsequent recitational use in ritual." Audition establishes the embodied, cognitive, and affective conditions of self-alteration essential for becoming a neyzen. How well one listens comes to index the whole transformation of a student, inseparable from modes of comportment, etiquette, and manners, all of which have an ethical import. Learning how to comport one's body, how to sit, how to walk, how to shape an utterance, how much to talk, and how to choose one's words are all part of the "listening" assemblage. If "İrşad [guidance] happens through the ear," as my teacher would often tell us, the artistic-ethical shaping of the learner, too, happens through the ear. The ear is the royal route to self-alteration.

APPRENTICESHIP BEYOND MUSIC

A further vital dimension of the learning experience involved its facilitation of firsthand exposure to a repertoire of practices other than music. Teaching expanded well into select places in the city. Visiting trade shops in Istanbul's old neighborhoods or the tombs of the dead members of the artist lineage, wandering around secondhand markets, and excursions to the city's Muslim places were part of the lessons. Attendance in such place-making activities fostered in students an embodied know-how about where to find a certain object, craftwork, or a certain food in the urban jungle of Istanbul; about how to discern the value of that thing; and about how to appreciate the labor invested in its making. Students were encouraged to constitute and use the city as a workshop, where purchasing the right goods for the right purposes was integral to developing artistic mastery. "From Hoca, I learned how to spend money and what to spend it on," remarked one of my fellow talebes, commenting on how he had become educated to value artisanal and craft skills.

The transformations fostered in becoming a neyzen involved, in another way, both new competencies and a new attitude toward Istanbul's urban environment.

In being visited, certain places in the city were deliberately brought to the attention of students, disclosed as something to be noticed and inhabited. A friend with whom I shared the evening ferry back home after our lessons told me that before coming to the school, she had always been oblivious to the calligraphic inscriptions scattered around Istanbul's urban landscape. Nor had she had any interest in visiting Sufi places. "I went to Bursa the other weekend and didn't leave a single tomb, a single *tekke* unvisited there," she remarked, pointing out how her sensory radar had changed. The altering of the self involves, then, a new attentiveness toward places, a capacity to reconstitute their significance and to shape the meanings of such places for oneself. As Christopher Houston says, the city "emerges for the perceiver in his or her acts of educated and embodied engagement with it, including, of course, with other beings, both human and non-human" (2015, 9). Thus, to reckon with the urban environment in new ways—for example, to perceive it against the grain of its concrete shaping by neoliberal capitalism—can be seen as an ethical modification that neyzens in the making went through.

Gender should also be considered here, given that the majority of talebes taking up apprenticeship are young men. (This male dominance was even more prominent among previous generations of learners.) The new ethical sensibilities fostered by the pedagogy involved a more expansive understanding of masculinity and a valuing of competencies that are often associated with women's work in Turkey. Take cooking, for example. "No matter whether you are a man or a woman, a neyzen should know how to cook," my teacher would instruct us. And hardly a day passed that he did not cook with and for his talebes, an expression of his care for them. Occasions of commensality also articulated to important dates in the Islamic calendar, as the hospitality would extend to the larger community of practice. For the majority of my male friends, the kitchen of the ney school was where they gained their first proper exposure to cooking, a significant mode of alteration in a patriarchal society.

The efficacy and long-term effects of these experiences of change become more pertinent if we consider that all the activities mentioned here, from sohbet to cooking to city visitations, were part of Salih Hoca's own learning under Sayın. Thus, even if the temporality of my fieldwork did not match neatly with the span of changes students go through in ney education, the relationship between my teacher's own student experience and his current teaching practice is living "proof" concerning the permanence of the skilled capacities he had acquired. Further, given that it was Sayın who provided my teacher with a "concrete" model of these capacities, a method by which they might be attained, and demonstrations about why they are valuable, there is something to be investigated here about what goes on within the hoca-talebe dyad and the transformative role that masters play in their students' trajectories of becoming.

MASTERS AS MODELS

In *An Anthropology of Ethics*, James Faubion makes an important observation about how individual actors come to occupy their ethical subject positions, a process he calls "ethical becoming." Placing a strong emphasis on pedagogy, Faubion argues that pedagogues do more than set out normative rules to be followed by others. Because they come to inhabit and maintain their subject positions so well, he says, they are able to fulfill the role of an *exemplar* of how to be and how to live (2011, 51–52).

This point is instructive for thinking about the pedagogical and affective workings of hoca-talebe intersubjectivity. What came out strongly in my autobiographical interviews with older lineage musicians is that it is in the act of surrendering to the authority of one's master—a kind of self-annihilation, so to speak—that the self is changed, gently but forcefully. To give oneself up to the hands of a master and to commit one's loyalty and obedience to them requires painstaking humility. But what makes the talebe capable of cultivating such intense behavior is the central role that the master occupies in their life as an exemplar, an existential guide, and a model-self for emulation. Exemplary masters inspire their students beyond their artistic excellence; they are capable of inciting in their talebes a desire to change, to become more like "them."

The admiration that talebes felt for their masters' virtuous qualities was often the prevailing mood of my conversations with them. A fellow talebe tells me how "listening to Salih Hoca speak, the way he chooses his words" has changed him. "Imagine for a moment that I'm the one sitting in Hoca's chair, addressing the class using exactly the same words," he says. "Would it still be the same sohbet?" What makes the teacher's spoken words have so much effect on him, he explains, is the "language of disposition" (*hâl dili*) that he speaks with. For him, words don't just come out of the teacher's mouth; they are "sediments" of his experiential knowledge.

I ask my teacher how he had been taught by Sayın. "Hoca taught us how to become a person, a complete person," he responds. "Learning how a neyzen's home should look like, what interests a neyzen should develop, and which activities a neyzen should take pleasure in were all part of learning," he says. He then recalls the "things" they did together as part of their lessons: learning how to sew, how to cook, how to make prayer beads, how to grow flowers, how to repair broken objects, how to make the art of water marbling (*ebru*), where to find the best *ebru* paint, and how much paint to buy. "He would want us to know where to eat the best *kurufasulye* [baked beans] or where to find the best coffee," he adds.

Neyzen Ömer Erdoğdular (1949–) underscores how the virtues of Sayın's generosity, hospitality, and kindness established him as a model to emulate: "When we used to go to his house, we were not even allowed to take a box of *lokum* [Turkish delight] with us. 'You will come empty-handed,' we would be told. It's that generosity that makes up the sound of Niyazi Sayın's ney," he remarks. Neyzen Özbek, too, draws attention to his teacher's humility when he says, "Even the way Hoca walks on the stage is a source of morals for us. He enters the stage in complete humility [*tevazu*]. His body says to his audience, 'I take you seriously' [*Bir muhatabım var*]." Now ninety-four years old, Sayın has been called *insan-ı kâmil* (a perfect human), *kutb-ı nâyi* (the musical-spiritual axis of his age), and *hezarfen* (a master of a thousand arts). These titles of recognition collectively bestowed upon him confirm that there is more to his artistry than musical excellence, as they acknowledge his mastery of the art of living (Şenay and Houston 2022).

These reflective comments reveal that in their comportment, demeanor, talk, and actions, masters are seen as worthy of emulation, enticing an inclination (*meyil*) for change. The motivating emotion that drives this inclination is admiration. Admiration of an exemplar, according to Linda Zagzebski, "leads to an imaginative ideal of oneself, which in turn produces emulation of the exemplar's motives and acts" (2017, 138). This imaginative ideal of oneself is what the mentor discloses, providing the talebe with a concrete image of how a self could be or what a self could become, reflecting back a possible future self or an alternative version of oneself. This is to suggest not a total replication of that person's actions and character traits but a wanting to be "the kind of person who would be capable of doing" something as virtuous as the exemplary person's acts in a similar situation (20). The exemplar can foster an "orientation" (Hojer and Bandak 2015, 3) and a new way of perceiving a situation, acting as a "counterfactual model" in the lives of talebes.

The shared presence of the hoca-talebe is an essential condition for emulation. Masters emphasize this repeatedly: "If you really wish to learn from a *mürebbi* [teacher] and spend a lot of time with that person, their smell permeates in you [*o kişinin kokusu sana siner*]." "The talebe must see her hoca, how they dress, what shoes they wear, how they live in their house." "Taking a lesson isn't all that important, but being in the presence of your hoca, sitting side by side with them, is." The underlining idea here is that personal qualities pass from person to person. In his work on the sohbet practice of another Istanbul-based Sufi order, Brian Silverstein makes a vital observation regarding this point. He notes that "the kinds of relationships formed in the act of oral transmission of texts and interpretations are considered liable to constitute a morally structured disposition in the devotee and are the object of careful cultivation through what I propose to call disciplines of presence" (2008, 135). The apprenticeship pedagogy can, too, be described as a "discipline of presence," as it fosters the intersubjective and affective conditions for the talebe to grow in her capacity to be influenced by the hoca—a self already altered—and to cultivate new ways of being and acting in the world.

CONCLUSION

Let me bring this chapter to a conclusion by refocusing on the questions of what the experience of alteration entails here and what the "self" is that is changing.

The slow process of change I have described gives us a sense of a "human-scale" alteration of the self, made possible by a series of phenomenological modifications (sensory, somatic, affective, and ethical) that the apprenticeship practice affords. Although not everyone takes up ney learning with an initial aim of self-alteration, for the dedicated practitioners with whom I worked, extended exposure to the learning practice is a deeply transformative experience, allowing new skilled-based capacities and new ways of attending to the world/self. These experiences are enabled by a concatenation of pedagogical elements, including the skilled acts of listening, imitation, and receiving knowledge through the ear, as well as learning through embodied participation in sohbet and in a wide range of nonmusical activities, all of which take place within the sociality of the hoca-talebe dyad. While I have approached the process of apprenticeship as the main technique through which this guided self-alteration happens, I have also sought to establish that, through the rich poetic images it reawakens of the ney, Sufi narratives act as a vital *affordance* of alteration by making the ney attractive or even seductive for many novices.

In another sense, this facilitated self-alteration is about personal change. While the phenomenal or perceived world changes for the neyzen, the world does not need to change for the individual to alter (unlike, say, in Houston's discussion in this volume of revolutionary activism). To be sure, the transformation of the self has always been an explicit focus of Sufi disciplinary practices, just as it has been in many other religious traditions (Shulman and Stroumsa 2002). The textual accounts of Sufism have indicated that the "self" in need of change is the *nafs*, a concept that carries a multitude of related meanings, including "ego," "lower self," and "the inferior aspect of the human psycho-physiological constitution," as Sara Sviri defines it (2002, 196). The idea here is that the *nafs* must be purified and tamed, enabling an alteration of the self from its "lowly instinctual nature to the ultimate state of subsistence in God" (196). Although the disciplining of *nafs* also finds explicit reference within the community of musical practice I have examined here, the ethnographic analysis presents us with an understanding of self-alteration that is not limited to the transforming of the psyche, egoist sentiments, or human desires. Transformation concerns here the perceiving and acting subject, including ways of being, living, and relating to other selves (including the city).

Further, this personal-level change transcends individual selves. As the snapshots from lessons illustrate, this learning activity is done in the company of and with others. The communal nature of the activities that learners come to participate in is remarkable. Thus, even if the hoca-talebe dyad is the core intersubjective relation in which selves are altered, social exchange with the community of practice and becoming a legitimate member of it are other enablers of change (Lave and Wenger 1991). Communities of practice extend both forward and backward in time as they connect the living to dead masters. By becoming a member of a neyzen lineage and by identifying their selves with a particular artist-kin group, ney players reimagine themselves as alternative communal selves.

The process of change delineated here follows a cumulative path, where the reconstruction of the self does not need to involve a discontinuity with the past. Skilled practitioners do not come to think of their changing selves along the lines of a radically different "old" and "new" self, a distinction that we often find in illness narratives, for example, whereby a sudden bodily change leads to a recognition of oneself in a totally new way (Frank 1993). There is a more continuous temporality at work that feeds into the alteration of the neyzen, a process never finished. Even the greatest master never ceases to be a talebe.

During my interview with him, Neyzen Sayın said to me, "I am eighty-seven years old now, but I am still learning. I am a talebe. 'From cradle to grave' [*beşikten mezara*], says our Prophet. I will continue to learn from cradle to grave."

In short, self-alteration through Sufi music pedagogy is processual, layered through time and unfolding in slow temporality. The analytical task of understanding the temporality of change also requires thinking about subject constitution as articulating—complementing or contradicting—existing perceptual capacities and ethical dispositions. This is why Husserlian phenomenology is particularly helpful for us given its particular stress on the temporal dimension of perception. As Dermot Moran asserts, "All perception takes place under a number of horizons which are implicit structural aspects of our original experience itself. . . . Perception is a temporal process; it does not take place wholly in the present but is oriented towards future experiences and at the same time is an experience of enduring or continuing from past experiences" (2000, 162). Accounting for self-alteration requires, then, recognizing multiple processes and practices that a self continues to be exposed to through time. This poses a challenge for anthropological fieldwork. Given that, at any one time, field research can grasp only a portion of a person's development or change, there are temporal constraints in studying the unfolding and efficacy of change in the longer term of someone's life. To avoid this constraint, I have moved back and forth between different hoca-talebe relationships and considered the subject positions of both actors.

This constraint can be overcome in another way—through submitting oneself as an ethnographer to the apprenticeship process. Self-alteration through musical apprenticeship not only develops over time and requires a long time, but it also needs learning from an "example." The alteration of the self cannot take place in any way but relationally. Apprenticeship under a master has a direct bearing on one's becoming not only because it provides the techniques of the self that configure the musical discipline as a means of artistic-ethical cultivation but also because it enables one to grow in one's capacity to be influenced by the other who has already been altered, a "sound" that has already been refined. Both exemplary masters and exemplary neys set out a model for how to "sound out well" in art and life, offering possibilities of self-alteration for those who engage with them.

NOTES

1. Here I use the terms *person, self,* and *subject* interchangeably.
2. This is the version of this tale that I heard from my own teacher. For a slightly different version of it, see Schimmel (2005, 13).

REFERENCES

Ahmed, Shahab. 2016. *What Is Islam? The Importance of Being Islamic*. Princeton, N.J.: Princeton University Press.
Bachelard, Gaston. 1983. *Water and Dreams: An Essay on the Imagination of Matter*. Translated by Edith R. Farrell. Dallas: Pegasus Foundation, Dallas Institute of Humanities and Culture.
Çetinkaya, Yalçın. 2019. "Mevlevî Düşüncesinde Ney ve İnsân-ı Kâmil Sembolizmi." *Rast Müzikoloji Dergisi* 7 (1): 1979–1992.
Duranti, Alessandro. 2009. "The Relevance of Husserl's Theory to Language Socialization." *Journal of Linguistic Anthropology* 19 (2): 205–226.
Faubion, James. 2011. *An Anthropology of Ethics*. Cambridge: Cambridge University Press.
Frank, Arthur W. 1993. "The Rhetoric of Self-Change: Illness Experience as Narrative." *Sociological Quarterly* 34 (1): 39–52.
Helminski, Kabir. 1981. *The Ruins of the Heart: Selected Lyric Poetry of Jelaluddin Rumi*. Putney, Vt.: Threshold Books.
Hirschkind, Charles. 2006. *The Ethical Soundscape: Cassette Sermons and Islamic Counterpublics*. New York: Columbia University Press.
Hojer, Lars, and Andreas Bandak. 2015. "Introduction: The Power of Example." *Journal of the Royal Anthropological Institute* 21 (S1): 1–17.
Houston, Christopher. 2015. "Politicizing Place Perceptions: A Phenomenology of Urban Activism in Istanbul." *Journal of the Royal Anthropological Institute* 21 (4): 720–738.
Husserl, Edmund. 1970. *Logical Investigations*. Atlantic Highlands, N.J.: Humanities Press.
Kirkwood, William G. 1983. "Storytelling and Self-Confrontation: Parables as Communication Strategies." *Quarterly Journal of Speech* 69 (1): 58–74.
Kondo, Dorinne K. 1990. *Crafting Selves: Power, Gender, and Discourses of Identity in a Japanese Workplace*. Chicago: Chicago University Press.
Lambek, Michael. 2010. "Towards an Ethics of the Act." In *Ordinary Ethics: Anthropology, Language, and Action*, edited by Michael Lambek, 1–63. New York: Fordham University Press.
Lave, Jean, and Etienne Wenger. 1991. *Situated Learning: Legitimate Peripheral Participation*. Cambridge: Cambridge University Press.
Marchand, Trevor. 2008. "Muscles, Morals and Mind: Craft Apprenticeship and the Formation of Person." *British Journal of Educational Studies* 56 (3): 245–271.
Messick, Brinkley. 1993. *The Calligraphic State: Textual Domination and History in a Muslim Society*. Berkeley: University of California Press.
Moran, Dermot. 2000. *Introduction to Phenomenology*. London: Routledge.
Nasr, Seyyed Hossein. 2007. *The Garden of Truth: The Vision and Promise of Sufism, Islam's Mystical Tradition*. New York: HarperCollins.
Schimmel, Annemarie. 2005. "The Role of Music in Islamic Mysticism." In *Sufism, Music and Society in Turkey and the Middle East*, edited by Anders Hammarlund, Tord Olsson, and Elisabeth Özdalga, 8–17. Istanbul: Swedish Research Institute.
Şenay, Banu. 2020. *Musical Ethics and Islam: The Art of Playing the Ney*. Urbana: University of Illinois Press.

———. 2022. "The Pleasures of Ambiguity: Pedagogy and Apprenticeship in an Istanbul Music School." *Journal of the Royal Anthropological Institute*, n.s., 28 (June): 632–650.

Şenay, Banu, and Christopher Houston. 2022. "Musical Intimacy, Model Citizenship, and Sufism in the Life of Niyazi Sayın." *International Journal of Middle East Studies* 54 (2): 225–242.

Shulman, David, and Guy G. Stroumsa, eds. 2002. *Self and Self-Transformation in the History of Religions*. Oxford: Oxford University Press.

Silverstein, Brian. 2008. "Disciplines of Presence in Modern Turkey: Discourse, Companionship, and the Mass Mediation of Islamic Practice." *Cultural Anthropology* 23 (1): 118–153.

Sviri, Sara. 2002. "The Self and Its Transformation in Sufism." In Shulman and Stroumsa, *Self and Self-Transformation*, 195–215.

Yen, Yuehping. 2005. *Calligraphy and Power in Contemporary Chinese Society*. London: Routledge.

Zagzebski, Linda. 2017. *Exemplarist Moral Theory*. Oxford: Oxford University Press.

2 · REIMAGINING SELF AND SELF-ALTERATION IN CONTEMPORARY NEW AGE, PAGAN, AND NEOSHAMANIC SPIRITUALITIES

KATHRYN ROUNTREE

Three decades ago, Paul Heelas (1991) coined the phrase *self-religion*. The term was quickly picked up and developed in various ways by other scholars (e.g., Hanegraaff 1996, 2002; York 1995; York 2001; Barker 1999; Clarke 2006) to characterize a plethora of new forms of spirituality that emerged out of the 1960s and 1970s counterculture dedicated to the pursuit of self-understanding, self-exploration, self-growth, self-help, self-healing, and self-empowerment.[1] Because of the historical moment in which this many-stranded phenomenon came to flourish and the highly eclectic nature of practitioners' beliefs and practices, it is perhaps understandable to construe this drive for self-development and personal maximization as a late modern / early postmodern religious expression related to the policy regimes of neoliberal capitalism. New Age discourses and practices have been referred to as "consumer religion/spirituality" (Heelas 2008, 169; Husemann and Eckhardt 2019), a "spiritual marketplace" or "supermarket" (Heelas and Woodhead 2005, 1; Redden 2016, 231), and the "commodified production of self-actualisation" (Rindfleish 2005, 343). Practitioners themselves, on the other hand, described their beliefs and activities as "alternative": a response to their alienation from and a critique of powerful religious and other cultural institutions that denied their right to a self-determined religiosity and failed to reflect their beliefs, values, concerns, or frequently—given that women predominated in many of the movements—gender.

Yet the trope of the "self-made man"—and it invariably was "man"—emerged before neoliberalism entered common usage in the 1970s and 1980s. It is an older, widely endorsed trope, at least in the modern West, where individuality has been most fervently celebrated (Seigel 2005, 3). *Self-making* refers to the taking of personal responsibility for making one's way and achieving one's goals in the world despite unpromising personal circumstances. Henry Clay used the term in 1842 in the U.S. Senate to describe individuals whose success lay with themselves—resulting from personal ambition, enterprise, and diligent hard work—rather than with outside conditions (Wyllie 1954). By the mid-1950s, the self-made man's "success" normally implied business success. In short, self-making and becoming "self-made" is not historically particular to the last half century, but it is in these years that demands and efforts to do so have undoubtedly ramped up.

Typically, public approval for self-making has been reserved mostly for social, economic, and political endeavors. In the field of religion, particularly Christianity, self-alteration tends not to be widely applauded unless, ironically, it takes a form of sel*fless*ness—contrition, repentance, meekness, humility, obedience, self-denial, or postponed self-gratification—none of which have much appealed to younger generations since the 1960s and 1970s.[2] The cultural aspirations of the "Me Generation" centered on self-realization, self-fulfillment, intellectual and spiritual enlightenment, and multiple forms of social, political, and other types of experimentation deemed narcissistic, hedonistic, selfish, or wrong by established centers of official power, particularly those of church and state.

This essay begins by looking at so-called self-religions, a term applied mostly to a diverse range of New Age spiritualities but sometimes also to other "alternative" paths, including contemporary Pagan movements and modern Western shamans or neoshamans (York 1995; York 2001; Possamaï 1999).[3] Modern Pagans are increasingly reconceptualizing the notion of the "self" in ways that take it beyond the bodily (human) relational, or reflective dimensions of individual being, a dominant vision of human being since the time of Descartes and Locke (Seigel 2005, 5). It is noteworthy that many who follow these paths, especially Pagans, have shunned the "New Age" designation, precisely because of its association with what they see as an unhealthy self-obsession.[4] Pagans point out that they are fundamentally earth centered, drawing inspiration from religions of the pre-Christian past, unlike New Agers, who emphasize a transcendent metaphysical reality and global awakening in the future (York 1995; Kelly 1992, 138).

In the second part of this chapter, my ethnographic focus is a group of modern Western shamans based mostly in Malta, a community of women I have been fortunate to come to know better in the past two years of intermittent lockdowns—despite living on the opposite side of the world—thanks to the increased use of Zoom and social networking platforms.[5] The group formed a decade ago following a series of workshops taught by three visiting shamans from the United Kingdom (one of whom was a Maltese woman). These three had studied with the Four Winds School of Shamanic Healing founded by Alberto Villoldo, who in turn had learned his shamanic techniques while living with Indigenous shamans in the Andes and Amazon,[6] and he now teaches them to westerners.[7] Around a third of the forty-four women in the group based in Malta are not Maltese by birth, and some live overseas (e.g., in Spain, Turkey, the United Kingdom, and Greece) and visit Malta occasionally.[8] The group comprises mostly professional (some now retired) women who have traveled, lived, and worked in many parts of the world and experienced a range of shamanic and other spiritual practices in such places as Peru, the United States, Scandinavia, Africa, India, Australia, Britain, and Ireland.

I originally joined this group in 2015 while undertaking ethnographic research on shamanism in Malta, and for the next five years, whenever in Malta, I shared their full moon rituals, attended by eight to fifteen people, held in members' homes, at a beach, or in the countryside adjacent to the Ħaġar Qim Neolithic temple (Rountree 2017, 2021). Between gatherings, group members interact via a private Facebook group created in 2014. This Facebook group helped me stay in touch with the members between trips to Malta.

During the COVID-19 pandemic, the group could not gather for rituals in one another's homes or outdoors. Despite this, and contrary to all our expectations, the group became closer during this period, and members frequently commented to this effect.[9] I illustrate below how relationships and interactions within the group—who refer to themselves as a tribe, sistren (group of spiritual sisters), and Medicine Circle—represent a microcosm of and are homologous to the vast meshwork of human and other-than-human relationships in which they see their lives embedded. While the group comprises only women and attracts like-minded women connected via friendship networks, their understanding of the collective Self is that it includes all beings, all individual selves, irrespective of their gender identities or lack of them.

RECONCEIVING SELF AND SELF-ALTERATION

The sistren posit—and more importantly experience—participation in a conscious, intersubjective, uppercase Self continuously co-constituted of and by all human and nonhuman, material and immaterial beings, including plant and animal spirits, ancestors and other spirit beings, guides, deities, and supernatural entities with no fleshly referents. This worldview replaces the all-too-familiar, static self/other dualism with an individual self / collective Self matrix of dynamic relationships characterized by openness, fluidity, mutuality, affinity, and constant change. This collective Self encompasses the consciousness of all individual selves and also preserves individuals' self-autonomy. Each individual's self-autonomy affects other selves and their self-autonomy. Within the ecology of selves (cf. Kohn 2013), all interconnect in a mutually influencing, ever-changing, collective consciousness of a collective Self. Humans are at neither the pinnacle nor the center of this ecosystem of multifarious beings: such an anthropocentric conceit is rejected. The individual self-alteration of any human or other-than-human being is connected with, impacts and is impacted upon, and causes and is caused by alterations in the collective Self. A discussion of personal "self-alteration" grounded in this worldview necessarily implicates also thinking about a larger, collective Self-alteration.

The notion of the individual human self as part of a collective whole is not novel, of course. Numerous thinkers and writers over the centuries have problematized individual selfhood in very different ways with very different agendas: Schopenhauer, Nietzsche, Marx, Durkheim, Heidegger, Foucault, and a great many others (Seigel 2005, 11–44). In 1891, philosopher and psychologist Alfred Fouillé wrote, "Nothing is so much singular as not to be multiple; nothing is so much my own that it is not also collective. . . . To the voice that says 'me, me,' the chorus responds 'we, we,' so that the law of the self's existence becomes the law of solidarity, of universal fraternity" (quoted in Seigel 2005, 514).[10] Others of Fouillé's contemporaries also emphasized the relational and highly fluid nature of the self, Théodule Ribot declaring that "the self only exists on condition of continually varying" (quoted in Seigel 2005, 514).[11] The sistren have come to their understandings of being-in-the-world in connection with other beings-in-the-world as a result of their deep love for—and phenomenological experiences of—inspirited nature and through their study of and affiliation with Indigenous shamanic cultures for whom the natural world is alive, sacred, and connected.

The ways in which the sistren came to see the world as they do, influenced by the worldviews of Indigenous shamans and in some cases by spending periods of time with them (though not as anthropologists), evoke the work of ethnographers whose research with Indigenous animist communities has led them to explore an anthropology beyond the human, a posthumanist approach that takes the discipline beyond the bounds of human selves and human relations and challenges human exceptionalism (Pyyhtinen and Tamminen 2011).[12] They include Nurit Bird-David's (1999) animism and relational epistemology among the Nayaka of South India, Eduardo Kohn's (2013) contention that selfhood is not exclusive to humans based on his work with the Runa of the Upper Amazon, Philippe Descola's (2009) work on the continuities and discontinuities between human and nonhuman selves among the Achuar of the Ecuadorian Amazon, and many others (e.g., Willerslev and Ulturgasheva 2012; Ingold 2006, 2011; Latour 2005; Hallowell 1960; Viveiros de Castro 1998; Haraway 2008).

Although obviously different from Indigenous animists in essential ways (for a start, they do not get the bulk of their food by hunting, fishing, trapping, herding, or gardening), the modern Western shamans I work with are, like Indigenous animists, "attentive to, and work towards making, relatedness" with other beings whose differences are absorbed into what Bird-David (1999, 73) calls "we-ness."[13] Their understanding of relationality with other beings, other selves, broadly resembles that of Indigenous animists from regions as diverse as Amazonia, Southeast Asia, and the circumpolar North, as summarized by Tim Ingold: "First, we are dealing here not with a way of believing *about* the world but with a condition of being *in* it. This could be described as a condition of being alive to the world, characterised by a heightened sensitivity and responsiveness, in perception and action, to an environment that is always in flux, never the same from one moment to the next. Animacy . . . is the dynamic, transformative potential of the entire field of relations within which beings of all kinds, more or less person-like or thing-like, continually and reciprocally bring one another into existence" (2006, 10).

As one of the sistren commented on a historical photograph of an Indigenous shaman posted on WhatsApp, "So much oneness. . . . Where does the human being and the landscape start? One. Living. Being. 🐚"

In the long anthropological tradition of being an ethnographer immersed in the community one is researching, I have also come to understand and experience the alteration of the personal self and collective Self in new ways. I quote Kohn (2013, 22): "As we learn to attend ethnographically to that which lies beyond the human, certain strange phenomena suddenly amplify, and in the process come to exemplify, some of the general properties of the world in which we live. . . . By methodologically privileging amplification over, say, comparison or reduction we can create a somewhat different anthropology, one that can help us understand how we might better live in a world we share with other kinds of lives." And I would add, "other kinds of selves." Before discussing further the sistren's ideas and experiences of the individual self, the collective Self, and their alteration, let us introduce other religious or spiritual paths that have been classified as self-religion, beginning with New Age spiritualities.

NEW AGE SPIRITUALITIES AND SELF-ALTERATION

Heelas locates the New Age as part of the "massive subjective turn of modern culture" (after Taylor 1991, 26), a turn he saw "very much bound up with the growth of subjective wellbeing culture, including wellbeing spirituality" (Heelas 2008, ix). New Age spiritualities are holistic, life-affirming, and on the whole, world-embracing (as opposed to world-rejecting). They integrate mind, body, and spirit; sacralize the body and subjective life; and emphasize lived spirituality. Their central ethic revolves around life, equality, and freedom, and their main thrust is toward practical application rather than doctrinal or textual adherence or declarations of faith (Heelas 2008).

Often known in its early days as the Human Potential movement, the New Age constituted a milieu that drew on a vast range of religious and secular sources from which individuals selected to create a personal path, each with different emphases and priorities. These included Buddhism, Hinduism, Sufism, Theosophy, Western esotericism, Indigenous religions, psychology and psychotherapy, meditation and creative visualization, the power of positive thinking, astrology, tarot and other forms of divination, clairvoyance and channeling, magic, belief in reincarnation, angels, spirit beings and other natural and supernatural entities, a love of nature, green values, environmentalism, the immanence of divinity within each person, and above all, healing of many kinds, especially alternative therapies, holistic healing, and self-healing.

Etic accounts of New Agers' purported self-interest frequently imply that their focus on "subjective well-being" means they are self-enclosed, solipsistic, and self-indulgent: in a word, selfish. Becoming "self-made" in a religious sense, it seems, is widely disapproved of or ridiculed, most vituperatively by certain scholars of religion (Lasch 1979). Ward (2006, 185) describes alternative spiritualities as "pampering to the need for 'good vibrations,'" presenting self-grooming as self-help and attracting those who are "sensation hungry." New Agers themselves frame their pursuits in terms of embracing personal responsibility, much in the mode of the archetypal self-made man or person. They emphasize the need to fix the self before fixing the world and in order to do so. This is summed up in the following: "Love yourself first, and everything else falls in line. You really have to love yourself to get anything done in this world" (Ball, n.d.).

New Age groups have always had a strongly religio-therapeutic strand running through their philosophies and practices. In several "alternative spirituality" Facebook groups I belong to, there are daily postings designed to encourage and assist self-development. Notably, though, these are geared as much toward self-acceptance as they are to self-alteration in the sense of self-improvement, providing affirmations along the lines of "You are great the way you are. You only need to wake up to the fact that you *are already* a perfect, eternal expression of Source / the Divine." Shirley MacLaine, self-professed "flint of New Age consciousness" and author of numerous books, refers to the "higher self" or soul as the "God force," saying, "We are that God force, we are perfect" (Easton 1987). Sometimes notions of self-improvement and the already perfect self are presented in the same breath: as I was drafting this paragraph, a posting to a Facebook group I belong to declared, "You are allowed to be both a Masterpiece and a Work in Progress simultaneously." Locating authority over the self within the self (instead of in an external self, such as a priest or church), locating the primary path to the sacred within the self (rather than a received doctrine or institution), and locating the agency to self-alter, self-heal, and self-transform within the individual self not only empower a self but also shift responsibility for the self to the self.

Nearly two decades after categorizing the New Age as self-religion, Heelas (2008, 3) doubts that New Age spiritualities are reducible to "an integral tool of capitalism," suggesting instead that they be seen as "spiritualities of life" that can be drawn on "to cultivate what it is to *be* alive.... Rather than the emphasis lying with the 'good life' of materialistic utilitarianism, the emphasis lies with the 'good life' of expressivistic humanism." "Fundamentally," Heelas says, "we are looking at a spirituality 'of' and 'for' *being* truly human" (17). A focus on one's inner spiritual life contributes to the cultivation of humanity, producing "people who can function with sensitivity and alertness as citizens of the whole world" (Nussbaum 1997, 8).

It is difficult to summarize the New Age except at a very high level of generality because of its multitudinous forms, the millions of mind-body-spirit activities run worldwide, and the fact that individuals create their own paths (Heelas 2008, 15). However, it is fair to say that New Age spiritualities characteristically begin with and work outward from the individual self, explicitly prioritizing the human self and human life. Other religious paths branded by scholars as self-religions include modern Paganisms, which do not, at least theoretically, elevate the value of the human self and human life over and above the lives of nonhuman selves. Although modern Paganisms are sometimes categorized under the umbrella of New Age spiritualities by outsiders and some scholars, Pagans themselves, including Pagan scholars, eschew such a categorization. Unlike followers of New Age spiritualities, Pagans claim their paths are nature based and earth centered, not human self–centered.

MODERN PAGANISM AND NEOSHAMANISM

Modern forms of Paganism began flourishing in the 1970s (although some, such as Druidry and Wicca, had earlier beginnings, and others claim ancient pre-Christian heritages), a decade or so before New Age movements, whose heyday was the 1980s. Unlike New Age movements, contemporary Western Paganisms—whose traditions include Wicca and eclectic witchcraft traditions, Druidry, heathenry, goddess spirituality, eclectic Paganism, neoshamanism, and a host of Native Faith movements (Rountree 2015)—have continued to proliferate and expand numerically in the twenty-first century.

I group modern Pagan and shamanic paths together here for the sake of economy and because although their interests, beliefs, and practices certainly overlap with those of the New Age (to a greater or lesser extent depending on the tradition and the individual), Paganism's core is a "this-worldly" orientation that values immanence over transcendence (York 1995, 136). The focus is this life in this body on this earth. While seeking inspiration from the beliefs and rituals of a variety of polytheistic traditions (e.g., Celtic, Nordic, Greek, Middle Eastern, Egyptian, Russian, etc.) and venerating a plethora of deities, all Pagans share a deep reverence for the natural world, the seasonal cycle (referred to as the Wheel of the Year), the animacy and connectedness of all life-forms, and the sacred cycles of birth, death, and regeneration experienced by all beings. In this respect, Pagans' and neoshamans' worldviews resemble those of Indigenous cultures worldwide (although, of course, Indigenous animisms are all culturally unique, as indeed are all polytheistic traditions, ancient and modern). Pagan author Starhawk says,

> To Pagans, all life is imbued with consciousness and all living beings are constantly communicating. The consciousness of a tree may be different from yours or mine; indeed, unless it is a very large and old tree, it may be less the consciousness of "this individual seedling oak" and more the consciousness of "oakness"—a group or collective sense of being.[14] But awareness, presence, is still there—in a tree, even in a rock or a mountain. . . . Pagan spirituality is centred in community. While many of our practices further personal growth and healing, our goals are centred not so much on individual salvation or enlightenment as on communal health and

balance ... where "community" includes the animals, plants, rocks, trees and waters that surround us, the broader human community around the globe, those who have come before us and those who will come after us. (Starhawk, NightMare, and the Reclaiming Collective 1997, 6–7)

Susan Greenwood (2020, 160) describes a shamanic worldview as perceiving all-that-is as a relational whole, where material and nonmaterial spirit dimensions are unified. Perception is expanded to "a form of panpsychism" (11) or "magical consciousness" where everything in the relational cosmos potentially has consciousness and "there is a reciprocity and correspondence between all things" (179). It is "the imagination that enables an opening of perception to a panpsychic worldview" (9), and the potential for this holistic mode of consciousness is panhuman.

The remainder of this chapter looks at how this relational worldview—or more properly, *world* (Kohn 2013, 10), which might be seen as the collective consciousness of a collective Self—operates in the context of social practices and is experienced as a phenomenological reality among the shaman sistren I introduced above.

THE SISTREN AND SELF-ALTERATION

In early 2020, the group's full moon rituals, previously held outdoors or in a member's home, necessarily moved online. Additional meetings and workshops were introduced, and a WhatsApp group with seventeen participants, a subset of the Facebook group mentioned above, was set up for those wishing to gather virtually via Zoom. The WhatsApp group quickly became a dynamic sacred space for sharing information about upcoming meetings and debriefing afterward, requesting healing for loved ones or oneself, and sharing all manner of musings, experiences, information, photographs, videos, lighthearted banter, and above all, unfaltering, loving empathy and support.

I already knew most of the members from our previous face-to-face encounters over the years and had written articles about the sistren (Rountree 2017, 2021). Joining this very active WhatsApp group and sharing in the Zoom gatherings during the pandemic meant that although I was based physically in New Zealand, I could now participate fully in the life of the sistren, as could several other members who were living permanently or temporarily in other countries.[15] Previously, this had only been possible when I/we visited Malta. The mandatory "social distancing," which physically isolated members living in Malta during lockdowns, actually had the effect of reducing social distance, or establishing a new dimension of social proximity, within the wider sistren, which especially benefitted those of us who lived geographically distant from Malta. Each member of the physically distributed sistren simultaneously continued to exist in other networks of relations and institutions in other communities in the countries where they lived and online. In the worldview of members, all these constellations of relationships form a vast web of connection that ultimately encompasses the whole planet.

Although unable to gather physically with one another during the pandemic, women were able to spend time with nonhuman beings in nature: walking and meditating in favorite places, singing with the wind, howling at the moon, reading a love letter to the earth, discovering special stones and inviting them to be part of a sacred altar, dancing with a much-loved tree, or in other ways, "talking with things," to use Bird-David's (1999, 77) phraseology, where "talking" is "shorthand for a two-way responsive relatedness." Sometimes nonhuman beings visited women's homes: one hosted a large cat snake behind her washing machine for several days, posting that she was "really grateful this snake appeared" because the local cats were annihilating the reptile populations, although she worried about the snake's ability to "continue its free wildlife" with "17 tigers" preparing to pounce upon it when it emerged.

In the reporting of these experiences to the WhatsApp group, nonhuman beings were often referred to with personal names and the pronouns one would use for human beings. Kinship terminology was used when referring to, for example, a sister tree, a mountain ancestor, Mother Earth, Father Sun, Grandmother Moon, Star Brothers, and Star Sisters. Going for a swim was described as "going for a dip in Mama Cocha" (Sea Mother).[16] When hiking or visiting beautiful, wild places, women posted pictures that were greeted by others with a flurry of comments. The following sample of responses to some land and seascape photos from one woman's journey indicates the group's strong sense of connection with one another and with the living, animate world:

- How your photos filled me with love for our mother. I am so glad you are walking with her.
- Wow, how astounding she is. Thank you so much for taking us on this journey with you.
- Cliffs breathing. Mother Earth heaving. . . . So wonderful you are there sister! Of course we are with you. 🖤 ⚚
- Mountains water greenery sand. . . . ahhh Pachamama 🤗
- Goddess in the undergrowth, wearing the new spring collection 😃
- How fabulous—I'm drinking it in!! 🥛

As well as delight and admiration, shared images often stimulated lengthier reflections and even original poetry.

When a member of the sistren requests healing for herself or a friend—a not uncommon occurrence during a pandemic—there is an instant flood of love and support. Women sit and meditate for one another, light candles and post photographs of them to the group; prayers, blessings, and practical support are offered, and a plethora of emojis representing love and care are posted. In the event of a friend or relative dying—human or special other-than-human, such as a pet—there is an outpouring of sorrow and love, prayers for a peaceful crossing of what Pagans refer to as the Rainbow Bridge, and reassurance that "there is indeed no separation." When my ninety-seven-year-old aunt died on the first day of spring 2020, women on the other side of the world who had never known—or even heard of—my aunt lit candles to honor and farewell her and posted lengthy messages of sympathy to me and gratitude for my aunt's life. When a group member was about to undergo surgery earlier this year, members of the sistren journeyed in shamanic consciousness to visualize a successful outcome:

- Seeing the op go perfectly and the surgeon's hands performing a more than excellent job and you recovering easily and swiftly. Much love and courage. 🫶🕊
- Also seeing you in excellent hands, all will go smoothly and perfectly. Sending you love and healing. 🌙 🫶
- Will ask my spirits to be with you dear [name] and know all will be well. All love to you.... For gentle courage and wondrous outcome. 💗💗💗🌙
- Also joining in the chorus of healing light, and seeing you surrounded by perfect love and harmony. 🕯💗🫶
- Dearest [name]. We are on the Ship and the sea is smooth.... When you alight this particular journey all will have gone perfectly 💗x
- Darling [name], yes, you are surely in the safest hands. Relax and trust sister pirate! We are all in the same boat, remember?! You are steeped in loving healing: ONE LOVE! XXX

The group's visualizations and expressions of love and empathy represented more than gifts of support; they became dynamically generative of the woman's experience of the surgery and of her altering self. She later posted that the messages had played over and over in her mind during the four-hour procedure (under local anesthesia), and inspired by the posts, she too had visualized the surgeon's "perfect hands." An otherwise anxious experience was instead calm and meditative, "steeped in loving healing," interrupted only by the surgeon's comments that "it was going very well and couldn't have gone better." Kohn (2013, 72) claims that "all thoughts are alive" and "thoughts grow by association with other thoughts [in a way that] is not categorically different from how selves relate to one another." A self, "whether 'skin-bound' or more distributed, is the locus of what we can call agency" (76). In the case I have just described, and in many others when healing has been needed, the group's thoughts—emanating from the sistren's distributed Self and supercharged with focused intent, will, emotion, confidence, visualization, candle lighting, and other rituals—have been mobilized to help a member of the group or someone whom one of them knew.

Because of the strong affinity and intimacy within the group—their use of empathic imagination and an often-articulated worldview that "everything is connected"—each woman's experience becomes, in a way, the group's experience.

An individual self alters and the collective group Self alters; the collective Self impacts and alters the individual self. The group constitutes a relational ecology of selves where individual selves emerge and "merge into new kinds of we as they interact" (Kohn 2013, 16). Kohn's depiction of a selfhood "distributed over bodies" rather than "coterminous with a physically bounded organism" is pertinent (75). All members participate consciously in a collective Self, a "we-ness" (Bird-David 1999, 78), a form of panpsychism (Greenwood 2020, 11), and what Sabina Magliocco (2012, 18) calls "participatory consciousness," where "a set of emotional, affective responses that cause a change in consciousness" emerges as a result of being and doing together in community. Ultimately, this "allows participants to switch to a more participatory view of the world" (18). Individual selves and the collective Self alter constantly as a result of participating in an evolving, intersubjective web of relationships among human and nonhuman beings, plants and animals, ancestors, spirits, deities, and other supernatural beings. When a photograph of a recent full moon was posted on WhatsApp, one of the sistren commented, "I see all the faces of the world in that [the moon's] face!"

Following a new moon ritual on November 3, 2021, just after the Pagan festival of Samhain (when the spirits of recently departed loved ones are especially remembered), one woman expressed the group's experience of we-ness thus: "Sistren, we are such clear reflections of each other as we journey on in this life! Such vital support esp with these constant challenges! Yes, trusting, but also acting. This month is so vulnerable and we need to light candles, smudge and honour the beings who r no longer with us physically. They will guide us and at times carry us to lighten our burden. 💝🤎 🕯️ 🐾🐾 ☆ ✨ 🕯️🕯️🕯️" Another responded, "Reading all these messages for me is like attending a healing session. All this amazing information inspires me and moves me forwards."

CONCLUSION

"Moving forward"—self/Self-altering—is inevitable. A self/Self, whether individual or collective, is never fixed or final, always in the process of being made, "becoming with" (Haraway 2008) others in a relational ecology of selves, irrespective of the source prompting alteration and whether individuals are conscious of altering or deem alteration desirable. Just as "the [individual] self is an active agent of its own realisation" (Seigel 2005, 6), so too is the collective Self inevitably and continuously Self-made through the agency of its parts.

Scholarly discourse on self-religion has considered the self exclusively as individual and human, as an expression of the "massive subjective turn of modern culture" (Heelas 2008, ix). Such a focus on the individual human self may be partly valid in regard to New Age ideologies, although it ignores the tendency of New Age philosophies to see self-alteration—likely to be couched as self-healing and self-acceptance rather than self-improvement—as only the first responsibility of the human individual, a necessary first step to "fixing" the world. In any case, the key ideas of (predominantly) New Age, modern Pagan, and neoshamanic movements have moved closer together in the twenty-first century, and in particular, deep ecological concerns are shared by all. In an interview with Oprah in 2014 (*Super Soul Sunday*), thirty years after riding the cresting wave of the New Age, Shirley MacLaine asserted, "We are all one" (MacLaine 2014), echoing the central refrain of the sistren: everything is connected, there is no separation, we are all one.

Limiting "self" (in academic discourse on self-religion) to the individual human self seriously misconstrues contemporary Pagan and shamanic worldviews, or rather *worlds* (Kohn 2013, 10), because it fails to acknowledge their relational epistemology, the understanding that selfhood does not belong exclusively to humans, and their reluctance to place human selves at the center or pinnacle of the world order. It also fails to acknowledge their relational ontology, the everyday lived experience of participating in a larger intersubjective Self, a "we-ness" within an environment of "nested relatednesses" (Bird-David 1999, 78). Entering into "conversation" (Bird-David's term for respectful engagement) with another being, human or other-than-human, "makes that being a self in relation with ourselves" (Bird-David 1999, 78; cf. Kohn 2013, 12). It is valid and interesting, perhaps, to discuss Paganism and shamanism in terms of Self-religion (uppercase), where "Self" is collective and "religion" is an everyday experience of being-in-the-world in connection with other beings-in-the-world, where all are alive, sacred, connected, altering, and being altered.

NOTES

1. In fact, all these movements' core ideas can be traced to the emergence of the Theosophical Society, founded in 1875, which sought to bridge Eastern and Western beliefs and emphasized the universal brotherhood of humanity, the self as divine, and self-knowledge/gnosis, blended with Hinduism, Buddhism, and the teachings of advanced spiritual beings known as the Masters of Ancient Wisdom.
2. There is a Christian tradition that values becoming or altering oneself to be more Christlike, but this implies that the authentic, individual human self is not acceptable as it is and needs to be replaced with or altered to become a Christlike self.
3. For readers unfamiliar with modern Paganism (sometimes referred to in scholarship as neo-Paganism), the Wikipedia entry "Modern Paganism" (https://en.wikipedia.org/wiki/Modern_Paganism) is a comprehensive, balanced, and well-referenced introduction to this diverse group of religious movements influenced by or derived from the various historical pagan beliefs of premodern peoples. Modern, self-identified Pagans use a capital *P* to distinguish themselves from historical pagans (who did not self-identify as such but were labeled thus by others) and to demonstrate that Paganism is a religion that requires capitalization in the same way that other religions are. Pagan studies is now an established multidisciplinary field of study within the academic study of religion.
4. Adam Possamaï (1999, 111) writes, "In 1996–1997, I interviewed 35 people who would 'commonly' be described as 'New Agers.' However, 71% of the participants criticised New Age, and 9%, even if positive towards it, did not consider themselves as 'New Agers.'"
5. As an earth-centered, animistic spiritual path or nature religion, modern Western shamanism is often classified loosely under the umbrella of contemporary Paganism; however,

practitioners are more likely to identify simply as shamans, broadly aligning their beliefs and practices with Indigenous shamans.

6. Alberto Villoldo's website is http://thefourwinds.com/.

7. I have discussed the complex and troubling issue of the cultural appropriation of Indigenous people's knowledge, traditions, and other cultural property elsewhere (Rountree 2017, 2021, 2023) and do not have the space here to digress.

8. A number of the non-Maltese members are British persons who have lived in Malta for many years. Other nationalities include French and Greek.

9. When embodied gatherings were finally possible again in 2022, the group chose to continue to meet online for their rituals but added some face-to-face social gatherings and rituals at Neolithic temples and members' homes and restaurants to their schedule.

10. Obviously *fraternity* becomes *sorority* in the ethnographic case I describe here.

11. In emphasizing the relational self, however, these "new psychologists" of the late nineteenth century were not thinking about social relationships with other-than-humans as part of a collective.

12. Andrew Kipnis (2015, 44) describes posthumanism as "analytic stances that grant agency to nonhuman entities and that downplay the differences between human and nonhuman agency."

13. Even so, it is important to acknowledge that the animism of the sistren and other modern Western shamans, given that they live in a world of capitalist and modern institutions and digital communication networks, functions in the first instance at the level of worldview and aspiration rather than being a taken-for-granted mode of living in the world in the way that communities of Indigenous animists do or did (Rountree 2012).

14. Starhawk's description of "oakness" here resembles Kohn's (2013, 76) discussion of selfhood being distributed through a collectivity.

15. When travel was permitted in and out of Malta in 2021, one group member normally resident in Malta went to the United Kingdom to spend several months with her partner; one visited her aging father in the United Kingdom; another who had recently moved from Malta to live in Gran Canaria, Spain, was able to join the Zoom meetings; and a new member—an English woman who lived in Turkey, a friend of someone in the group—joined the sistren and was warmly embraced.

16. Mama Cocha is the ancient Incan goddess of the sea.

REFERENCES

Ball, Lucille. n.d. "Love Yourself First and Everything Else Falls into Line." BrainyQuote.com. Accessed November 12, 2021. https://www.brainyquote.com/quotes/lucille_ball_127076.

Barker, Eileen. 1999. "New Religious Movements: Their Incidence and Significance." In *New Religious Movements: Challenge and Response*, edited by Bryan Wilson and Jamie Cresswell, 15–32. London: Routledge.

Bird-David, Nurit. 1999. "'Animism' Revisited: Personhood, Environment and Relational Epistemology." In "Culture—A Second Chance?" Supplement, *Current Anthropology* 40 (S1): S67–91.

Clarke, Peter Bernard. 2006. *New Religions in Global Perspective: A Study of Religious Change in the Modern World*. London: Routledge.

Descola, Philippe. 2009. "Human Natures." *Social Anthropology / Anthropologie Sociale* 17 (2): 145–157.

Easton, Nina. 1987. "Shirley MacLaine's Mysticism for the Masses: She's the Super Saleswoman for a Fast-Growing New Age Movement." *Los Angeles Times*, September 8, 1987. https://www.latimes.com/archives/la-xpm-1987-09-06-tm-6352-story.html.

Greenwood, Susan. 2020. *Developing Magical Consciousness: A Theoretical and Practical Guide for the Expansion of Perception*. Abingdon: Routledge.

Hallowell, Irving. 1960. "Ojibwa Ontology, Behavior and World View." In *Culture in History: Essays in Honor of Paul Radin*, edited by Stanley Diamond, 19–52. New York: Columbia University Press.

Hanegraaff, Wouter J. 1996. *New Age Religion and Western Culture: Esotericism in the Mirror of Secular Thought*. New York: E. J. Brill.

———. 2002. "New Age Religion." In *Religions in the Modern World: Traditions and Transformations*, edited by Linda Woodhead, Paul Fletcher, Hiroko Kawanami, and David Smith, 287–304. London: Routledge.

Haraway, Donna. 2008. *When Species Meet*. Minneapolis: University of Minnesota Press.

Heelas, Paul. 1991. "Western Europe: Self-Religions." In *The World's Religions: The Study of Religion, Traditional and New Religion*, edited by Peter Clarke, 167–173. London: Routledge.

———. 2008. *Spiritualities of Life: New Age Romanticism and Consumptive Capitalism*. Oxford: Blackwell.

Heelas, Paul, and Linda Woodhead. 2005. *The Spiritual Revolution: Why Religion Is Giving Way to Spirituality*. Malden, Mass.: Blackwell.

Husemann, Katharina C., and Giana M. Eckhardt. 2019. "Consumer Spirituality." *Journal of Marketing Management* 35 (5–6): 391–406. https://doi.org/10.1080/0267257X.2019.1588558.

Ingold, Tim. 2006. "Rethinking the Animate, Re-animating Thought." *Ethnos* 71 (1): 9–20.

———. 2011. *Being Alive: Essays on Movement, Knowledge and Description*. London: Routledge.

Kelly, Aidan. 1992. "An Update on Neopagan Witchcraft in America." In *Perspectives on the New Age*, edited by James R. Lewis and Gordon J. Melton, 136–151. New York: State University of New York Press.

Kipnis, Andrew. 2015. "Agency between Humanism and Posthumanism: Latour and His Opponents." *HAU: Journal of Ethnographic Theory* 5 (2): 43–58.

Kohn, Eduardo. 2013. *How Forests Think: Towards an Anthropology beyond the Human*. Berkeley: University of California Press.

Lasch, Christopher. 1979. *The Culture of Narcissism: American Life in an Age of Diminishing Expectations*. New York: W. W. Norton.

Latour, Bruno. 2005. *Reassembling the Social: An Introduction to Actor-Network-Theory*. New York: Oxford University Press.

MacLaine, Shirley. 2014. "Shirley MacLaine on Her Lifelong Spiritual Quest." Oprah Winfrey Network. March 20, 2014. YouTube video, 1:31. https://www.youtube.com/watch?v=k5LqaA6K4TI.

Magliocco, Sabina. 2012. "Beyond Belief: Context, Rationality and Participatory Consciousness." Archer Taylor Memorial Lecture 2010. *Western Folklore* 71 (1): 5–24.

Nussbaum, Martha. 1997. *Cultivating Humanity: A Classical Defense of Reform in Liberal Education*. Cambridge, Mass.: Harvard University Press.

Possamaï, Adam. 1999. "Diversity in Alternative Spiritualities: Keeping New Age at Bay." *Australian Religion Studies Review* 12 (2): 111–124.

Pyyhtinen, Olli, and Sakari Tamminen. 2011. "We Have Never Been Only Human: Foucault and Latour on the Question of the Anthropos." *Anthropological Theory* 11 (2): 135–152.

Redden, Guy. 2016. "Revisiting the Spiritual Supermarket: Does the Commodification of Spirituality Necessarily Devalue It?" *Culture and Religion* 17 (2): 231–249.

Rindfleish, Jennifer. 2005. "Consuming the Self: New Age Spirituality as 'Social Product' in Consumer Society." *Consumption Markets & Culture* 8 (4): 343–360. https://doi.org/10.1080/10253860500241930.

Rountree, Kathryn. 2012. "Neo-paganism, Animism, and Kinship with Nature." *Journal of Contemporary Religion* 27 (2): 305–320.

———, ed. 2015. *Contemporary Pagan and Native Faith Movements in Europe: Colonialist and Nationalist Impulses*. New York: Berghahn.

———. 2017. "The Spirits Are Cosmopolitan Too: Contemporary Shamanism in Malta." In *Cosmopolitanism, Nationalism, and Modern Paganism*, edited by Kathryn Rountree, 245–268. New York: Palgrave Macmillan.

———. 2021. "Negotiating Indigenous/Global Relationships in Contemporary Shamanism: The Case of Malta." In *Contemporary Indigenous Cosmologies and Pragmatics*, edited by Françoise Dussart and Sylvie Poirier, 88–110. Alberta: University of Alberta Press.

———. 2023. "Towards a Cosmopolitan Animism." In *Animism and Philosophy of Religion*, edited by Tiddy Smith, 341–364. New York: Palgrave Macmillan.

Seigel, Jerrold. 2005. *The Idea of the Self: Thought and Experience in Western Europe since the Seventeenth Century*. Cambridge: Cambridge University Press.

Starhawk, M. Macha NightMare, and the Reclaiming Collective. 1997. *The Pagan Book of Living and Dying: Practical Rituals, Prayers, Blessings, and Meditations on Crossing Over*. San Francisco: HarperSanFrancisco.

Taylor, Charles. 1991. *Sources of the Self: The Making of the Modern Identity*. Cambridge, Mass.: Harvard University Press.

Viveiros de Castro, Eduardo. 1998. "Cosmological Deixis and Amerindian Perspectivism." *Journal of the Royal Anthropological Institute* 4 (3): 469–488.

Ward, Graham. 2006. "The Future of Religion." *Journal of the American Academy of Religion* 74 (1): 179–186.

Willerslev, Rane, and Olga Ulturgasheva. 2012. "Revisiting the Animism versus Totemism Debate: Fabricating Persons among the Eveny and Chukchi of North-Eastern Siberia." In *Animism in Rainforest and Tundra: Personhood, Animals, Plants and Things in Contemporary Amazonia and Siberia*, edited by Marc Brightman, Vanessa Grotti, and Olga Ulturgasheva, 48–68. New York: Berghahn.

Wyllie, Irvin. 1954. *The Self-Made Man in America: The Myth of Rags to Riches*. New Brunswick: Rutgers University Press.

York, Michael. 1995. *The Emerging Network: A Sociology of the New Age and Neo-pagan Movements*. London: Rowman & Littlefield.

———. 2001. "New Age Commodification and Appropriation of Spirituality." *Journal of Contemporary Religion* 16 (3): 361–372.

3 · WOUNDED BY GRACE
Becoming a Prophet in an Evangelical Revival in Solomon Islands

JAAP TIMMER

Christian commitments and their personal and social ramifications have received significant attention in anthropology over the last few decades (Bialecki 2018). For Melanesia, there has been an intense interest in conversion, especially the engagement between missionaries and Melanesians (Barker 2019b), and whether and how that conversion changes people's practices, ethics, and social imaginaries (Robbins 2004; Eriksen 2008). Overall, religious conversion in these studies mostly appears to refer not to an immediate distinct shift in self-identification but rather to a gradual acceptance of and participation in some form of Christianity (Lambek 2018, 125). Observations and debates scale up to the collective level too—over whether gradual acceptance, private or collective, has meant more the Christianization of Melanesian society or the Melanesianization of Christianity. Further, given the various waves of Christianity through the region, individual and social alteration may also be caused by "secondary conversion" (Barker 2012), as more recent charismatic and Pentecostal revivals critique and contradict earlier forms of Christian life (Eriksen and MacCarthy 2019).

Crucially, anthropological studies are conflicted over whether charismatic Christianity alters Melanesian personhood (Robbins 2004; Hirsch 2008; Mosko 2010), enabling the formulation of new moralities and the formation of new selves. For some, Pentecostal movements are understood as societal transformations heralding a radically new order and new identities (Robbins, Schieffelin, and Vilaça 2014). Others argue that the agentive force of Christianity (including Catholicism) in such contexts requires an investigation of the extent to which newly "imported theologies and mythologies become inflected by Melanesian values, orientations, and narratives" (Barker 2012, 78) that are already affected by Christianity. In brief, as John Barker puts it, "it is difficult to separate out the enduring qualities of Christianity from the diverse historically shaped institutional and theological formations in which it is embedded" (2019a, 283).

In this essay, I explore the self-alteration of the charismatic leader of a religious movement on the island of Malaita in Solomon Islands in a context of lively revival in 1970 that continues into the present. I show how it should be seen in light of a long tradition of engagement with different forms of Christianity and a postcolonial sociocultural context while considering the synergies and contradictions that converts work through over time. Prominent older studies in the region confirm this. For instance, for the island of Malaita, Ben Burt notes that the South Sea Evangelical Church (SSEC), especially since the spiritual inspiration resulting from that 1970 revival, "created local forms of Christianity appropriate to their own cultural traditions and contemporary circumstances" (1994, 246).

What do these cultural traditions and contemporary situations include? One is a history of spiritual inspiration since the advent of Christianity in the region as well as ways in which ancestral spirits continue to be present (Burt 1994, 241). Contemporary references include the long resistance against British authority in the form of the Maasina Rule movement, which united Malaitans along a shared idea of self-rule (Akin 2013; Timmer and Frazer 2023). In the neighboring autonomous province of Bougainville in Papua New Guinea too, an Island-wide Catholic Charismatic Renewal and fresh anti-colonial sentiments inspired individual and collective renewal and political change in the 1980s (Hermkens 2020). As a result of the anti-colonial sentiments and people's disappointment in the "normal" European time of failing development and nation-building projects, the promises of apocalyptic times have become attractive. This attraction is, however, informed not just by Christian notions of the millennium but also by the sociocultural context in which they emerge (McDowell 1988, 122).

Below I investigate the decades-long self-alteration of Reverend Michael Maeliau, a minister of the SSEC and the leading prophet of the politico-religious movement called the All Pacific Arise (APA, formerly known as the All Peoples Prayer Assembly). In the context of secondary conversions following the 1970 charismatic revival, Maeliau began to receive messages from God, revelations of a prophetic nature concerning the past, present, and future of Malaita. Becoming and being a prophet in this context involves a prophet-leader receiving revelation from and speaking on behalf of God while being in control of a movement (Trompf 1977, 9). They take advantage of and are informed by what Garry W. Trompf sees as a Melanesian prophetic tradition: "Even when certain messages may be palpably syncretic . . . or heavily garbed in Christian vocabulary, they are mouthed by Melanesians in an indigenous, non-imitative manner" (9).

Over a period of years, Maeliau has lived out a new understanding of himself in constructing APA by building on key elements of cultural traditions and with strong links to Israel as well as to other eschatological movements around the globe. As prophet and theologian, Maeliau has used this evangelical revival to redefine both himself as a prophet and Malaita as a Christian nation, presented as possessing certain key continuities with its past forms. Over the years, he has designed (for APA) an evangelical and Pentecostal theology that focuses on preparing the *nation of Malaita* and all other nations for their return to Jerusalem in anticipation of the coming of the kingdom of God in light of the outpouring of the Holy Spirit. As part of its theology, under Maeliau, APA has advocated that Malaita become a constitutional theocracy as a purified nation (see Timmer 2015; Bond and Timmer 2017). APA's theology builds on the notion that the coming of Christ's reign is expanded through the gift of the Holy Spirit "in the last days" (Acts 2:17) toward "the ends of the earth" (13:47), including to the divinely named Solomon Islands.

Over the years, APA emerged as a Pacific-wide evangelical fellowship that accepts as its God-given mandate the task to take the gospel from "the ends of the earth" back through the nations to Jerusalem. Based on early European accounts of Solomon Islands, messages hidden in the Bible, and prophetic landmarks, the movement discerns that Malaita will take center stage in this return of the gift of the gospel. Besides training sessions for empowering people with an understanding of God's redemptive purpose for each nation and a so-called twenty-four-hour prayer watch, APA began to organize and became involved in prayer assemblies throughout the region, and its leaders regularly join prayer assemblies in Israel. During these gatherings, representatives from "the nations" gather for worship, spiritual warfare, and prayer. In Solomon Islands, the movement attracts thousands of people, and throughout the Pacific, its popularity is growing.

As we will see, Maeliau's self-alteration can be contextualized within the flow of continuing cultural change, constant revisions of internal and external theological frames, new readings of the European historiography of the exploration of the Pacific, and the idea of the island of Malaita being a Christian nation before European colonialism.

FIRE IN THE ISLANDS!

According to the book *Fire in the Islands!*—a history of the mission activities of the SSEC on Malaita, including the "acts of the Holy Spirit" (Griffiths 1977)—a dramatic revival transformed evangelical Christianity starting in 1970. Alison Griffiths sees this revival as relieving people of at least thirty years of God's "absence" in the region (169–170). During the revival, lives were remade and people became "sensitive to the spirit who is holy" (12). Revelations and prophecy have always been part of Malaitan evangelism since the beginning of Christianization in the early twentieth century (Burt 1994, 240; Barr 1983, 111–112), but during this revival, people appeared ready to develop particularly drastic new spiritual sensitivities. Individuals became open to revelations from God about the future role of Malaita during the approaching end-time, including a new interest in possible lineal descent from Israelites.

The interest in such "Hamitic" origins dates back at least to the 1960s, when the evangelical theology of Herbert W. Armstrong and its British and U.S. Israelism were broadcast in Solomon Islands, as well as by decades-long ponderings about why their country is named Solomon Islands. Could islanders be Israelite too? This environment was pregnant with ontological questions. With the cup being full to the brim, as it were, the revival was for many the last drop, but it still needed an authoritative voice. Here theologian Michael Maeliau came in as a broker among possible new pasts for Malaita, biblical and present-day Israel, and the future that will arrive with the end of time.

Caroline Humphrey would say the revival constitutes a "decision-event" for individuals, facilitating "the overturning of accustomed patterns of intelligibility and the advent of a radically new idea" (2008, 357). According to Humphrey, individuals recompose themselves through decision-events, archiving past and plural identities and fixing on a new momentous one (374). But in Malaita, as in anywhere else, this did not happen overnight, highlighting the importance of considering the subject in a more long-term situation of innovation and improvisation (358). The revival put things in motion and created fertile ground for Maeliau's endeavor to institute a new regime, beginning with his establishment of APA.

During many years of fieldwork with this movement, it has become clear to me that Maeliau has become a person with an increasingly sharpened and pervading sense of who he is, "such that this idea dominates other possible ways of being and orients subsequent action" (Humphrey 2008, 374). According to his own testimony, this alteration was triggered by God revealing himself to him, exposing him to his commands. In other words, this cooperative divine- and self-alteration involves constant communication with the Spirit, as it regularly "comes down." The revival, thus, is always new, giving him, on his account, the confidence to overturn the future and the past of Malaita and to work, as demanded by his vision, for its new role as a nation, as seen in the fulfillment of scripture.

Crucial for our understanding of self-change in this context is "to give due weight to intentionality, to motivation, and to self-examination in people's projects of self-alteration" (Houston 2022, 494). Maeliau's project of self-alteration originates partly from a sense of humiliation by church and state structures since colonial times, which he makes sense of in both theological and cultural terms. Next, his generation of a fresh set of notions from the charismatic revival vitalized a self-conscious process of culturally driven alteration that sanctioned members of APA to act as agents of change.

One source of people's sense of agency is the one I have already mentioned above—it derives from the notion of Israelite origins for Malaitan society that is thus (precolonially) founded on Mosaic law. At the same time, people wonder about the significance of the early Spanish explorer Álvaro de Mendaña y Neira's idea that he had discovered the land of Ophir (where King Solomon sourced materials for his fabled temple) when he and his crew stumbled upon Islas Salomón in 1568. Over time, people engaged in "kinshipping," establishing historical relationships between Malaitan genealogies and ancestors in the Old Testament. Alongside the drawing of family trees (see below), people mapped possible migration routes. To renew these roots within God's plan for the nations, social and ethical holiness is required for the return to Jerusalem to build on that foundation.

In the openness to the Holy Spirit that the revival in Malaita created, Maeliau's self-alteration is related to a discontinuity brought about not solely by being reborn during the revival but also by his working with experiences and narratives that promise to control the flow of change. Much of his self-alteration is cultural. It is not a break that is caused by the kinds of social upheavals described in Humphrey's (2008) analysis of the event. Maeliau owns the narrative: it reflects *his* path as a Black theologian in search of a Melanesian worship as a break from White theology and from church-based gatekeepers of religious meaning. For this break, he sought a return to the original spirituality of Malaita, and from the elements he finds, he builds a new past for Malaita as a Christian nation.

MR. OPHIR AND HIS DESCENDANTS

One key teaching Maeliau introduced toward this goal is a technique of charting descent in straight lines that does not conflict with alternative historical accounts, thus reconciling divergent genealogies. He calls this "family treeing," and besides the aim of settling conflicts over land, it seeks eventually to unite all Malaitans under one ancestor, Ophir son of Joktan, the second son of Eber (Genesis 10, Table of Nations), who brought the tabernacle to Malaita (Maeliau 2018a). The charismatic revival on Malaita thus asserted the establishment of unbroken links between Indigenous genealogies and Hebraic origins. These genealogies give a mythical time to Malaita that legitimizes APA's theological foundation in Judaism:

> In the book of Genesis chapter 10:29 was, the first mention of the name Ophir, as being one of the sons of Joktan. That was seven generations from Noah. Joktan's brother was called Peleg, during whose time the earth was divided. Before this, the earth was just one mass of land and one ocean. During this time the continents were divided and the islands were formed....
>
> Mr Ophir and his descendants migrated eastward. Ophir's descendants migrated as far as, at least, the Solomon Islands. From the book of Job in the Bible was the mention of the Land of Ophir. Job was a counterpart of Abraham. At this time trade with the Middle East was already going on with the land of Ophir [Malaita]. Its gold dust was known to be the finest on earth....
>
> Then there was silence until the time of King David and King Solomon when sailing boats were sent to fetch gold from the Land of Ophir for their building programs including the building of the Temple. Then again there was a period of silence, until around the sixteenth century when serious search was made to find the exact location where the Land of Ophir was. In 1568, Captain Mendana [*sic*]... came to the Solomon Islands and named it after King Solomon.
>
> The first Ophirites were the first people group who populated the Western Pacific, now known as Melanesia. They were dark skinned in colour. These included

Australia, Indonesia and Malaysia. Contrary to popular opinion Adam and Eve were black in colour of their skins. Medical science confirms that you cannot add colour to your skin, you can only lose it. So the original people of the Pacific were the Melanesians. Melanesia means dark skinned. (Maeliau 2018a, 4–5)

There are numerous similar narratives that trace origins to other figures in the Old Testament. Maeliau has been instrumental in fabricating these narratives and the identities they underwrite. Maeliau changed Malaita culture not just by formulating new histories based on the Bible and European historiography but also in keeping with elements of its customary ways. Maeliau's historicity (and theology) hinges on the ancient (precolonial) shrines in the mountains of Malaita where ritual communication with ancestors once took place. Over the last few decades, these shrines have become the locus of Christian worship and the place where Maeliau delivers prophecies to leading people. These prophecies give shape to APA's leadership and stimulate a social ethic of equality, work, family-based economic management, and participation in the world with like-minded groups on behalf of the kingdom of God.

APA sees prophethood as relevant for all believers regardless of social position and uses prophecy to confront the present condition of economic and social inequality, individualization, and loss of (customary) morals. At the same time, it respects and instrumentalizes a tradition of "priesthood" in which particular male leaders known as *wane ni fo'a* have privileged ritual access, which brings prestige and power (see below). Contemporary "priests" are APA prophets, and this understanding has kept Maeliau's ascendance as the leading prophet in line with this framing.

CALLED BY GOD

During a prayer gathering on the western shore of the Sea of Galilee, in the town of Tiberias, on December 14, 2012, I gained a sense of how Maeliau communes with God, being led and enlightened by him. We were at a social gathering with his group from the Pacific and with several like-minded evangelicals from First Nations in Canada and the United States. After lunch, people retreated to the hall of the guesthouse to pray and talk. The prayers focused on blessings and guidance as the key spiritual work and modality of agency. The long prayer sessions marked the two-week-long tour that for Maeliau revolved around the fourth meeting of the movement's so-called Jerusalem Council, one of the pillars for organizing the "New Jerusalem" on Malaita.

Two days before, Maeliau had been mingling with others in the group quite casually, in contrast to the start of the tour when he led most prayers charismatically and often told people what to think of the Holy Land and its connections with such apparently gentile nations as Solomon Islands. After the prayer that afternoon, people began to chat in small groups about the spiritual journey through Israel and what it meant to them to be in Tiberias, the capital of Galilee and one of the four holy cities of Judaism. Some spoke about dipping in the water the next day to engineer a divine encounter, while others were planning to buy gifts for relatives and friends back home.

Sharing a small round table with his close friends Elijah Titus and Ezekiel, both from Papua New Guinea, and me (from Australia), Maeliau spoke to us about the signs he saw that the Holy Spirit was moving in his homeland.

"But look at them," he said. "Many in this group are so busy with walking the pages of the Bible and collecting souvenirs when visiting Israel that they forget about the Holy Spirit and the revelation of the glory of the Lord. They do not seem to realize what this means for the ends of the earth, especially my island of Malaita, where the Holy Spirit is present, full-time, to prepare my nation for the climax of all things." The people at the table fell silent, and Maeliau pulled out his laptop from his bag, opened it on the table, and closed his eyes. I thought he had fallen into a light sleep, but in fact, he was connecting with God through the internet for some important "download." The download concerned guidance for the constitution of the state of Malaita, on which he was working for the Jerusalem Council. He stood up and addressed the gathering with a short speech about the revelation of the glory of the Lord.

People were reminded that Maeliau was still the movement's leading prophet and, as prophets do, must commune with God. He retreated to his room. At breakfast the following day, I asked him about connecting with God through the internet. Maeliau explained,

> There are all these messages out there—you can call them revelations—they just come through. It is often hard to make sense of them. It requires patience. God instructs us to do things, and they happen more often here in Israel than back home. Perhaps the internet connections in Solomon Islands are not good [Maeliau laughs loudly]. Over there we need to do rituals, some small, others big. A big one was when we fasted for a period of forty days. We prayed as prayer warriors to move the angels and the spirits to ask God what he had promised in Psalms 2, verse 8: "Ask of me, and I will make the nations your heritage and the ends of the earth your possession."

We continued to talk about the forty days of fasting. "We were all holy," Maeliau emphasized, upon which I asked if the transformation he experienced the day before was like becoming a prophet. He responded, "It is; it is like becoming Moses! Since God's first revelation to me, I have become more holy. Then, following the realization that this is all in our past and on our island, I began to realize that it is all connected, everything: our history, the Bible, God's revelation, our nation, and the end-time. Well, you know that story. It is the story of me *becoming a new man, a prophet* [my emphasis]. They call me Papa Michael now [Maeliau laughs]." I suggest we can only make sense of this development by seeing

Maeliau himself as a historical actor who through being called by God (and as a theologian) allowed himself to be gradually *wounded* by grace in a process of self-alteration that will always be hidden and "remain a deeply wondrous enigma and mystery" (Barth 1963, 72–73). In this process, he changed from being an SSEC minister and aspiring Black theologian to a new man and a prophetic leader of a religio-political movement.

CONSTRUCTING A MELANESIAN THEOLOGY

Michael Maeliau was born on September 6, 1946, in north Malaita, and he passed away on October 14, 2021. Maeliau completed a college diploma at the Bible College of New Zealand (now known as the Laidlaw College) in 1974 and in the same year obtained a diploma in divinity from the Melbourne College of Divinity. In 1975, soon after he married Martha Safina Atomea, he took up the position of lecturer at the Christian Leaders' Training College (CLTC) in Banz, Papua New Guinea (Timmer 2022). By that time, the CLTC had seen many students from the SSEC in Malaita who had participated in the revival in their region. They contributed to "a sense of urgency that something similar should also occur in Papua New Guinea" (Macdonald 2019, 396). Maeliau, educated in that environment, became inspired by accounts of the Remnant Church in Malaita narrated to him by Erustus Wane'efo from the Kwara'ae region (Maeliau 1976, 5n). The Remnant Church was founded among the Kwara'ae-speaking people in the 1950s around the idea that Malaitans are members of a lost tribe. The church was instituted by Zebulon Sisimia, who was inspired by the Holy Spirit to find a religious solution to colonial domination (Burt 1983, 338).

In an essay on the Remnant movement that he wrote for the CLTC, Maeliau identifies legal parallels between Malaita and Jewish traditions and concludes that the movement stayed close to traditional ways (1976, 5). Around the same time, Aruru Matiabe, a Huli from highland Papua New Guinea, was a source of inspiration for Maeliau too, and he witnessed a Huli revival (Maeliau 1987, 126). In 1978, Maeliau was asked to preach in the Baiyer River region of the Western Highlands of Papua New Guinea. He reports on this in some detail in an essay titled "Searching for a Melanesian Way of Worship" (1987). Witnessing the shaking of bodies, tongues hanging out, and people's panting, Maeliau was reluctant to understand the phenomena using any of the labels he had learned during his theological education (125). An answer to a prayer to God gave solace: "This was exactly how these people used to worship to their 'devils' [ancestors]" (126).

With this insight and reflecting on his Papua New Guinea experiences and similar events back home in north Malaita, including the body movements of his daughter to express her excitement about his return home, Maeliau concluded that it is in these embodied practices that authentic Melanesian worship is to be found. They are the "natural expression of the Melanesian peoples, their spontaneous response to the objects of worship given the spiritual heritages of their pre-Christian past" (Maeliau 1987, 119). In that writing, Maeliau makes an early allusion to similarities with worship in Jewish culture (120) that, on his account, will "arise spontaneously out of the revival movements" (126).

In a later reflection on his time in Papua New Guinea, Maeliau told me that the revivals in that region made him realize that characteristic Malaitan worship, and perhaps all Melanesian worship, is originally Jewish: "But I still had to figure out whether those roots were just there or if some people had brought them from Israel to Malaita. Eventually, God revealed to me that Malaitans originate from Israel" (Michael Maeliau, pers. comm., June 29, 2012). As discussed above, in his last booklet, *The Land of Ophir*, Maeliau (2018a) eventually concludes that Malaitans are Ophirites.

When Maeliau returned to Solomon Islands, he became an ordained minister of the SSEC and later the president of that church. He also became the president of the Evangelical Fellowship of the South Pacific. Maeliau was in Honiara, the capital of Solomon Islands, when the revival happened. When he returned to Malaita, he carried with him theological knowledge, an eyewitness account of revivals in Papua New Guinea, more detailed knowledge of local religious movements that emerged on Malaita since British rule, and connections with a worldwide prayer movement (see below). Back home, he began to self-consciously engage with his own society, seeking to effect both its transformation and his own. The transformation of his society envisions a new moral community founded on pre-Christian prophethood and the manifest presence of the Lord. It should become a holy group that, united, worships the presence of God, experiences the eruptions of revelations, joins prayers and songs, and revitalizes the ancestral shrines of original worship in expectation of God's divine intervention in their group. This divine intervention involves the renewal of the individual, the family, and foremost, the new nation and state of Malaita.

In early 1986, a group of elders of the SSEC met to consider starting a new congregation in one of the suburbs of Honiara. During prayer time, Maeliau began to receive a vision from God. This end-time prophetic vision foretold the story of a massive wave that begins in Solomon Islands, travels around the globe, and ends up in Jerusalem. The vision begins with a valley that fills with crystal clear (unpolluted) water, which develops into a flood and later becomes a cloud. The cloud travels to Australia and returns to Solomon Islands, from where it goes eastward to all the nations in the South Pacific. As the cloud reaches Papua New Guinea, it changes into a three-pronged powerful current that heads eastward toward the West Coast of the United States. When it arrives in the United States, the central current continues toward the East Coast, then turns around 180 degrees and develops into a mighty wave that eventually stretches from the North to the South Pole.

The wave then rolls back and travels westward. The wave is so great that it submerges all the nations in its path and is so high that it floods even Mount Everest. It covers everything in its path as it moves over the Pacific and Asia until a circle encompassing the globe is complete. With the completion of the circle, the wave zooms in on Jerusalem and shoots up into the heavens like a huge pillar. As it reaches high in the sky, it opens up like a great big mushroom that gradually spreads until it envelops the earth. At this point, a voice comes out from the cloud, saying, "And the glory of the Lord shall cover the earth as the waters cover the sea."

This vision has inspired followers to reflect on the Sermon on the Mount (described in Matt. 5:7 and Luke 6:17–49; see Acts 1:8), in which Jesus refers to the uttermost parts of the world as the geographical ends to which God's word should be spread. For most Christians in Malaita, this has become the most significant aspect of the sermon. In Maeliau's historical reflection on this vision, the Lord raised him up together with a prayer movement from Melanesia (Maeliau 2018b, 4). Some of these truths resonate with the theology developed around the Jerusalem House of Prayer for All Nations' Worldwide Watch prayer network initiated and run by U.S. pastor Tom Hess from his base on the Mount of Olives. The Jerusalem House has operated a 24-7 prayer and worship practice since 1987 with the aim to call all nations to Jerusalem to prepare for the full restoration of Israel since it was "reborn" as a nation in 1948 (Hess 2008, 1–2). Following a number of contributions of Maeliau to Hess's prayer meetings, Solomon Islands was allotted a Worldwide Watch mandate "to take up the dish and the towel, to be a servant of all (John 13) and to guide the return of the nations from the Pacific region through the Golden Gate" (Hess and Hess 2012, 279).

BECOMING A MALAITAN PROPHET

Following some fifteen years of engagement with Hess's movement and a growing following in Malaita, Maeliau began to communicate what he named his Deep Sea Canoe revelations, said to be similar to revelations from ancestors (or even God) during sacrifice rituals on mountaintops in the interior of the island in the past. For Maeliau, traditional prayer mountains feature as key local sites where these narratives of the past coalesce. They are formations of rocks reminiscent of a tabu-sanctum (*gwa bi'u*), or "shrine," on mountaintops where spiritual leaders, or tabu-speakers (*wane ni fo'a*), used to sacrifice to the ancestors (Hogbin 1939, 105–110). In his narrative of self-alteration, Maeliau has a lot to say about prayer mountains in terms of their centrality to prophecy.

It is at shrines, although not exclusively, that prophets receive and interpret revelations from God. Malaita has seen a steady growth in the number of prophets. In and around APA, there are now tens of prophets. Prophets are relatively new in Malaita, and many people wonder whether they are like their former priests. Many see that the mountain shrines on Malaita are like the mountain on which the temple was built in Ezekiel 42. They represent the history of Malaitans who have tried hard to remain faithful to the covenant. In addition, people construct theologies that further kindle comparisons between their lineages and Hebrew people, each of which has a tradition of strong horizontal social bonds and vertical links with ancestors and God. At the horizontal level, divine grace fits classical anthropological depictions of Melanesian societies in which the person is embedded in social and reciprocal relations with other humans and nonhumans (Strathern 1988). Similarly, people take up theologies that promise the restoration of some desired social unity, often in response to perceived current individualism and related widespread concerns about the deterioration of morals and loss of traditional ties.

With respect to verticality, some people reinterpret pre-Christian offerings to their ancestors, claiming that at the end of the genealogy that was recounted during those offerings, priests would add "God." Those past priests are currently often associated with Levites as a special people who devote themselves to spiritual pursuits, providing the rest of the community with a strong moral compass. It is therefore no surprise that in the movement's theology, key elements are revealed from above and give a sense of sovereignty to the group, as servants of God, to contribute to the messianic era.

For the individual, people connected to the movement often talk about the "one new man." A key source of inspiration for this is the book by George Annadorai (2001) titled *The One New Man in Christ*. Annadorai and Maeliau were fellow travelers in prayer congregations organized within the international network of prayer groups of Hess. During these prayer sessions, Maeliau would receive further revelation on how to partner with God. In his ongoing partnership with God, the new man enables for others new understandings of the present and invites possibilities for imagined futures—"as a resurrection from the dead" (Maeliau 2018b, 20)—which in turn impel new pasts and stimulate new forms of social organization. Since people began to see Maeliau as a leading prophet—or Papa Michael, as they began to call him—he began to feel comfortable forging a new past and new identity for Malaita.

MORE FIRE NEXT TIME?

By way of conclusion, let me suggest that Maeliau's self-alteration is an experiential narrative that is continually reinstituted to speak to Solomon Island's changing environment. It has, thus, continued to be instrumental in personal and social renewal for many in north Malaita in response to culture change and an uncertain political environment in which Malaitans tend to feel discriminated against by individuals and parties that dominate the central government in Honiara. In that process, Maeliau and his audience continually represent the drama of Christian conversion, both in the Bible and in the history of their region, in cultural frames of kinshipping and communication with ancestors. Geoffrey M. White writes about this in his reflection on conversion and revivals on the island of Santa Isabel, Solomon Islands, in the following terms: "The various local [and regional] histories of conversion offer . . . attempts to incorporate or mediate Christian knowledge through stories of transformation that recenter the process of change within localized histories of person and place" (1991, 246). For APA, conversion also mobilizes people to participate in a global world of religious movement.

Maeliau's historicity, which connects European and biblical narratives with changing landscapes of kinship and memory, has greatly stimulated people to situate their history more confidently in biblical pasts and see a covenanted role in the time that remains. Here Nigerian theologian Nimi Wariboko's (2012) explanation of "Pentecostal time" in *The Pentecostal Principle* sheds useful light on this relationship to the past and to the future. Being in time for believers involves a particular openness to the plan of God and "means to be in the grip of a penchant for newness in order to bend the arc of existence toward the not-yet. In this curving exercise, space is continuously created (expanded). Like the universe it creates its own space and expands into it" (156). Maeliau's self-alteration is well seen in this light as a series of events that overcame a wounded theologian self, paving the way for a new man, who, like Paul, is both in possession of and possessed by the revelation (Annadorai 2001, 18) and is, at the same time, the local prophet in the tradition of Malaitan priests. The case also confirms observations around cargo cults in the Melanesian cultures, in which "the role of the divine . . . is less a guarantor for the reproduction of society than as a source of cultural creativity" in cultures in which "the scope of human order has palpable limits" (Jorgensen 1994, 133).

Wariboko emphasizes such palpability is a result of the theological demand for new beginnings such as we see with Maeliau becoming a prophet and a new man: "More is expected from every moment and every life, and there is a radical openness to alternatives and surprises. The restlessness of all en-spirited life is recognized, understood, and grasped" (2012, 197). This highlights the significance for believers of the possibility of the radical new during the time that remains within chronological time. It may simultaneously add a different, alternative vitality, a temporal orientation that is nonidentical with respect to the dynamics of progress, development, justice, modernity, history, present, and so on.

This means that Maeliau's self-alteration into a prophet can only be understood when we think outside and beyond the frameworks of a singular time of development and progress. While it may be tempting to see APA time as a resistance to the modern state and to the West's modernity, the picture is less simple. Above all, Maeliau is unfolding an internal, local theological dynamic with evolving perceptions of the activities of God and Malaitan ancestral spirits in a culture in which the human order has always been unfinished. At the same time, Maeliau's self-altering trajectory cannot be characterized as a change only reserved for him. In APA, no one writes or owns a whole book, as it were. Works are collective, like sacred texts. Every Malaitan involved in the movement, including Maeliau, has taken on the transformation of their society toward a proper Christian nation.

Members of APA continuously seek to engage as new individuals with their variable relationships to living kin, ancestors, and a future nation. In other words, much of the momentum of APA is understood as generated from the divine within Malaitan culture itself, in a human order that is, like all human orders, always unfinished (cf. Jorgensen 1994). Moreover, conversion in this case is experienced as an increased interest in past, present, and future social relations. What I have shown in this chapter is that the self-alteration of Maeliau led to substantial changes in his and his followers' conceptualizations of the core domains of Malaitan culture. Here spirits and spiritual power are transmitted to the group and believed in as a group, and it does not matter that this group has now been extended to ancestors in the Old Testament and fellow evangelical travelers around the globe.

On top of that, Maeliau's openness to new ideas and, above all, to the divine power is expressed in his self-alteration. Over the years, though, Maeliau's openness toward the spirits became less radical. Things are not as turbulent as before, and we see the emergence of increasingly more schematic and decontextualized ecclesiological themes of a gospel and liturgy. The last publication by Maeliau (2021), entitled *The Revelation of the Glory of the Lord*, illustrates this. In contrast to his two histories of Malaita in *The Land of Ophir* (Maeliau 2018a) and *The Lion of the Tribe of Judah* (Maeliau 2018b), this latest book outlines an orthodoxy. It may be time, especially now that Maeliau is forever on the other side of the shrine, for a new prophet to ascend the mountain to ignite an even greater fire of openness to new gateways against this established order and the increasing centralization of power and control over revenues in Honiara.

ACKNOWLEDGMENTS

I am grateful to people in north Malaita, the Armitage family in Brisbane, and travelers from the Fourth Jerusalem Council gathering in Israel in December 2012 for their help with the research that underpins this chapter. Feedback on my presentation of an early version of this chapter by Christopher Houston has been very helpful. Jojada Verrips offered stimulating remarks, and I also thank Anna-Karina Hermkens and Daniel Tranter-Santoso for their helpful comments and suggestions. This research was supported under the Australian Research Council's Discovery Projects funding scheme (150102312) and has received funding from the European Union's Horizon 2020 research and innovation program under the Marie Skłodowska-Curie grant (agreement no. 754513) and the Aarhus University Research Foundation.

REFERENCES

Akin, David W. 2013. *Colonialism, Maasina Rule, and the Origins of Malaitan Kastom*. Honolulu: University of Hawai'i Press.

Annadorai, George. 2001. *The One New Man in Christ: Unveiling and Unleashing the Ultimate Revelation of All Time*. Singapore: Teach His Word.

Barker, John. 2012. "Secondary Conversion and the Anthropology of Christianity in Melanesia." *Archives de Sciences Sociales des Religions* 157:67–87. https://www.jstor.org/stable/41419264.

———. 2019a. "Converts, Christian and Anthropologists: A Critique of Mark Mosko's Partible Penitent Thesis." *Australian Journal of Anthropology* 30 (3): 277–293. https://doi.org/10.1111/taja.12330.
———. 2019b. "Missionaries in the Melanesian World." In *The Melanesian World*, edited by Eric Hirsch and Will Rollason, 77–91. Oxon, U.K.: Routledge.
Barr, John. 1983. "A Survey of Ecstatic Phenomena and 'Holy Spirit Movements' in Melanesia." *Oceania* 54 (2): 109–132. https://doi.org/10.1002/j.1834-4461.1983.tb00340.x.
Barth, Karl. 1963. *Evangelical Theology: An Introduction*. Translated by Grover Foley. New York: Holt, Rinehart & Winston.
Bialecki, Jon. 2018. "Christianity." In *The International Encyclopedia of Anthropology*, edited by Hilary Callan, 1–5. Hoboken, N.J.: John Wiley & Sons.
Bond, Nathan, and Jaap Timmer. 2017. "Wondrous Geographies and Historicity for State-Building on Malaita, Solomon Islands." *Journal of Religious and Political Change* 3 (3): 136–151. https://doi.org/10.1080/20566093.2017.1351169.
Burt, Ben. 1983. "The Remnant Church: A Christian Sect of the Solomon Islands." *Oceania* 53 (4): 334–346. https://doi.org/10.1002/j.1834-4461.1983.tb01997.x.
———. 1994. *Tradition and Christianity: The Colonial Transformation of a Solomon Islands Society*. Chur, Switzerland: Harwood Academic.
Eriksen, Annelin. 2008. *Gender, Christianity and Change in Vanuatu: An Analysis of Social Movements in North Ambrym*. Aldershot, U.K.: Ashgate.
Eriksen, Annelin, and Michelle MacCarthy. 2019. "Charismatic Churches, Revivalism and New Religious Movements." In *The Melanesian World*, edited by Eric Hirsch and Will Rollason, 345–358. Oxon, U.K.: Routledge.
Griffiths, Alison. 1977. *Fire in the Islands! The Acts of the Holy Spirit in the Solomons*. Wheaton, Ill.: Harold Shaw.
Hermkens, Anna-Karina. 2020. "Charismatic Catholic Renewal in Bougainville: Revisiting the Power of Marian Devotion as a Cultural and Socio-political Force." *Australian Journal of Anthropology* 31 (2): 152–169. https://doi.org/10.1111/taja.12360.
Hess, Tom. 2008. *The Watchmen: Being Prepared and Preparing the Way for Messiah*. 4th ed. Jerusalem: Progressive Vision; Jerusalem: Jerusalem House of Prayer for All Nations.
Hess, Tom, and Kate Hess. 2012. *House of Prayer for All Nations: The World Wide Watch*. Rev. ed. Jerusalem: Progressive Vision.
Hirsch, Eric. 2008. "God or Tidibe? Melanesian Christianity and the Problem of Wholes." *Ethnos* 73 (2): 141–162. https://doi.org/10.1080/00141840802180330.
Hogbin, H. Ian. 1939. *Experiments in Civilization: The Effects of European Culture on a Native Community of the Solomon Islands*. London: Routledge & Kegan Paul.
Houston, Christopher. 2022. "Alternative Me? Anthropology and Self-Alteration." *HAU: Journal of Ethnographic Theory* 12 (2): 482–498. https://doi.org/10.1086/720356.
Humphrey, Caroline. 2008. "Reassembling Individual Subjects: Events and Decisions in Troubled Times." *Anthropological Theory* 8 (4): 357–380. https://doi.org/10.1177/1463499608096644.
Jorgensen, Dan. 1994. "Locating the Divine in Melanesia: An Appreciation of the Work of Kenelm Burridge." *Anthropology & Humanism* 19 (2): 130–137. https://doi.org/10.1525/ahu.1994.19.2.130.
Lambek, Michael. 2018. *Island in the Stream: An Ethnographic History of Mayotte*. Toronto: University of Toronto Press.
Macdonald, Fraser. 2019. "Melanesia Burning: Religious Revolution in the Western Pacific." *Journal of the Polynesian Society* 128 (4): 391–410. https://www.jstor.org/stable/26912174.
Maeliau, Michael. 1976. "The Remnant Church—(a Separatist Church)." Unpublished manuscript. Copy in possession of author.

———. 1987. "Searching for a Melanesian Way of Worship." In *The Gospel Is Not Western: Black Theologies from the Southwest Pacific*, edited by Garry W. Trompf, 119–127. Maryknoll, N.Y.: Orbis.

———. 2018a. *The Land of Ophir*. Honiara, Solomon Islands: Provincial Press.

———. 2018b. *The Lion of the Tribe of Judah*. Honiara, Solomon Islands: Provincial Press.

———. 2021. *The Revelation of the Glory of the Lord*. Self-published, Kindle Direct.

McDowell, Nancy. 1988. "A Note on Cargo Cults and Cultural Constructions of Change." *Pacific Studies* 11 (2): 121–134. http://lir.byuh.edu/index.php/pacific/article/view/2811/2719.

Mosko, M. 2010. "Partible Penitents: Dividual Personhood and Christian Practice in Melanesia and the West." *Journal of the Royal Anthropological Institute* 16 (2): 215–240. https://doi.org/10.1111/j.1467-9655.2010.01618.x.

Robbins, Joel. 2004. *Becoming Sinners: Christianity & Moral Torment in a Papua New Guinea Society*. Berkeley: University of California Press.

Robbins, Joel, Bambi Schieffelin, and Aparecida Vilaça. 2014. "Evangelical Conversion and the Transformation of the Self in Amazonia and Melanesia: Christianity and the Revival of Anthropological Comparison." *Comparative Studies in Society and History* 56 (3): 559–590.

Strathern, Marilyn. 1988. *The Gender of the Gift: Problems with Women and Problems with Society in Melanesia*. Berkeley: University of California Press.

Timmer, Jaap. 2015. "Building Jerusalem in North Malaita, Solomon Islands." *Oceania* 85 (3): 299–314. https://doi.org/10.1002/ocea.5110.

———. 2022. "All Pacific Arise." World Religions and Spirituality Project. Accessed January 4, 2023. https://wrldrels.org/2022/09/24/all-peoples-prayer-assembly/.

Timmer, Jaap, and Ian Frazer. 2023. "The Religious Self-Alteration of Shem Irofa'alu during the Anti-colonial Maasina Rule in Solomon Islands (1944–1953)." *Oceania* 93 (1): 23–40. https://doi.org/10.1002/ocea.5356.

Trompf, Garry W. 1977. Introduction to *Prophets of Melanesia: Six Essays*, edited by Garry W. Trompf, 1–10. Port Moresby, Papua New Guinea: Institute of Papua New Guinea Studies; Suva, Fiji: Institute of Pacific Studies, University of the South Pacific.

Wariboko, Nimi. 2012. *The Pentecostal Principle: Ethical Methodology in New Spirit*. Grand Rapids: Eerdmans.

White, Geoffrey M. 1991. *Identity through History: Living Stories in a Solomon Islands Society*. Cambridge: Cambridge University Press.

PART II SELF-ALTERATION AND POLITICAL ACTIVISM

4 · FABRICATING THE NEW MAN AND WOMAN
Self-Alteration through Revolutionary Socialism

CHRISTOPHER HOUSTON

Socialist movements hope and assert that revolution generates a new world. Through it, humanity acquires a changed collective ontology, and participants alter their selves. Leftist revolutionary activism wagers all, then, on the contention that radical *social* change is a prerequisite for genuine self-knowledge and self-alteration. In doing so, it runs against the grain of a century of psychiatric care whose dominant models of self-alteration privilege individual and psychological factors and downplay the sickness of the social order.

How do revolutionary political projects imagine and pursue self-alteration? In this essay, I analyze three very different events and portrayals of revolutionary socialism, as well as the forms of self-alteration they enable. The first takes place in the Soviet Union in the years 1931–1933 and concerns the fabled building of the White Sea–Baltic Sea Canal, as well as its collectively written "live history" edited by Maxim Gorky. The second occurs in Algeria and revisits alterations in individual practices and collective consciousness experienced by those pursuing the socialist war of national liberation against the French, as described by Pierre Bourdieu in his book *The Algerians* ([1958] 1962).

The chapter then brings these accounts of revolution and of their fabricating of new men and women into dialogue with a third activism, the militant politics of Turkey in the late 1970s. Elsewhere, I have described how the years 1976–1980 were a time of intense urban activism and political creativity in Istanbul (Houston 2020). Revolutionary (*devrimci*) political organizations, legal and illegal, flourished in the city, radicalizing students, workers, and professional associations. Here was an attempt to make a city socialist from "below," unlike the 1924–1933 period in Russia, where through radical architecture and planning, the new Soviet state and communist government sought to construct a salvific socialist city. This sprawling revolutionary movement came to a jarring halt with the military insurrection of September 12, 1980, leading to an unprecedented phase of martial law and criminal state terror. Unlike in Algeria, the revolutionary enterprise in Turkey resulted not in victory but in defeat.

Despite profound differences among these three events and situations, the comparison reveals at least two binding ties among them. The first is the way militants in each new revolutionary enterprise reanimate the significance and meaning of the revolutions that precede their struggle, injecting its histories, practices, and outcomes into their own tempestuous debates over strategy and ideology. Heroes or heretics, socialist actors—Vladimir Lenin, Che Guevara, Ben M'hidi—are made to live on again in the fractious practices of every subsequent revolutionary situation. In claiming political figures and even whole revolutions for themselves, militant groups graft themselves into prestigious socialist lineages.

A second core commonality exists at the ideological level—in activists' shared conviction that only *collective* social revolution can lead to profound *individual* self-change. For these movements, without a (post)revolutionary society, any individual character development, personal ethical modifications, altered self-knowledge, or phenomenological *epoche* (see Houston 2022b) is minor and insignificant. As Leon Trotsky puts it in *Literature and Revolution*, only in the classless society established by the proletarian revolution will "social construction and psycho-physical self-education ... become two aspects of one and the same process" (cited in Cherstich, Holbraad, and Tassi, 66).

Why this must be so is most comprehensively elaborated in Bourdieu's other sociological-cum-political writings. For him, persons are constituted by their society. Objective social structures fabricate and socialize in each member schemes of perception and appreciation, bodily postures and stances, and modes of cognition. Self-alteration, thus, is impossible without a transformation of the structures that condition consciousness. Revolutionary practice is the necessary exception to "normal" exploitative social life. Without it, and in the usual run of events, the classed and gendered conditions of existence deposit in "agents" durable dispositions whose generation of practices in turn leads to the reproduction of those material conditions. Accordingly, short of a revolution, even consciousness-raising by subordinated individuals changes little (Bourdieu 2001).

According to an emerging anthropology of revolution (Ghamari-Tabrizi 2021; Cherstich, Holbraad, and Tassi 2020), the socialist conviction that only systematic reform can fabricate the new man and woman testifies to a belief both in the malleability of human beings at birth and in their intractability once local social practices and structures lay down in them a socially fabricated habitus. In postrevolutionary society, political strategies to remake such intractable selves often manifest in violent and psychologically intrusive methods of thought reform, self-criticism, and transformation of conscience (ethics). Igor Cherstich, Martin Holbraad, and Nico Tassi analyze Maoist conceptions of and techniques to produce "revolutionary personhood," noting "ever more penetrating attempts by the revolutionary process to reformat individuals, moulding them into 'new people' (*xin min*), in the idealized image of Mao himself as well as other selected models of revolutionary citizens" (2020, 81). Similarly, through compulsory labor, the Belomor Canal experiment sought to "reforge" consciousness in prisoners.

Nevertheless, below I also show that contrary to the totalistic logic of revolution and of postrevolutionary society, in Turkey, it was not a new order established by a revolution that enabled men and women to alter but, more significantly, revolutionary political activism itself. Militants were both pedagogues and students at the same time. The alternative (mis)use of place by their factions effected a transformation in militants' embodied subjective perceptions of "the world" (e.g., of the city and its places, of other people, of machines and objects, of its violence and social order, etc.). In the same way, political action facilitated an intersubjective encounter with the "working class" that modified partisans' ethical senses. In short, activism afforded militants insights into various factors that constitute what Edmund Husserl ([1913] 2012) calls the "natural attitude"—in the process, neutralizing its taking of things for granted and generating in turn what we can call a political *epoche*.

SELF-ALTERATION AT THE WHITE SEA CANAL

I begin with the "I. V. Stalin White Sea–Baltic Sea Canal," a massive infrastructure project of 227 kilometers built in just twenty months by more than one hundred thousand convict prisoners, at the cost of thousands of laborers' lives who died from overwork, sickness, and work accidents.[1] A celebrated development in Stalin's first five-year plan to transform the agrarian Soviet Union into an industrial powerhouse, the digging of the canal, with its forty-four dams, was also germane to the regime's "war on nature." The White Sea–Baltic Sea Canal project can be contextualized by placing it within the wider history of both the most revolutionary period of the new Soviet state and its most utopian futurism; when alongside brutal coercion, it sought to inspire and mobilize citizens into giving their allegiance to its romance of making things new and equal. Soviet revolution thus involved an ethical appeal: a promise to enable people to act as more virtuous subjects.

The White Sea–Baltic Sea Canal has generated a conflicted literature, from Aleksandr Solzhenitsyn's (1973) condemnation of its brutality in his *Gulag Archipelago* to Maxim Gorky's celebratory *Stalin's White Sea—Baltic Canal: History of Construction 1931–1934*, edited by him and two others in 1934, translated into English in 1935, and banned in the Soviet Union in 1937 (Gorky, Averbakh, and Firin 1935). Gorky's work originated from a 1933 regime-sponsored visit to the finished canal project by a large delegation of writers, who did interviews with convict-workers in the presence of camp authorities. An early 1936 review of the English translation in the *Geographical Journal* found that "the main interest of the book is to be found in the description of the methods of education applied in the labour camps, methods which are said to have transformed the professional criminals into enthusiastic workers, and the class enemies into convinced followers of proletarian ideals" (F. L. 1936, 559).

The psycho-politics of the canal have been of continuing interest in more recent studies.[2] Nearly all of them zero in on the word and act of *reforging* (in Russian, *perekova*), the primary metaphor used by the Stalinist regime to describe the process whereby prisoners were recast through communal labor. According to Julie Draskoczy, reforging was central to Soviet penal philosophy during the construction of the White Sea–Baltic Sea Canal, where authorities desired to reform the population of the work camps into "dedicated believers and practitioners of Soviet ideology" (2012, 31).

Were all prisoners allowed to take part in the destructive-creative process of self-reforging? The literature makes it clear that in the work camps, some selves were not considered remakeable. The remodeling project thus was selective, and "political" prisoners or "socially alien" elements were perceived as enemies committed to the interests of their bourgeois or landlord class. By contrast, criminals were asserted to be made, not born, and in Marxian fashion, Soviet criminology saw them as products of their social conditions. Indeed, according to Draskoczy (2012), in the unstable and poverty-struck conditions of the Soviet Union in the 1920s, many of the criminal prisoners at the canal had been orphaned early in life, describing in their camp-written autobiographies their falling into the path of crime as an act of survival. That was one reason, too, for the Bolsheviks' instituting of a five-year maximum prison sentence for crimes.

Methods of reforging were twofold. The first was through the redemptive path of *physical labor* and duress in a work collective, coupled with socialist *work competition* between brigades of workers, a work-for-extra-food rationing system, and early release for "heroic" labor performance and self-reform. The other was through "art" and education, with many of the camp programs being prisoner run. For Draskoczy (2014, 19), the prison was a site of "intense creativity." In it, autobiographical writing, costumed plays, musical performances, literacy programs, technical and professional courses, writing competitions, and production of a camp newspaper appropriately titled *Reforging* were all aspects of reeducation. "Educators" were often criminal mentors who took a special interest in fostering the journeying of new convicts along the path of self-reform. This autobiographical self-confession conformed to what Oleg Kharkhordin (1999) identifies as the secularization by the Bolsheviks of Orthodox ecclesiastical rites of public penance, whereby self-criticism and later self-denunciation became a central aspect of Stalin's purges.

Which part, if any, of this remolding was self-willed? We can never know. In her book *Belomor: Criminality and Creativity in Stalin's Gulag*, Draskoczy (2014) analyzes unpublished prisoner-written autobiographies, poems, and short stories from the Belomor Canal labor camp collected in the Russian State Archive for Literature and Art. She notes that the camp was a disorganized place, with relative freedom of movement and a lack of barbed wire and tall fences (197). More significantly for the question of inmates' agency, she underscores the "diversity of prisoners' reactions to the enforced ideological programs, [as well as] the complexity of their reactions and the many sources of their motivations" (Draskoczy 2012, 47).

SELF-ALTERATION THROUGH ANTI-COLONIAL SOCIALIST STRUGGLE IN ALGERIA

A second description of collective and individual alteration through engagement with revolutionary socialism involves Bourdieu's analysis of the "awakening" of consciousness experienced by participants through their prosecution of war against the French colonial system. Bourdieu describes a twofold movement of Algerian resistance to French settler colonization through which people made themselves "new men and women." The first he names "colonial traditionalism" ([1958] 1962, 155), whereby forms of behavior that were once naturalized and taken for granted by locals—dubbed "traditional traditionalism"—are now purposely selected to express opposition to the colonial order and its values. Bourdieu uses the example of the veil, "consciously utilized" by Algerian women as a "language of refusal" (156, 157) to assimilate. In short, given the relentless social upheaval caused by destructive colonialism, Algerians were compelled "to make a conscious examination of the implicit premises or the unconscious patterns of [their] own tradition" (144).

A second phase of resistance and self-change begins with the existence and activities of a revolutionary organization (the FLN, or National Liberation Front), a revolt that Bourdieu tellingly describes as issuing in the "end of a world." In moving from resistance to rebellion, the practices of colonial traditionalism through which a dominated caste had symbolically defended its integrity were rendered "valueless" (Bourdieu [1958] 1962, 157). Among conduct that now lost its significance was veiling. In their place, "each Algerian may henceforth assume full responsibility for his own actions and for the widespread borrowings he has made from Western civilization; he can even deny himself a portion of his cultural heritage without denying himself in the process" (157). This transformation in attitude results in profound modification in the Indigenous social system, including altered relationships to European education, housing, and medical services. Perceived no longer as Trojan horses to penetrate native populations or as gracious gifts, they are now understood as "prerogatives won by right of conquest" (160).

The revolutionary struggle also provided a counteractive *mood* to the feelings of anguish, shame, humiliation, and despair that the colonial overthrow of a vital social order had caused. For Frantz Fanon ([1961] 1963), too, and contrary to psychiatry's individualizing of pathology, colonialism produces sickness and madness in its victims. Both Bourdieu and Fanon (see below) thus ascribe a central *affective* dimension to the process of decolonization, as the war transformed intersubjective relations between the dominant French and dominated Arab castes/races. Europeans "no longer cast a spell over the Algerian" (Bourdieu [1958] 1962, 161). Rather, Algerians "regard as scandalous injustice all that they formerly endured as ineluctable and inescapable necessity" (161). The cultural *unmaking* of Algerians is reversed by their remaking via revolution. For each analyst, then, *self*-awareness and autonomy are inaugurated only through participation in this revolutionary project to destroy the social structures of the colonial order.

Jeffrey Alexander (1995) informs us that *The Algerians*, the 1962 English translation of Bourdieu's 1958 book *Sociologie de l'Algerie*, had added to it a second section written by Bourdieu in 1961 ("The Revolution within the Revolution"). The two halves are radically different.[3] The first half presents an ethnographic reconstruction of precolonial, original Arab and Kabyle societies—preliterate, timeless, functionally integrated, deaf to their own self-composition, and devoid of individuals with any genuine personal life. Call them Bourdylia.

By contrast, the second half of the book makes a sensitive historical and social analysis of the revolutionary political situation in Algeria witnessed by Bourdieu at the time of writing. Identifying and condemning the continuing "social vivisection" of Algerian society by the colonial system, Bourdieu writes about anti-colonial revolt as an efficacious mode of both collective and individual self-alteration and new self-knowledge. The regular reappearance of Bourdylia in his later work in a new, more abstract language of habitus, dispositions, doxa, symbolic violence, and so on, each of which mandates against self-alteration, demonstrates that Bourdieu has forgotten or rejected what Alexander (1995, 197) calls these early "phenomenological-Marxist" arguments.[4]

Nevertheless, despite these differences, there is some overlap between "The Revolution within the Revolution" and Bourdieu's mature work. Alongside his agentive analysis of the revolutionary project of individual and collective self-alteration in the second half of *The Algerians*, he also implies that given the objective processes and underlying conditions of colonialism, the Algerian people's resistance and pursuit of anti-colonial war was singularly determined. He writes, "Individual conflicts were based on an objective situation which conditioned all the dramas that went on in men's consciousness" ([1958] 1962, 149). For Algerian combatants, once they committed to revolutionary war, liberation from the colonial order could only come through victory. War and revolution were systemic necessities, "as if they could not have been otherwise" (Humphrey 2008, 358). In short, even as war is a "cultural agent" of change, Bourdieu underplays the acts and decisions whereby particular people decide to "wage war." It is in these dynamic processes that revolutions are co-made, caused both by unfolding historical developments and by subjective personal commitments to political autonomy and action.

What significant contrasts can we identify in the Soviet and Algerian projects and accounts of socialist self-alteration, even if for both of them revolutionary action enables the birth of a new person? Most important is the radical difference in the causal force that engenders subjects' self-reconstruction. In the Soviet

Union, it is the revolutionary regime that takes responsibility for providing the infrastructure, inspirational and coercive, that enables and obliges people to reforge themselves. Labor camps like those associated with the White Sea–Baltic Sea Canal condense and intensify this obligation, as "criminals" are forced to participate in mechanisms that might remake them. Sheila Fitzpatrick (1999) suggests that in less magnified ways, however, all Soviet citizens shared the experience of the canal's inmates of destructive-creative reforging, being likewise simultaneously addressed by the *institutions* of the new Soviet state and monitored for participation in those institutions' attempted creation of altered personalities.

By contrast, although for Bourdieu war is the final cause of the destruction of both the colonial order and the Indigenous cultural system, it is also Algerians' willing embarkation upon revolutionary activism, terrorist violence, and the independence struggle itself that becomes a powerful mode of both individual and collective self-alteration. Unlike at the White Sea–Baltic Sea Canal, Algerian people's forging of a new "political conscience" in themselves becomes the very precondition of the establishment of the revolutionary Algerian state.

REVOLUTIONARY SELF-ALTERATION IN ISTANBUL

How can we connect the Algerian and the Soviet projects to the alterations of the self enabled by participation in revolutionary politics in Istanbul in the late 1970s? Most significantly, militants themselves constructed relations among all three events. Turkish revolutionaries composed the historical meanings of the Soviet revolution, of socialist China, and of other anti-imperialist movements from countries around the world, including Algeria. One outcome of their doing so was that Istanbul's revolutionary politics fractured gratuitously between pro-China and pro-Albanian Maoist groups (e.g., People's Liberation, or HK), pro-Soviet parties (e.g., the Turkish Communist Party, or TKP), and several "third-way" mass movements inspired by Che Guevara–style anti-imperialism and popular uprising, the largest and most significant being the Revolutionary Way (or *Dev Yol*).[5]

Below I focus on perceptual truths, activist practices, *and* pedagogical processes by which both novice and experienced militants in revolutionary organizations in Istanbul in the 1970s sought to modify their own spatial, ethical, and social perceptions. Fieldwork for this research involved both archival work and intimate conversations with more than fifty ex-militants, men and women, all of whom were active in various leftist political organizations in the 1970s. For activists in some groups, their experiences of political activism were understood as personally transformative, being a foretaste of the socialist organization of society to come. The attempted carving out of "liberated zones" in some of Istanbul's poorest informal settlements was apprehended as the gaining of a foothold on the future. By contrast, according to the theory of other groups, individual self-alteration during the phase of revolutionary struggle could at best be only partial, even as factions educated partisans toward a new awareness of their historical formation, class interests, and collective fate. *Complete* self-alteration awaited the arrival of a socialist society animated by radically different imaginary significations and structured by new pedagogical institutions.

Despite these differences, all groups sought to educate militants in an alternative attentiveness to their lives and to the lives of others. One concern was to enable novice activists to perceive that their situation was neither immutable nor particular to themselves and that their common existence could be changed through political action as a member of an oppressed class. Personal and collective self-alteration thus was to be best achieved by changing the classed world that crafted you and others as subordinated persons. To use the language of phenomenology, organizations drew activists' attention to their own political intersubjectivity and to its bond to an unequal city.

Developing this new *class* self-awareness was difficult in 1970s Turkey, but not because of any lingering "traditional traditionalism" (as described by Bourdieu [1958] 1962) that first had to be destroyed in prospective recruits. Activists were already intimately familiar with radical social movements. Most significant, of course, was the Turkish Republic itself, founded as a powerful "state-social movement assemblage" (Houston 2022a, 386) in 1923 by militants of the Committee of Union and Progress (the so-called Young Turks). In its rupture with the Ottoman past, the republic itself was revolutionary, and Kemal Atatürk was its first militant.

In pursuing political change in Istanbul in the 1970s, then, revolutionary activists were forced to deal with the legacy of the Kemalist state's own self-proclaimed cultural revolution. This included the Kemalists' overt propagation of Turkish nationalist consciousness and affect in the imagination of its citizens, as well as the repetition of their never-ending enlightenment revolution. Kemalism's third significant "arrow" was the corporatist contention that the Turkish nation was classless, composed of functional groupings among whom antagonistic relations did not exist, and presided over by a modernizing party (Atatürk's Republican People's Party) that claimed both to protect the interests of the Turkish nation *and* to be its sole legitimate representative.

In short, because these perceptual truths of Kemalism "vibrated" in militants' en-minded bodies, the disputed meanings of this first (Kemalist) revolution generated difficulties for them in creating unified action. On the other hand, it also acted as a goad to action, being a powerful political affordance. What was the result? Perceiving in Kemalism a nationalist, anti-imperialist revolution, some parties sought its restitution. Others maintained that it was a bourgeois revolution made against a feudal ancien régime and thus advocated its transcending. A third position asserted that it had established a fascist oligarchy and advocated its overthrow. Maoist factions focused on mobilizing peasants, supporting their land occupations while seeking to restart the republic's aborted land reforms. Socialist parties concentrated on organizing proletarians. Revolutionary Kurds pursued national self-determination alongside a socialist struggle against Western imperialism. Kemalist radicals conspired with sections of the military to ferment a progressive "colonels" coup and a national front.

Yet across all these disputed political practices, activists modified their self-understandings through the acquisition of mastery in a new *language*. Militants learned to speak "socialist." Language socialization allowed partisans to resubjectify themselves through skillful adaptations of existing speech genres, such as putting leftist poems to music, bestowing "traditional" folk songs (*türkü*) with new lyrics, performing revolutionary theater, creating and chanting slogans, and rewriting obituaries. Indeed, participation in activist groups involved induction into a new sonic world. Interviewees reported that they heard genres of music and even particular musical instruments as politically charged. Partisans learned to listen to songs to know which group was occupying the ferry or bus or marching down the street. They remembered that the period was a time for *speaking out fearlessly* in meetings and at organized events in the evenings. In any week, one group or other would organize a "campaign" in celebration of an important figure or event. Speechmaking, then, became a valued skill.

Alongside this education in language, sound, and practice, revolutionary activists and their factions sought to reorient and alter their political selves in other ways as well. Militants devised protest repertoires that forced the issue of the collective enemy (i.e., the police, or the fascists, or rival "revisionist" leftist groups) upon embodied consciousness. Marking space visually and sonically through graffiti, slogans, posters, and pirate speeches was a challenge to other groups and a sign of spatial authority. Pasting notices was a good form of corporeal alteration. One activist said to me, "First, fourteen-to-fifteen-year-old youths would hang up posters and get arrested and perhaps beaten. By seventeen or eighteen, they would develop into hardened militants."

Equally importantly, modifications in perceptions of the city and of the self came about through militants becoming teachers of revolutionary practices and ideas to one another, as well as to the targets of their group's consciousness-raising—to workers employed in Istanbul's bourgeoning import-substitution industrial plants, to inhabitants of the informal settlements that dotted the edges of the city, and to high school and university students. Bülent recounted how as a member of a communist theater group, he went to strikes to perform plays for the picket line or protesters. "Workers used to look at us as we acted, very stereotypical characters in the plays; the worker, the bourgeoisie, the police, and so on. Watching us, I wondered what they thought," he said.

Alongside militants' learning of revolutionary texts, organizations encouraged their practical work in Istanbul's massive shantytowns (*gecekondu*). Partisans' attempted building of relations between what they called the resistance districts and themselves became a rite of passage for tens of thousands of leftist students. For student-militants, working in informal settlements—perceived as sites of unfolding revolution—was a process of character formation. They were also politically violent places where self-defense was necessary to protect oneself against attacks by anti-communist "commandos." Given the high possibility of a violent encounter in the city, one vital activity involved the assembling of a microgeographical knowledge of places and the developing of a political-spatial intuition to minimize risk.

According to interviewees, activist work in squatter settlements involved a huge range of practices, including selling the group's journal there, teaching literacy classes, protecting the gecekondu from attacks (e.g., on its coffeehouses), and providing services (holding health clinics, bringing medicine, giving legal advice, building roads and stairs, digging house foundations, organizing piping and public water taps, and pouring concrete). "I took a woman to have an abortion—I was sixteen!" said Özlem. Importantly, some student activists themselves were from the first, more established gecekondu suburbs settled in the 1950s and 1960s. As part of their "people's war," students from different groups devised their own curricula of small novels and books to teach reading. For those from the Turkish People's Liberation Army (THKO) and the Turkish Revolutionary Path (TDY), for example, it included Leo Huberman's (1953) *The ABC of Socialism* and Stalin's ([1906] 2020) *Anarchism or Socialism?*

Another way of thinking about these practices and perceptions of self-alteration is to consider their contribution to militants' developing ethical sense. Revolutionary organizations were communities of practice, modifying militants' ethical perceptions. For example, partisans' self-educating involved cultivating a *mood* that would enable them to sense and be affected by aspects of shantytown existence—for interviewees, this was a fostered sympathy that perceived urban misery as an effect of the oligarchy's exploitation and neglect. At the same time, their work there unfolded among the maelstrom of intersubjective interactions with people, which also brought them into friction with other explicit intentions of socialist class struggle. Revolutionaries were "caught" trying to solve the problems of the poor, seeking to educate them in what Henri Lefebvre (1996) calls the "right to the city," inciting them in making a revolution, and protecting them against "fascist" violence visited upon settlements by their own presence there.

All endeavors were significant in understanding the modified ethical perspectives of revolutionary subjects in Istanbul. Place breakdown provoked a questioning of spatial order and of its hierarchical divisions, as well as sensitivity toward existing conventions of urban engagement, bodily movement and comportment, and socially gendered relationships. For both male and female student-militants from Istanbul's more middle-class suburbs, successful propaganda and solidarity work in the gecekondu required conscious performance and mastery of a new embodied style. Serdar (*People's Voice*, or *Halk Sesi*) remembered the Yılmaz Güney film titled *Arkadaş* (Friend), where someone from the slums asks the hero why he has long hair: "He cuts it. I cut mine. We didn't want to do anything that would separate us from the people." Dilek (TKP) told me the story of a university student who came to the union building for lunch where she was a lawyer: they were all eating together, and she noticed him hardly touching his food. "Why aren't you eating?" she asked him. "I am trying to get used to being hungry," the student said, "like the workers."

In the squatter settlements, talking, eating, sitting (on the floor), and even smoking were intuited as ethical performances and as props critical for the success of communicating militants' messages. For example, activists perceived that smoking Marlboro cigarettes would set them apart from the people: "Revolutionaries smoked *Birinci*. Sometimes we even took off the filter, as it was seen as a luxury" (Özlem, People's Liberation Party-Front of Turkey, or THKP-C). In the process of intense social interaction with shantytown inhabitants, activists exhibited exemplary behavior according to certain existing normative practices and ideals, even as they sought to add fresh meanings to them. The longish skirts worn by female activists conformed to the sexual ethics of both gecekondu residents and militant groups, who discouraged flirting between members. Certain phrases summarized the "techniques of the body" (Mauss 1973) pursued by female activists: "Revolutionary girls don't use makeup" and "Revolutionary girls don't dress up."

Ethical self-cultivation, then, was also fostered through revolutionaries' politicization of gendered and sexual conduct, which simultaneously became a spatial tactic and an embodied politics. Marriage and relationships took on political meanings, as Şahin (*Birikim* journal) recounted: "I married in 1979, partly so I could set up another activist house. For a wedding present, I asked my mum and dad for eight *divan* [sofa beds]. Ten or eleven people would stay and eat every night: I remember doing lots of dishes with two, three other people." Female militants would sometimes stay overnight at the organizations' houses in the gecekondu with other males. "That's why the newspapers said things about our morals, but no one thought of having sex in that time," noted Ayda (*Dev Yol*). "We said 'sexual relations were bourgeois.'" Indeed, militants themselves discouraged sexual relations among comrades and policed displays of affection: "If you so much as touched a hand, it meant you were together, married. Only if you were engaged could you hold hands, otherwise it was politically shameful" (Levent, *Dev Yol*).

In this intense period of ethical and social self-formation, revolutionary activists and groups also gave new meanings to the deaths (and lives) of those killed by police, state gendarmerie, or "civil fascists." Constructed as both martyrs (*şehit*) and witnesses (*şahit*)—the Arabic root of the two words is the same—it was the dead more than any living factional leaders or ideologues who became exemplary and motivating figures of revolutionary action and life.

The short obituary for Kemal Karaca published in *Devrimci Yol* (newspaper) on May 1, 1977, is a case in point. Printed next to a black-and-white picture of the slain Kemal, the text reads, "While fighting militantly and sacrificially against the oligarchy, our heroic brother KEMAL KARACA was treacherously and deceitfully struck down. Let your memory lead our struggle, let your life be our honor! Once again, a thousand times again, we condemn provocation." Obituaries showed that becoming a revolutionary was intimately related to developing a "sacrificial subjectivity" (Bozarslan 2012, 4). In doing so, militants' own dramatic practices of activism were ethically and emotionally directed to something beyond themselves, such as the struggle for the emancipation of the working class and of the urban poor through the defeat of the violent oligarchy. Every death of an "anarchist" testified to the evils of fascism and to what must be sacrificed to oppose it.

Other "mourning genres" also sought to augment the affective capacities of activists needed for pursuing revolution. For example, there were the declarations (*demeç*) made by bereaved parents or siblings and published in newspapers alongside more extensive coverage of murderous events, declarations that were less standardized than obituaries and much more affecting. We see this in the statement of a father made in response to the killing of his son in a National Movement Party and police attack on leftist students at the Atatürk Education Institute in the town of Uşak, published in the newspaper *Devrimci Yol*. He wrote,

> Our son was a 25-year-old young man. Haydar often went to meetings and marches. We would say, "son, be careful, they can kill you, they can shoot you." "If I don't go, if you don't go, who will save this country?" he would reply. He would tell us that if we were unified, the oligarchy couldn't kill us, couldn't oppress us, and that they feared our unity. Of course, we didn't understand all this. But now we know it very well. We saw the police and the gendarmerie attack the school where our son studied with our own eyes; we lived the event. We saw how they took away our son's corpse.
>
> We are not saddened by Haydar's death, by his dying for this cause. We raised our son for these days. Every oppressed mother and father should raise their children for this path. We are no longer scared of the oligarchy's police and gendarmerie. We are on the path of Haydar. If one Haydar dies, then another one is born. The new Haydar, his brother's son, was born three days before his death. (*Devrimci Yol* 1977)

Because the dead cannot speak for themselves, in writing their obituaries, the living—their comrades, their families, and their organizations—were tasked with composing the meaning of a revolutionary's life. In giving their deaths, revolutionaries themselves were altered. They became model ethical figures of self-sacrifice, pathfinders for the living who followed in their footsteps. In that sense, once changed, "martyrs never die."

COMPARATIVE MODES OF REVOLUTIONARY SELF-ALTERATION

Above I have discussed three very different revolutionary movements and historical moments, identifying in them circumstances and strategies whereby their protagonists made aspects of themselves anew. Importantly, although some of this alteration was revealed and described by militants themselves, the political context conditioning their self-telling varied widely in the three situations. Maxim Gorky's edited book on the reforging of criminals at the Belomor Canal has long been criticized as shamefully unethical for the compromised nature of the interviews with prisoners upon which it was based. Bourdieu's eyewitness account of the Algerian revolution was made during his years of living and researching in Algeria, although in typical fashion, he never includes any personal narratives of local militants or situates himself as a presence in the text. By contrast, my interviewing of activists about their memories of 1970s revolutionary Istanbul occurred *decades* after the 1980 military coup d'état and its show trials destroyed their parties. Clearly, the positions of the authors of these accounts vary widely. Gorky is a revolutionary insider, Bourdieu is an anti-"colonial" anthropologist, and I am a "white-Australian" scholar of Turkish politics. Nevertheless, despite this comparison of very different societies at very different points in time, we can make these examples synergize and draw meaning out of one another.

One significant factor influencing accounts and processes of self-alteration in all three situations is the fateful historical significance given by activists (and writers) to different "revolutionary" regimes—Kemalism in Turkey, the colonial state in Algeria, and the communist party in Russia. For Bourdieu, French colonialism's active destruction of the social order of local societies, and its overthrow in turn by the Algerian revolution, was a prerequisite for the emergence of a reflexive Algerian "self" and thus for any consequent *self*-alteration. Activists in Turkey sought to revitalize, transcend, or oppose the political revolution of the Atatürk Republic fifty years after its foundational militancy. Revolutionaries against the revolution, partisans constituted themselves in relation to other rival processes of subject formation. By contrast, at the Belomor Canal in the Soviet Union, self-alteration was forcibly enacted by the people-party-state, for the people-party-state. In all three situations, the central *purpose* of self-change was not to benefit the singular person but to emancipate the class of which the militant was a member.

Although the creation of new men and women was a stated aim of the revolutions, we can describe in a different vocabulary and more synthetic manner the ways in which *participation* from "below" in leftist praxis enabled experiences of self-alteration for activists. To take Turkey as an example, in 1970s Istanbul, militants ardently pursued—as well as passively experienced—changes of perspective, of language, of perception, of skill, of knowledge dependent on intersubjective encounter, of affective consciousness, and of ethical action. We can also call their self-mobilization a striving for "epistemic agency" (Guenther 2017), given that organizations were encountered as places of learning for student activists, workers, and gecekondu inhabitants who sought to join them. As in all forms of political activism, becoming a revolutionary was arduous even as militants embraced its demanding path.

In short, in Turkey and Algeria, activism in revolutionary groups provided subjects with a hard-won alternative historical perception of the world and its parts. Using the language of phenomenology, we can say that revolutionary self-education sought to neutralize the naive attitude that assumes the existence of the historical world as an objective, external reality divorced from one's intentions toward it. Instead, by displacing activists' ways of understanding the everyday world of experience, revolutionaries taught one another to *attend* to the anthropology of the existing social order, as well as to the morality of its poverty and wealth. As individuals' orientations toward the world changed—say by their living through the spatial convulsions wrought by urban militancy or by a diminution of their bodily capacities by state torture—so also did different properties of places, situations, emotions, and people, once at the margins of perception, come into audibility.

Yet, clearly, in Turkey bitter conflict over revolutionary aims and methods meant partisans of rival factions and groups did not all attend to the same things. These disputes reflected major disagreements over the analysis of both global and national situations, as well as the different experiences of those situations by revolutionaries from ethnic or religious minorities. One central arena of dissent concerned the act and purpose of *revolutionary violence*.

For militants, the very perceptual modifications enabled by activism facilitated a retrospective realization that one's class situation had been generated by the *violence* of political-socio forces that one was now opposing. Accordingly, partisans were forced into a decision about the role of counterviolence in resisting that fate. In the main, violence was justified and enacted in either a defensive or a strategic-pragmatic mode. For example, in Istanbul, *Dev Yol* partisans, who fostered linkages with people living in the informal settlements, were overexposed to paramilitary violence from the anti-communists and ultranationalists in the urban struggle over the shantytowns. In response, militants organized neighborhood "defense committees," self-authorized to check the identities of people wishing to enter to protect residents against National Movement Party death squads.

But revolutionary violence could serve righteous purposes too, as in the just assassination of a state torturer or of a murderous policeman. And it could be strategic as well, pursued to expel rival factions from schools, lodgments, or suburbs to occupy them in turn. Indeed, in both Algeria and Turkey, more explicit justifications for acts of revolutionary violence were connected to the inspirational blueprint of Che Guevara's successful revolutionary experience in Cuba, as well as to Regis Debray's (1967) formulation of it in his book *Revolution in the Revolution? Armed Struggle and Political Struggle in Latin America*, translated into Turkish in the very same year. According to Debray, exemplary military acts of guerilla bands, by providing a *focus* for popular but suppressed discontent, can catalyze, speed up, or jump-start a general insurrection against the existing regime. Turkish *focoism* gained a mass dimension in the second half of the 1970s. "Armed propaganda" became one of its strategic practices, constituting both a mode of revolutionary action and a mode of relationship with the people.

Nevertheless, for a minority of militants, the act of revolutionary violence was desirable for another reason. It enabled the creation of a new relationship with oneself, a belief that also appeared at the Belomor Canal as the fiery metaphor of *reforging* shows. According to Hamit Bozarslan, in the poetry of influential Turkish revolutionary Mahir Çayan, there is a personalization of revolution that portrays it as creating a "new man." For Çayan, "the responsibility for slavery also lies with the slave himself and it is only his resistance that will allow him to become a free man. Violence is the main key to reach this goal" (Bozarslan 2012, 6).

The assertion resembles Fanon's ([1961] 1963) claim made in *The Wretched of the Earth*. In arguing that in Algeria the liberation of the colonized and racialized masses can only be achieved by armed struggle, Fanon's investigation of the violence of racist colonialism and of its effects on the personality of the colonized subject analyzes why at both the collective and the individual levels the event of anti-colonial violence is self-altering. The practice of violence "binds [colonized people] together as a whole, since each individual forms a violent link in the great chain, a part of the great organism of violence which has surged upwards in reaction to the settler's violence in the beginning." For the individual, "violence is a cleansing force. It frees the native from his inferiority conflict and from his despair and inaction; it makes him fearless and restores his self-respect" (73).

Here we find a key distinction between Fanon's and Bourdieu's analyses of the situation of revolt in Algeria, as well as between their diagnoses concerning the alteration of the self. Fanon and Bourdieu agree that in the process of decolonization, "no conciliation is possible" (Fanon [1961] 1963, 32).[6] However, one glaring difference between their analyses is Bourdieu's use of the term *caste system* to describe colonialism compared to Fanon's concentration on "race." For Bourdieu, freedom requires economic independence, given racism is a secondary product of the exploitative colonial system. By contrast, for Fanon, *Black liberation* occurs only by destroying the "rhythms" that corrupt colonialism imposes upon the "brains" of the colonized.

CONCLUSION

Education in political practice and theory that modifies militants' worldly intentions, transforming the oppressed through the event of (anti-oppressor) violence, and reforging prospective revolutionaries through art and hard labor: all have been pursued as revolutionary modes of self-alteration.

In each case, their temporalities are different. In her essay on animal rights activists in India, Naisargi Dave notes that for activists, social movements "are full of becomings: they are defined and made by them" (2017, 164–165). Yet Dave also describes animal rights activists as commonly narrating how in a critical *moment* of sighting a suffering animal, they "stake their commitment to a way of life . . . after which nothing can ever be the same" (152). In the same way, for Fanon, revolutionary violence heralds "instant" personal and social change, becoming a radical act that might heal the "mental disorders" ([1961] 1963, 203) caused by racism and the colonial system.

By contrast, *apprentice activism* is slow, modifying the self through the steady altering of militants' perceptions of the world. In Istanbul, militants worked with and committed themselves to political groups, trade unions, civil society associations, and socialist parties for years, as the recent self-identification of activists as the "1968–1978 generation" shows. Rival answers to Lenin's revolutionary question "What is to be done?" gave on to dispute over rival temporalities involved in altering activists' selves.

But the Turkish event suggests the significance of one further issue concerning the temporality of revolutionary struggle. How much time will be afforded revolutionaries for social-self alteration before the counterrevolution and its modes of making subjects begin?

NOTES

1. See Morukov (2003) for the administrative history of the canal project.
2. See, for example, Fitzpatrick (1999), Kharkhordin (1999), and Draskoczy (2012, 2014).
3. There is no indication in the 1962 English text that it is made up of two sections written three years apart.
4. See, for example, *Outline of a Theory of Practice* (Bourdieu), *The Logic of Practice* (Bourdieu 1990), and *Masculine Domination* (Bourdieu 2001).
5. *Maoist* in the Turkish context meant pro-Chinese rather than pro-Soviet.
6. In his preface to Fanon's book (published in the same year as Bourdieu's *The Algerians*), John Paul Sartre, too, agrees that natives in Algeria have only one choice: "servitude or supremacy" ([1961] 1963, 11).

REFERENCES

Alexander, Jeffrey. 1995. *Fin de Siècle Social Theory: Relativism, Reduction, and the Problem of Reason*. London: Verso.
Bourdieu, Pierre. (1958) 1962. *The Algerians*. Boston: Beacon.
———. 1977. *Outline of a Theory of Practice*. Cambridge: Cambridge University Press.
———. 1990. *The Logic of Practice*. Translated by Richard Nice. Cambridge: Polity.
———. 2001. *Masculine Domination*. Boston: Polity.
Bozarslan, Hamit. 2012. "Between Integration, Autonomization and Radicalization. Hamit Bozarslan on the Kurdish Movement and the Turkish Left." *European Journal of Turkish Studies* 14. http://journals.openedition.org/ejts/4663.
Cherstich, Igor, Martin Holbraad, and Nico Tassi. 2020. *Anthropologies of Revolution: Forging Time, People, and Worlds*. Berkeley: University of California Press.
Dave, Naisargi. 2017. "Witness." In *Unfinished: The Anthropology of Becoming*, edited by Joao Biehl and Peter Locke, 151–172. Durham, N.C.: Duke University Press.
Debray, Regis. 1967. *Revolution in the Revolution? Armed Struggle and Political Struggle in Latin America*. Middlesex: Penguin.
Devrimci Yol. 1977. "Mektup." Letter. May 1, 1977.
Draskoczy, Julie. 2012. "The *Put'* of Perekova: Transforming Lives at Stalin's White Sea-Baltic Canal." *Russian Review* 71 (1): 30–48.
———. 2014. *Belomor: Criminality and Creativity in Stalin's Gulag*. Boston: Academic Studies.
Fanon, Frantz. (1961) 1963. *The Wretched of the Earth*. Reprint, New York: Grove.

Fitzpatrick, Sheila. 1999. *Everyday Stalinism: Ordinary Life in Extraordinary Times, Soviet Russia in the 1930s*. Oxford: Oxford University Press.

F. L. 1936. "Review of the White Sea Canal." *Geographical Journal* 87 (6): 559.

Ghamari-Tabrizi, Behrooz. 2021. "Revolution." In *A Lexicon for Dark Times*, edited by Veena Das and Didier Fassin, 166–184. Durham, N.C.: Duke University Press.

Gorky, Maxim, Leopold Averbakh, and S. Georgievich Firin, eds. 1935. *The White Sea Canal: Being an Account of the Construction of the New Canal between the White Sea and the Baltic Sea*. English edition by Anabel Williams-Ellis. London: John Lane.

Guenther, Lisa. 2017. "Epistemic Injustice and Phenomenology." In *The Routledge Handbook to Epistemic Injustice*, edited by Ian Kidd, Jose Medina, and Gaile Pohlhaus, 195–204. New York: Routledge.

Houston, Christopher. 2020. *Istanbul, City of the Fearless: Urban Activism, Coup D'état, and Memory in Turkey*. Berkeley: University of California Press.

———. 2022a. "Urban Activism and Social Movements in Turkey." In *Handbook on Modern Turkey*, edited by Joost Jongerden, 385–397. Oxford: Routledge.

———. 2022b. "Why Social Scientists Still Need Phenomenology." *Thesis Eleven* 168 (1): 37–54. https://doi.org/10.1177/07255136211064326.

Huberman, Leo. 1953. *The ABC of Socialism*. New York: Monthly Review.

Humphrey, Caroline. 2008. "Reassembling Individual Subjects: Events and Decisions in Troubled Times." *Anthropological Theory* 8 (4): 357–380. https://doi.org/10.1177/1463499608096644.

Husserl, Edmund. (1913) 2012. *Ideas: General Introduction to a Pure Phenomenology*. Reprint, London: Routledge.

Kharkhordin, Oleg. 1999. *The Collective and the Individual in Russia: A Study of Practices*. Berkeley: University of California Press.

Lefebvre, Henri. 1996. *Writings on Cities*. Malden, Mass.: Blackwell.

Mauss, Marcel. 1973. "Techniques of the Body." *Economy and Society* 2 (1): 70–88.

Morukov, Mikhail. 2003. "The White Sea-Baltic Canal." In *The Economies of Forced Labour: The Soviet Gulag*, edited by P. Gregory and P. Lazarev, 151–162. Stanford, Calif.: Hoover Institution Press.

Solzhenitsyn, Aleksandr. 1973. *The Gulag Archipelago 1918–1956*. New York: Harper & Row.

Stalin, Joseph. (1906) 2020. *Anarchism or Socialism?* Mumbai: Sanage Publishing House.

5 · TRANSCENDENTAL TERROR

Zen Self-Transformation through White Supremacist Atrocity, from Nazi Germany to Utøya and Christchurch

MAX HARWOOD

TWO VIGNETTES

i.

> His body was fighting against it; his muscles were twitching. He felt he would never be able to go through with it. A hundred voices in his head were screaming: Don't do it! . . . He forced his right hand down to his thigh, unfastened the holster, took hold of the pistol. . . . Screams filled the air. . . . From now on, he thought, everything would be easy.
>
> —*One of Us* (Seierstad 2016, 308–309), a narrative nonfiction account of the 2011 Oslo and Utøya terrorist attacks

In September 1941, Heinrich Himmler, Reichsführer of the Schutzstaffel (or SS), faced a macabre dilemma. As Nazi forces swept through Ukraine as part of Operation Barbarossa, the former chicken farmer had received troubling field reports. Although the mass killings of civilians by Himmler's Einsatzgruppen (SS death squads) were well underway, some soldiers were reported to be going mad (Shirer [1961] 2011, 961, 966). In his description of Himmler's deliberations, Richard Rhodes ([2002] 2004) describes how "both the men doing the killing and the leaders ordering and directing it had to find a way to stomach it. For the killers, a conditioning process was necessary" (81).

At the peak of Nazi atrocities in the Ukrainian Ostfront, over thirty thousand Jewish civilians were murdered by gunshot in just two days at Babyn Yar (Dawson 2012, 8). And despite this egregious feat of mass murder, Himmler was apparently troubled by the psychological strain of the work on his soldiers. This concern would later be echoed by SS functionary Otto Ohlendorf. On trial for his life at

Nuremberg, Ohlendorf testified about the methods of execution preferred by the Einsatzgruppen to minimize the psychological burden for the SS. "I never permitted the shooting by individuals but ordered [instead] that several of the men should shoot at the same time, in order to avoid direct personal responsibility," he said. Commenting specifically on the brutality of the mass killings he supervised in Moldova, Ohlendorf also asserted that "both for the victims and for those who carried out the executions, it was, psychologically, an immense burden to bear" (Shirer [1961] 2011, 958–959).

Ironically, Himmler himself had experienced this "immense burden." According to the memoirs of Karl Wolff, after Himmler personally supervised the execution of around one hundred civilians (including women and children), he was reported to have almost collapsed at the sight and retched uncontrollably. Following this display, Antony Beevor (2012) writes that attending SS commander Erich von dem Bach-Zelewski begged Himmler to find a solution to the increasing madness that was gripping his own soldiers. "Look at the eyes of the men in this Kommando!" Bach-Zelewski said to him. "These men are finished for the rest of their lives!" (232). Soon after, Bach-Zelewski himself was hospitalized for stomach pain and chronic nightmares—perhaps symptoms of that "immense burden" that would not leave him (232).

Ultimately, Himmler's firsthand experience with his "dilemma" led to an even darker consequence. This anecdote of the bespectacled Reichsführer gagging at the sight of the consequences of his own orders is often framed as a grim prelude to the final solution (Dawson 2012, 177–183). However, Himmler's dilemma existed alongside a long-standing spiritual aspiration that predated the mass killings of 1941. Though never realized, Himmler had been preoccupied with a long-term ambition to spiritually imbue and psychologically strengthen the SS, as had other key luminaries of the Third Reich (Bieber 2015, 1). As this chapter describes, throughout their tenure as the "exterminators of bed bugs and rats" in Western Europe and Russia (Beevor 2012, 232), Himmler and others admired and aspired to apply so-called Eastern wisdom to the murderous military ethos of the SS (Victoria 2013a, 2014). In this vague, orientalist enterprise that looked narrowly to D. T. Suzuki's contentious mixing of Japanese Zen, the Bushido code, and European fascism, Himmler dreamed of spiritually transforming his soldiers, creating resilient, perfect mass killers.

ii.

March 2019.[1] Brenton Tarrant, an Australian man, sits in a parked car in Christchurch, New Zealand. It is the early afternoon, with dull skies overhead. He is dressed in black tactical combat gear, including a ballistics helmet with a camera mounted on the front. On the passenger seat next to him is a semiautomatic Mossberg shotgun. He takes the helmet off and points the camera at himself, which has begun live streaming to an inestimable audience on social media. He speaks calmly, with a forced amiability that suggests a guarded personality or perhaps someone who rarely speaks to others. Eventually, he puts the helmet back on.

Still live streaming, he drives to Al Noor Mosque, blaring a far-right meme-inspired playlist, much to the delight of his viewers. He parks discreetly in a laneway adjacent to the mosque. When random pedestrians cross in front of his vehicle and hesitate, the man behind the windshield offers them a friendly, black-gloved wave with a thumbs-up for them to walk by. They do not seem to notice Tarrant's outfit or the firearm on the front seat. In a few moments, he walks around the car to open the trunk. For those watching online, all this is seen in the first person.

As Tarrant surveys the contents of the trunk, we see semiautomatic rifles equipped with high-capacity magazines, as well as red jerricans of fuel rigged up as crude explosive devices. The rifles are black but scrawled with distinct, hyper-white text that is legible, despite the patchy bitrate of the stream. "REFUGEES WELCOME TO HELL" says the thermoset handguard, while "LEPANTO 1517" is scrawled on the lower receiver. Racial obscenity mixed with historical crusade. Draping the first of the two semiautomatic rifles over his shoulder, Tarrant closes the trunk and briskly walks around the corner. In just a few seconds, he is striding up the short pathway to the mosque entrance, where three men are standing in oblivious conversation. Just as they notice him, the barrel of the shotgun lifts suddenly into the frame.

INTRODUCTION

This is the imminent moment preceding the 2019 Christchurch mosque terrorist attack. It is described here to preface a necessarily partial examination of Anders Breivik's and Brenton Tarrant's "projects" of self-alteration that prepared the way for both the Oslo/Utøya and the Christchurch massacres. While the pain and suffering inflicted by both terrorists on others begin there, for the terrorists themselves, the murders were a chilling apogee—a climax of radical self-alteration that had commenced years earlier. Accordingly, this essay studies these terrorists' self-alteration "projects," which in turn reveal how the transformation of both men evokes the phantasmagorical and inconclusive historical efforts by Nazi Germany to infuse a weaponized "Eastern" spiritualism into the SS as a means of transforming them into resilient and proficient mass murderers.

Following a limited cultural analysis that frames both terrorists' manifestos and their biographies as salvageable objects of ethnographic reconstruction, this chapter investigates their phenomenological transformation. To do so, it revisits Brian Victoria's (2006, 2013a, 2013b, 2014) account of the Nazis' own aspirations to "inject" the tenets of Japanese Imperial-state Zen into the SS via the early teachings of D. T. Suzuki and others. The essay examines the self-transformation of the 2011 Oslo/Utøya and 2019 Christchurch terrorists by "poetically" linking their alteration into White supremacist and fascist killers with Nazi fascination for Japanese military practices and its use of so-called Eastern wisdom as a spiritual weapon.

In doing so, this essay does not suggest that the Utøya and Christchurch terrorists were consciously inspired by these militarized spiritual ambitions. Nevertheless, it analyzes the all-encompassing "living death" of Breivik and Tarrant (Harwood 2021) as an uncanny and inadvertent realization of Himmler's own dreams: their developing of a Zen-like, transcendental transformation that enabled hitherto nonviolent individuals to irrevocably alter themselves for the express purpose of committing mass murder.

ON ANTHROPOLOGY, PHENOMENOLOGY, AND REPLACEMENT THEORY MASS SHOOTERS

In his most famous work on the nature of existence, Martin Buber contemplates his question of questions: "It is said that man experiences his world. What does that mean?" ([1937] 2013, 4). For anthropology, understanding the lived experience of others—that is, both the subjective experience of another's reality and the objective experience of living within human societies—is at the heart of the discipline's raison d'être. Alongside this premise, it has also been argued that anthropology offers unique contributions to critical terrorism studies—including presenting interdisciplinary ethnographies that explore the subjectivity of violent extremists (Sluka 2009).

A sufficiently motivated anthropologist, then, can apply their training to understand the personal, social, and ideological worlds that partly produced Anders Breivik and Brenton Tarrant. Both men epitomize antagonistic digital White nationalist subculture (Harwood 2021), with its layers of historical, political, and spiritual meaning. Nevertheless, engaging with their actions and words is an ethically and pragmatically fraught endeavor. That is, while theories of cultural anthropology are capable of illuminating the dimensions of terrorists' practices and histories themselves, the practice of the discipline (i.e., ethnographic fieldwork) is unviable when it comes to engaging with so-called replacement theory mass shooters.[2] Further, their identification is inherently retrospective. Indeed, lone-actor terrorists like Breivik and Tarrant are only known to researchers in the wake of their attacks, and so anthropologists are left with few practical tools with which to ethnographically assess their subjective milieu in any traditional sense.

To address the retrospective nature of this pseudoethnographic study, I have previously framed my analysis of replacement theory terrorist subculture as a particular form of salvage anthropology (Harwood 2021, 27). Salvage anthropology is a subset of forensic cultural anthropology, in which the anthropologist uses ethnographic research methods to survey the unencounterable (e.g., deceased, historical) subject and/or cultural setting (Hester 1968, 132–146). Therefore, if Breivik and Tarrant are regarded as appropriators and translators of a particular social and cultural milieu that is inherently unencounterable, then a salvage anthropology—or "reconstruction" of their social and cultural world—is the anthropologist's only practical recourse.

Not accidentally, both Breivik and Tarrant left behind significant salvageable materials in the form of elaborate written manifestos: *2083: A European Declaration of Independence* (hereafter called the Compendium; Breivik 2011) and *The Great Replacement* (hereafter called TGR; Tarrant 2019). In the spirit of this new salvage anthropology, these manifestos are "imperfect Rosetta Stone[s] that partially decrypt the world [of] white nationalism, as well as offering a culturally relativist interpretation [of Breivik's and Tarrant's] terrorist actions" (Harwood 2021, 27). Moreover, while these intricate confessional texts speak to a variety of audiences, they also provide a unique phenomenological lens into the deliberate self-alteration of hitherto nonviolent men into resolutely focused ideological mass murderers.

Following Bourdieu (cf. Houston 2022), we note that phenomenological frameworks of individual perception are often beneficial in anthropology, as they seek to understand the subjective experience and everyday reality of ourselves and others. As Kalpana Ram and Christopher Houston (2015) explain, "Phenomenology is an investigation of how humans perceive, experience, and comprehend the sociable, materially assembled world that they inherit at infancy and in which they dwell" (1). In the context of anthropological analysis, phenomenology provides a framework to understand the individual constitution of *external* reality as a means of ethnographically documenting the *subjective* experience of the "other."

However, how "best do we describe relations between the self and the collective" (Houston 2022, 38) if we cannot speak with them? The exploration of the subjective experience of an other's reality is contingent on an analysis of some*thing*—perhaps salvaged biographical artifacts and the subsequent ethnographic reconstruction of the self that forged them. In this essay, the salvaged artifacts are Breivik's and Tarrant's manifestos, and phenomenology is the framework with which to ethnographically view them. This reconstructs a *kind* of subjectivity for the anthropologist, thus mimicking the traditional ethnographic encounter with an interlocutor and their world. And while advocates of phenomenology's use in anthropology are quick to recognize "the limits to knowing consciousness" (Ram and Houston 2015, 11), there is inherent value to be found in regarding ethnographic informants' subjectivity as the "constitutive 'horizon' of experience" (11).

In short, although both manifestos were clearly devised in the hope of converting and inspiring, if read critically and carefully, they permit the ethnographer to inhabit a salvaged subjectivity. Read as autobiographical texts, Breivik's (2011) sprawling Compendium and Tarrant's (2019) comparatively lean TGR present a comprehensive "horizon" that enables social scientists to partially understand the personal, cultural, and political experiences of the replacement theory massshooter self—including subjective processes of radical self-alteration.

IMPERIAL-STATE ZEN, NAZI GERMANY, AND "MASTERY OF DEATH"

As Himmler grappled with his "dilemma" in September 1941, he might have regarded the twenty-first-century transformation of young men from hitherto passive—albeit racist—ideologues into White nationalist mass killers as a literal *triumph des willens*. Surely this was clear evidence that—through training and determination—even a lone actor could fortify their "spiritual welfare" and remain psychologically resilient when exterminating the "bed bugs and rats" that threatened the Aryan people (Beevor 2012, 232). For Himmler, the possibility of such self-alteration would not have been unfamiliar territory: the SS head was well known for his passionate reverence of Eastern spiritualism, to the degree that it was apocryphally said that he always kept a leather-bound copy of the Bhagavad Gita in his jacket pocket (Žižek 2003, 30).

However, Nazi intellectual fascination with "Eastern wisdom" was not limited to Hinduism. By 1941, the translated writings of D. T. Suzuki (the Japanese Buddhist philosopher and outspoken Nazi sympathizer) had already influenced the highest ranks of the Third Reich (Victoria 2006, 2013a, 2013b, 2014). Suzuki's ([1938] 1959) work *Zen and Japanese Culture* was particularly well received in Germany at a critical moment for national socialism—with Suzuki describing Zen in the book as "a religion of iron will" (Victoria 2014, 4). Importantly for the SS, the text also outlined Zen's role in Japanese military power, with Suzuki writing, "Good fighters are generally ascetics or stoics, which means to have an iron will. When needed, Zen supplies them with this" (4).

Indeed, at the height of Showa Statism, Zen was one of many spiritual tools of Japanese Buddhism (Nihon Bukkyo) that had been weaponized and taught to the Imperial Japanese Army (IJA). Remade as "Imperial-state Zen" (Victoria 2006, 111) as part of Showa Japanese militarism, Victoria describes how by the end of the 1920s, "institutional Buddhism had firmly locked itself into ideological support for Japan's ongoing military efforts" (79). This included spiritual support for the IJA troops and state-crafted spiritual education for Japanese soldiers to learn the virtues of Zen during wartime (117–119). By integrating Imperial-state Zen into IJA training, the Ministry of War (Rikugun-sho) hoped to enhance their soldiers' capacity for extreme violence, which included the indiscriminate slaughter of civilians throughout the Asia-Pacific. In short, it was hoped that the IJA's ranks would become spiritually indifferent to all forms of death—most famously even their own (122).

This instrumental mixing of Zen principles into the Japanese war effort was then transmitted to Germany by way of Suzuki's publications and lectures throughout the Showa period—and it was not long before key members of the Third Reich took notice. By the late 1930s, Suzuki had toured Europe and openly declared that "Zen could be wedded to almost any form of political ideology, fascism included" (Victoria 2006, 9) and that through Zen, "mastery of death" was possible for any warrior (123). Thus, while Himmler may have had a personal admiration for the tenants of Hinduism, Nazi fascination with Suzuki's perverse reading of Nihon Bukkyo and Zen's specific role in spiritual militarization was comparatively clear cut.

In fact, Hitler himself had expressed admiration toward the "Japanese religion" (Speer 1970, 96), and in 1935, he specifically directed Himmler to explore remodeling the SS on the Bushido, or Japanese samurai (Victoria 2014, 32). Though the führer's outlandish suggestion was never realized, the sentiment was pervasive throughout the Third Reich's short history. Even as the war turned against Germany in late 1942, Nazi diplomat Prince Albrecht of Urach again encapsulated Germany's reverence for Suzuki's militarization of Zen, writing that "the active and yet stoic Buddhism of the Zen-sect perfected and refined the ethos of the Japanese warrior . . . giving him the highly ascetical note that [is] the essential feature of Japanese soldiery" (Albrecht quoted in Victoria 2014, 35). Albrecht was alluding to a new weaponized "spiritualism" that had been activated within the Japanese soldier—something the Germans both feared and admired (Bieber 2015, 7).

Of course, neither Himmler nor his acolytes would live to see their musing on a spiritually empowered SS tested in war. And yet over half a century later, two White supremacist terrorists would unknowingly revitalize some of the broad ideas of Suzuki's teachings and Imperial-state Zen, as well as inadvertently embody aspects of the unrealized Nazi designs for the "spiritual welfare" of the SS.

THE TRANSFORMATION OF ANDERS BREIVIK AND BRENTON TARRANT: "HOW DOES ONE COMMIT SUCH AN ACT?"

> The individual is capable of pursuing an idea or plan of action with considerable determination and with no assistance from others. Indeed, he can be single-minded to the point of obsession. . . . For the more than 18 months he lived in New Zealand preparing for the terrorist attack, he remained resolutely focused.
> —New Zealand Government (2020, 167).

In the wake of mass shootings, public discourse invariably returns to that agonized question: How is such an act committed? A near decade apart and on opposite sides of the globe, two men—Anders Breivik and Brenton Tarrant—committed elaborate acts of political mass murder. They had never met, and their victims were unlucky representations of separately imagined grievances. Nevertheless, both men were motivated to kill by the same Nazi-inspired ideology: historical White nationalism and its derivative progeny, the great replacement conspiracy theory (Harwood 2021).

While this shared extremist ideology explicitly linked both men within the annals of lone-actor White nationalist terrorism, it is valuable to consider the personal journeys that ultimately led them to commit separate acts of mass murder. Indeed, both the 2011 Oslo/Utøya and the 2019 Christchurch attacks were prefaced by eerily similar projects of self-alteration. These personal, deliberate metamorphoses seemingly empowered (at least in part) both men to kill dozens of civilians. In fact, neither Breivik nor Tarrant had any history of violence (criminal or otherwise) prior to their massacres. Instead, over many years, they both discreetly transformed from unremarkable, law-abiding civilians (albeit hardened racists) into violent extremists with a singular purpose. This is a rare escalation of "abstract" racist discourse and "partisan" (Tarrant 2019, 12, 14, 17) identity politics into real-world acts of violence.

The most compelling evidence of Breivik's and Tarrant's self-alteration is to be found in the biographical sections of their respective manifestos. Once they commit their lives to mass murder, there is a distinctly transcendental quality in both their actions and writing: a Zen-like state of "living death" (Harwood 2021) that appears to have resulted in a toxic alchemy of an extreme dehumanization of others and a near-total social withdrawal.[3] This transcendental quality of their experience is crucial, as it not only is evocative of the Nazis' historical designs for spiritually resilient killers but also dovetails neatly with the observed bodily and moral alterations that both men exhibited prior to their attacks. Thus, while the evidence for this project of self-alteration is empirically twofold—that is, significant physical and psychological changes—the Zen-like transcendental nature of both men's "living death" suggests an insidious, weaponized spiritual element as well.

THE "DOCTRINE OF EMPTINESS" AND "LIVING DEATH"

Toward the end of his tome-like Compendium, Breivik interviews himself. Across sixty-four pages, the Norwegian's affected candor serves to answer the questions that he imagined devotees would ask. Throughout this prelude to his climactic "Knights Templar Log," Breivik offers mostly personal insights but also counsels future White nationalist lone-actor terrorists. Within the "interview," he emphasizes the loneliness of the "operation" and the challenges of self-imposed isolation. "You can basically live a normal life if you chose to," Breivik writes. "You just have to be extra careful. I have been practising certain rituals and meditation to strengthen my beliefs and convictions" (Breivik 2011, 1384). These "rituals and meditation" speak to both his and Tarrant's all-encompassing self-alteration into committed violent extremists, a transformation to which there are distinct social, material, physiological, and moral components.

To begin with the social element, both men were minimally contactable in the months leading up to their respective massacres, as they deliberately withdrew to remote rural residences far from family, friends, and even the vicinity of their planned attacks. This physical withdrawal was as methodical as it was extreme. Not only did they largely break off almost all contact, but Breivik and Tarrant were also ethereal in their new abodes—instead practicing a deliberate, articulated hermitage aesthetic. This contrasted sharply with their relatively active online social lives—as they withdrew dramatically from the "real" world, both men keenly inhabited a distinct, virtual milieu: a vibrant, multiplatform far-right "digital" monastery that was teeming with kinfolk.

For Breivik, his "digital" monastery was mainly counter-jihad websites and far-right European nationalist forums. Tarrant found an active community in the fringe imageboards of 4chan, 8chan, and the wider Islamophobic memesphere (Harwood 2021, 43). For both men, participation in this online extremist "monastery" was a vital social media "virtual community" (Wilhelmsen 2022, 121) that supplanted their former social worlds, calcifying their radicalization and accelerating their plans. Indeed, it was in this digital milieu that Tarrant likely first discovered Breivik's Compendium, which he cites as the "true inspiration" and political affordance for Christchurch (Tarrant 2019, 18). This retreat into a virtual White nationalist cloister also saw both men eschew the material trappings of their former lives. In this new reality, the only physical possessions retained were those relevant to the "operation." Minimal contact with the outside "real" world was de rigueur. Simultaneously, life online ramped up and continued until (and, in Tarrant's case, during) the attacks themselves. This was a transcendental, Zen-like state of "living death," a mindset unique to the subculture of great replacement theory terrorists (Harwood 2021).

In this new phenomenological horizon, everyday reality is diffused in favor of a new subjectivity—a mindset cultivated in part by their dwelling solely in that "digital" monastery of online White nationalist subculture, which encourages a fundamental reimagining of the past that then informs a new "imagined" present. As George L. Mosse (1996) notes, "The so-called new man of national socialism was deeply rooted in the past" (163), and as will be later examined, the consequent "imagined present" articulated in both Breivik's and Tarrant's manifestos was largely predicated on a spurious epic of White nationalist history—an ancient ethno-religious saga in which both men wholeheartedly believed they were participating (Harwood 2021, 36–40).

This experience of "living death" in a new "imagined" present is also evocative of IJA professor Furukawa Taigo's teachings, who as a contemporary of D. T. Suzuki emphasized Imperial-state Zen's value of "leading a plain and frugal life" (Victoria 2006, 120). Taigo also argued that this lifestyle "appealed to the straightforward and unsophisticated warrior temperament" and that it comported gracefully with Japanese Zen's "doctrine of emptiness" (120) for warrior monks. While Breivik explicitly called his social withdrawal part of a wider "overcoming" of his learned ethics and morality via a kind of enlightenment (Breivik 2011, 1384), Tarrant's own embrace of this "emptiness" seemed to have been more logistically pragmatic (i.e., so as not to arouse suspicion). However, it also reflected the findings of New Zealand investigators, who emphasized the Australian's unusual determination, obsessively singular focus, and hardened resolve once he had committed to planning his attack (New Zealand Government 2020, 167).

Thus, this warrior monk–like existence was particularly apparent in the case of Tarrant. Indeed, the Australian's resolute tenacity is evocative of Suzuki's 1942 description of Zen's contribution to "the warrior spirit," in which he wrote that "once [the warrior] sets his goal, it is intuition that allows him to rush towards it, having transcended advantage and disadvantage, profit and loss" (Victoria 2002, 120). Like Breivik before him, Tarrant sacrificed his financial and personal life, channeling all available resources toward his massacre, and took great pains to be hidden upon arriving in New Zealand beginning in August 2017. Moreover, from the moment he arrived in the country (nearly two years before the attack), Tarrant lived a remarkably isolated and minimalist lifestyle. When police burst into his rented Dunedin duplex following his attack, they found it nearly empty: the only furnishings were a desk, a computer, a chair, and a mattress (New Zealand Government 2020, 184). His neighbor, with whom he shared a thin wall, told police that she never heard a sound from his side of the duplex.[4]

In short, though he lived in the small community for just under two years, Tarrant was rarely seen or heard, an example of Taigo's militarized "emptiness," contrasted with a relatively active online social life in a virtual extremist milieu. Similarly, Breivik had also expunged the trappings of ordinary social life in the years before Oslo/Utøya, dedicating every waking moment to his planned terrorist attack from around the mid-2000s onward (Breivik 2011, 1380–1381), as well as increasing physical withdrawal from his former life as the attack took logistical shape. In his Compendium, Breivik describes the sacrifices he made to his personal life as he trained, prepared, and planned. For example, in a three-year period leading up to the attack, Breivik states, "I lived very ascetic and relatively isolated. . . . [This] would also contribute to detach[ing] myself from my 'old life.' . . . It's a process I used in order to isolate myself . . . in preparation for the coming operation" (1380–1381).

MATERIAL TRANSFORMATION: BUSHIDO DECORUM AND CRUSADER COSPLAY

At the height of Showa Statist reform, Taigo and Suzuki both articulated the militarized nexus between the Bushido (samurai) code and Japanese Zen (Victoria 2006, 118–119). As the religion was gradually integrated into the IJA, Taigo wrote that those Imperial-state Zen warriors who embraced Bushido should emphasize "an esteem for order and proper decorum" (118–119). Perhaps the most vivid element of Breivik's and Tarrant's self-alteration is to be found in their own exhibition of a new sartorial "order and proper decorum"—specifically the elaborate costumes and symbol-laden uniforms worn by both men when they "came out" to the world as their new, warrior monk selves. Most dramatic in this instance was Breivik (figure 5.1), who at the coda of his manifesto poses in various custom-made "Knights Templar" uniforms in what appear to be professional portrait photos (Breivik 2011, 1095).

These images suggest a dual temporal framework generated by Breivik and Tarrant—namely, both the histrionic "imagined past" and the subsequent "imagined present" that vexes replacement theory White nationalists (Harwood 2021, 28). As a

FIGURE 5.1. Breivik posing in custom-made Knights Templar outfits (L: formal; R: military dress). Source: Breivik 2011.

realm of ethno-nationalist memory, this "imagined past" is equivalent to those political mythologies that Benedict Anderson (2006) regards as essential to maintaining one's felt unity with the national whole—that subjective "sense" of belonging to a nation as a citizen (1–7). Importantly, this dual framework of historical "imagining"—past and present—is also underpinned by shared features in both Breivik's and Tarrant's biographies. First, from their adolescence, both men harbored a pronounced racism for the non-Whites present within their communities (especially Islam, but Tarrant's first articulation of hardened racism was directed toward Indigenous Australians).[5] Second, following their mutual discovery of the great replacement conspiracy theory, both men were inspired to transform from "mere" ideological racists into violent political extremists (Harwood 2021, 34).

While modern great replacement theory is largely concerned with immigrant birth rates and the enabling of White cultural erasure by "Marxists" in western Europe and the Anglosphere (Cosentino 2020, 73–77), underpinning the conspiracy is an elaborately "imagined" White nationalist history imbued with esoteric racial spiritualism (Weiss 1987, 193–236). Breivik's and Tarrant's writings exhibit a fixation on this "imagined past"—that is, their belief that they are part of a millennia-old conflict between Christianity and Islam (Harwood 2021, 36) and that they are spiritually duty bound to take extreme action against "invaders" and their traitorous enablers. In this new horizon of political, cultural, and historical White nationalist subjectivity, both men grasped at radical affordances that elevated them beyond ordinary civilians. Indeed, each modified themselves into gallant ethno-nationalist soldiers, defending the very existence of their civilization. Most notably, Breivik's self-declared membership in the Knights Templar is a clear link to his "imagined past" as well as his militarized self-alteration. Though a delusion, he nonetheless transposes this new "inner" self onto his "outer" body via his elaborate sartorial creations.

Similarly, Tarrant wielded firearms adorned with handwritten names, memes, Nordic runes, 4chan insults, racial epithets, and key historical dates all related to his own "imagined past" of great replacement White nationalism (Harwood 2021, 46–47).[6] These crude inscriptions are a summary of his manifesto and succinctly clarify his actions in the wider context of his ethno-nationalist imaginings. However, his graffitied weapons also operate as effective propaganda. In the attack's live stream, the decorated firearm is center stage, with Tarrant himself relegated necessarily behind the camera. The symbolic power of weapons used to "remove" the "invaders" was also important for Breivik, who named his rifle Mjølnir (after Thor's hammer) and his pistol Gungnir (after Odin's spear), with assorted Nordic runes and crusader symbols engraved into both firearms (Seierstad 2016, 178–179). Although Breivik's weapons were never seen by the public, their ritual christening and decoration speak to his fixation on esoteric Aryanism, a specious pseudohistorical niche also valued by the Nazis (Goodrick-Clarke 2002).

Breivik's penchant for arcane Aryan symbols was also shared by Tarrant, who adorned himself in various White nationalist signs and ciphers to signal his own "order and proper decorum" of this grand history—most prominently of which is the Sonnenrad, or black sun wheel (figure 5.2). This black segmented circle is a supposedly ancient European or Nordic symbol, popularized in Aryan race subculture beginning in the early twentieth century. Like the adoption of the Eurasian swastika, the ancient Sonnenrad was also plucked from relative obscurity by the Nazis for the purposes of White nationalist propaganda (Goodrick-Clarke 2002).

Given its ideological heritage, the Sonnenrad not only adorns Tarrant's manifesto but was also worn over his chest (in the form of an iron-on patch) throughout the Christchurch attack. As a distilled political semiotic, this is Tarrant's "imagined" history, politics, and personal self-alteration combined. Along with his graffitied firearms, his "new" self (with its specific cultural lineage and ideological pedigree) is on full display. However, for both men, this is more than crusader cosplay. Between Breivik's surreal regalia and Tarrant's explicit use of esoteric White nationalist symbology, we (as their audience) are shown the "order and proper decorum" of both terrorists' new phenomenological "horizon"—an integration of the "imagined" history of White nationalism into the material world.

FIGURE 5.2. Artwork depicting Tarrant in the style of a Christian saint. Source: 4chan.

It is a means of signaling their political allegiance as well as their new affordances, "legitimising fantasy and ratifying [their] place in the annals of crusader history" (Harwood 2021, 46).

Indeed, both men regard themselves as living symbols of the ongoing Christian Crusades. And in the years since their massacres, both terrorists have been venerated in a style befitting religious icons. Memes of Tarrant often depict him in robes—a Christian warrior monk in fresco, resplendent in symbols of his attack (the Sonnenrad, the headcam, the decorated rifle, the manifesto)—and his hands are often fixed in Christian chironomia (figure 5.2). Breivik has been similarly beatified as the Justiciar Knights Templar who hitherto only existed in personal fantasy. In one 4chan meme (figure 5.3), Breivik is rendered in full medieval heavy armor, sword in one hand as his rifle fires into the bodies of mostly non-White toddlers with the other. These depictions raise the question of art imitating life—but the purposeful wearing of such clothes (which included symbols of esoteric White nationalism) suggests a prescient anticipation. Here there is a deliberate material alteration of the killers into new, iconic political beings before their attacks—with the attendant artworks that followed a potent validation that both men's transformation was at least aesthetically certified in their "imagined" history.

BODILY AND MORAL SELF-ALTERATION: DRUG-INDUCED ZEN AND "NO INNOCENTS IN AN INVASION"

In his gendered analysis of masculinity and the Third Reich, Mosse (1996) notes how the "new man" of fascism "was to be inspired by the war experience, and indeed he lived in a state of permanent war. . . . The constant wearing of uniforms, the marches, the emphasis on physical exercise, on virility, these were [all] part of the battle against the enemy" (160). In his Compendium, Breivik writes, "You are going have [sic] to go through a 'physical transformation period' to prepare yourself as a Justiciar Knight before you engage in armed resistance" (Breivik 2011, 900). What the self-styled chevalier meant by this was not figurative. In what may

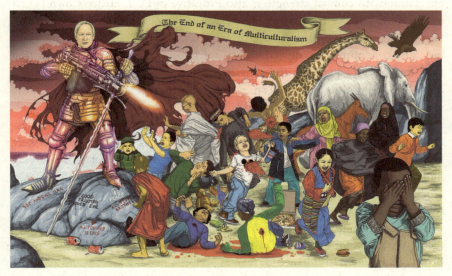

FIGURE 5.3. Artwork depicting Breivik in full Knights Templar armor as he massacres children of "multiculturalism." Source: 4chan.

be the most literal aspect of this salvaged ethnographic analysis, there are striking cosmetic and pharmacological elements to both men's transformation—an unsubtle remaking of the physical self into new, hypermasculine warrior monks of White nationalism.

Most notably, both Breivik and Tarrant openly abused anabolic steroids in preparation for their attacks, literally altering their physiques into new, combat-strengthened forms (New Zealand Government 2020, 197, 212–213). Ostensibly, this produced a toughened build that would enhance their somatic performance as mass killers, but Mosse also reminds us of the long-standing "fascist preoccupation with the human body as representative of the proper spirit" (1996, 169). As notably image-conscious White nationalists, this ideological fixation appears to have continued in the self-alteration of Breivik and Tarrant. And while Tarrant does not address his use of steroids in TGR, Breivik dedicates numerous sections of his Compendium to advising new recruits on best practice steroid "cycling" to become warrior knights (Breivik 2011, 883–886, 903–906). Moreover, Breivik also took his "physical transformation" to the extreme by also undergoing a series of cosmetic facial surgeries, including a rhinoplasty to apparently make his nose appear more Aryan (Seierstad 2016, 91).

While this plastic surgery may speak to vanity couched in Mosse's "fascist preoccupation," Breivik's steroid use is of particular significance, as he links it candidly to his self-alteration into a logistically effective Justiciar Knights Templar. In a lengthy description of how to efficiently move around in medieval "heavy armor" for his attack, Breivik brags about his newfound strength, writing, "I can wear 50kg of armour, transforming me into a human tank . . . as long as [I] use a suitable steroid cycle" (Breivik 2011, 883–886). This marrying of sartorial affectation with combat strength is also evocative of D. T. Suzuki's own fascist interpretation of the relationship between warrior Zen and Bushido, in which he echoes the positions of Furukawa Taigo and the IJA. In this narrow reading, Suzuki admires the "rugged virility" of Japan's historical warriors, writing that "the soldierly quality, with its mysticism and aloofness from worldly affairs, appeals to willpower [sic]. . . . Zen in this respect walks hand in hand with the spirit of Bushido" (Victoria 2006, 121).

Achieving a kind of hypermasculine "rugged virility" in the context of the fascist physical ideal was also a high priority for both Breivik and Tarrant. Both were fitness fanatics, with Tarrant's preterrorist occupation as a personal trainer serving him well in this enterprise. As Mosse (1996) recounts, "Physical exercise played a crucial part in forming the fascist man" (162), and the refashioning of the physical self was a long-standing ideal of fascism, "especially National Socialism, [both of which] demonstrated the awesome possibilities inherent in modern masculinity" (180). But while Tarrant limited his performance-enhancing drug use to steroids, Breivik also wanted to enhance his mental performance as a killer—and achieved this by imbibing a homemade stimulant mixture of ephedrine and caffeine during his mass shooting on Utøya island.[7] This was presumably taken as a means for gaining quick reflexes but also for attaining an altered state of consciousness and an elevated mood throughout the massacre. Indeed, once he had started shooting, Breivik's own description of his mindset is relayed by Asne Seierstad (2016), who writes, "As the adrenalin pumped round his body, he was suffused by a feeling of calm. His will had triumphed over his body. The barrier was down" (310).

Given Breivik's desire to literally alter his mind during his attack, it is important to finally consider the *moral* transformation of both men as the closing salvaged piece of ethnographic analysis. In the widely popular German translation of Suzuki's ([1938] 1959) *Zen and Japanese Culture*, the scholar-monk describes how in the history of Japan, Zen had "passively sustained" the country's warriors both morally and philosophically. As Victoria (2006) notes, "They were sustained morally because 'Zen is a religion which teaches us not to look backward once the course is decided.'... Philosophically, they were sustained because '[Zen] treats life and death indifferently'" (Suzuki quoted in Victoria 2006, 121). Thus, when surveying the writings and actions of Breivik and Tarrant, perhaps most shocking to the reader is the callous indifference to life and death—particularly given the scale of their attacks and their indiscriminate targeting of unarmed civilians, including teenagers and small children.

Ironically for interested anthropologists, both men frame much of their justification for mass murder on the grounds of a cruel moral relativism. For example, as part of their commitment to the great replacement conspiracy theory and its accompanying White nationalist mythos, both Breivik and Tarrant describe experiencing a historically informed moral "enlightenment" that altered their preestablished moral and ethical horizons. In their manifestos, this Imperial-state Zen-like indifference to life and death takes the shape of dramatic, catalytic paradigm shifts that incite their transformation from law-abiding civilians into actively planning terrorists. For Breivik, it was his government's foreign policy that first tipped him over the edge. He writes that—in the wake of watching the 1999 NATO bombings of Serbia on Norwegian television—he knew that he would have to eventually do something (Breivik 2011, 1380).

Likewise, Tarrant dedicates a large section of his manifesto to various trigger points for his radicalization—all of which are European. The most prominent is Ebba Akerlund, an eleven-year-old Swedish girl who was murdered by Islamic extremists in downtown Stockholm in 2017. Tarrant fixates on Ebba, writing that her death was the moment he decided to commit mass murder: "I could no longer turn my back on the violence. Something, this time, was different" (Tarrant 2019, 7). Throughout TGR, Ebba is a political refrain for whom Tarrant seeks vengeance, an avatar for his new moral self. This would be horrifically exhibited in his retaliatory, deliberate point-blank execution of a three-year-old boy in Christchurch—Ebba's death weaponized by Tarrant to create a new moral affordance.[8]

Similarly, Breivik goes to great lengths to defend the murder of White teenagers, categorizing his European "targets" into a priority hierarchy of "A/B/C traitors." In this dehumanized grading system, category "A" traitors are heads of state, whereas category "C" traitors are "low-level" civilian enablers of multiculturalism, such as the teenage attendees of the Utøya Island Labour Party summer camp (Breivik 2011, 938–939). "There are no innocents in an invasion" is Tarrant's (2019, 13) moral axiom, summarizing his and Breivik's shared logic that sees any child as an enemy in waiting. Thus, when fused with their wider experience of "living death" (with its attendant spiritual, historical, and political affordances), this new moral horizon not only permits the murder of small children—it explicitly encourages it.

CONCLUSION

To return to that agonized question: How is such an act committed? This chapter has offered a limited anthropological answer via a salvaged ethnographic analysis of the significant projects of self-alteration pursued by the 2011 Oslo and 2019 Christchurch terrorists. By situating Breivik's and Tarrant's manifestos and "living death" in the wider context of White nationalist "imagined" history—including Nazi fascination with Imperial-state Zen as a spiritual weapon—one can better understand the myriad historical, political, and ethical *affordances* that underpin modern replacement theory terrorism. And while the merits of studying "hate" are debatable (Harwood 2021, 27–29), it is not the place of anthropology to hastily diagnose pathological behavior. In doing so, it would overlook the equally significant social, physical, and moral changes that composed both Breivik's and Tarrant's dramatic, multidimensional self-alterations.

Indeed, by the time of their attacks, both men wholeheartedly believed that they had metamorphosized into perfect and virtuous White nationalist warrior monks—new murderous representatives of a continuous historical political project. Thus, when reading their manifestos in the context of this White nationalist history (real and "imagined"), it appears that Breivik and Tarrant unknowingly embodied that militarized "doctrine of emptiness" advocated by the IJA and envied by the Third Reich—a weaponized spiritual creed whose fascist disciples spuriously claimed was "the foundation of all Buddhism" (Victoria 2006, 119). However, this transformation is not only evocative of Imperial-state Zen but perhaps something new entirely. Through this metamorphosis, Breivik and Tarrant also believed that their violent actions would summon their epic, "imagined" history and force it onto the "real" world—bending *outer* reality to the whims of their *inner* crusader reveries.

And so the transformation was complete, and dozens were murdered. Both men are now imprisoned for life in solitary confinement—an eerie reflection of the "living death" hermitage that prefaced their attacks. Incarcerated, Tarrant is reportedly despondent, while Breivik is said to have become "more" insane.[9] Perhaps, in the years that have followed, both men have discovered that they are condemned to remain on the other side of this transformation—there is likely no going back. This is because terrorist self-alteration is seemingly phenomenologically reciprocal: it is predicated on an abstract, *inner* subjectivity attacking an empirical, *outer* reality—and in this case, both have survived. Thus, even if these two homicidal entities were capable of yet another transformation and were to genuinely repent, what would the world see?

NOTES

1. The following reconstruction is drawn from the *Report of the Royal Commission of Inquiry into the Terrorist Attack on Christchurch Masjidain* (hereafter the NZRCI Report; New Zealand Government 2020) and the author's personal review of Brenton Tarrant's live stream.
2. For example, see Sluka (2008) and Gonzaléz in MacClancey (2019).
3. The NZRCI Report suggests that ordinary socialization may have tempered Tarrant's views (New Zealand Government 2020, 232).
4. Mahtani (2019).
5. See New Zealand Government (2020, 168).
6. 4chan is an anonymous imageboard well known for its offensive content generation and harboring of far-right extremist communities.
7. See Arieli et al. (2022) and *BBC News* (2012).
8. See Tarrant's formal sentencing remarks in High Court of New Zealand (2020, sec. 13).
9. Langbach (2022).

REFERENCES

Anderson, Benedict. 2006. *Imagined Communities: Reflections on the Origin and Spread of Nationalism*. 3rd ed. London: Verso.

Arieli, Michael, Aviv Weinstein, Uri Ben Yaakov, Ronnie Berkovitz, Alina Poperno, Hagit Bonny-Noach, and Robert P. Granacher. 2022. "Psychoactive Agents and Mental Disorders in Lone-Actor Terrorism." In *Lone-Actor Terrorism: An Integrated Framework*, edited by Jacob C. Holzer, Andrea J. Dew, Patricia R. Recupero, and Paul Gill, 57–84. New York: Oxford University Press. https://doi.org/10.1093/med/9780190929794.003.0005.

BBC News. 2012. "Breivik: Court in Norway Hears Killer Took Stimulants." May 31, 2012. https://www.bbc.com/news/world-europe-18282760.

Beevor, Antony. 2012. *The Second World War*. New York: Little Brown.

Bieber, Hans-Joachim. 2015. "Zen and War: A Commentary on Brian Victoria and Karl Baier's Analysis of Daisetz Suzuki and Count Dürckheim." *Asia-Pacific Journal* 13, issue 20 (no. 2): 1–15.

Breivik, Anders. 2011. *2083: A European Declaration of Independence*. N.p.

Buber, Martin. (1937) 2013. *I and Thou*. Reprint, London: Bloomsbury. ePub.

Cosentino, Gabriele. 2020. "From Pizzagate to the Great Replacement: The Globalization of Conspiracy Theories." In *Social Media and the Post-truth World Order*, 59–86. Cham, Switzerland: Palgrave Pivot. https://doi.org/10.1007/978-3-030-43005-4_3.

Dawson, Greg. 2012. *Judgment before Nuremberg*. New York: Pegasus.

Goodrick-Clarke, Nicholas. 2002. *Black Sun: Aryan Cults, Esoteric Nazism and the Politics of Identity*. New York: New York University Press.

Harwood, Max. 2021. "Living Death: Imagined History and the Tarrant Manifesto." *Emotions: History, Culture, Society* 5 (1): 25–50. https://doi.org/10.1163/2208522X-02010112.

Hester, James J. 1968. "Pioneer Methods in Salvage Anthropology." *Anthropological Quarterly* 41 (3): 132–146. https://doi.org/10.2307/3316788.

High Court of New Zealand. 2020. "Sentencing Remarks of Mander J." Courts of New Zealand, August 27, 2020. https://www.courtsofnz.govt.nz/assets/cases/R-v-Tarrant-sentencing-remarks-20200827.pdf.

Houston, Christopher. 2022. "Why Social Scientists Still Need Phenomenology." *Thesis Eleven* 168 (1): 37–54. https://doi.org/10.1177/07255136211064326.

Langbach, Tor. 2022. "Det er lett å være enig i at Breivik fremstår som gal. Men mye er vanvittig i denne verden." *Aftenposten*, February, 9, 2022. https://www.aftenposten.no/meninger/debatt/i/Bj4dPe/det-er-lett-aa-vaere-enig-i-at-breivik-fremstaar-som-gal-men-mye-er-vanvittig-i-denne-verden.

MacClancy, Jeremy, ed. 2019. *Exotic No More: Anthropology on the Front Lines*. 2nd ed. Chicago: University of Chicago Press.

Mahtani, Shibani, Wilma McKay, and Kate Shuttleworth. 2019. "Hiding in Plain Sight: In Quiet New Zealand City, Alleged Gunman Plotted Carnage." *Washington Post*, March 22, 2019. https://www.washingtonpost.com/world/asia_pacific/hiding-in-plain-sight-in-quiet-new-zealand-city-alleged-gunman-plotted-carnage/2019/03/21/1846de9e-4a7b-11e9-8cfc-2c5d0999c21e_story.html.

Mosse, George L. 1996. *The Image of Man: The Creation of Modern Masculinity*. New York: Oxford University Press.

New Zealand Government. 2020. *Ko tō tātou kāinga tēnei: Report of the Royal Commission of Inquiry into the Terrorist Attack on Christchurch masjidain on 15 March 2019*. Vol. 2. n.p.: New Zealand Government. https://christchurchattack.royalcommission.nz/the-report/download-report/download-the-report/.

Ram, Kalpana, and Christopher Houston. 2015. "Introduction: Phenomenology's Methodological Invitation." In *Phenomenology in Anthropology: A Sense of Perspective*, edited by Kalpana Ram and Christopher Houston, 1–25. Bloomington: Indiana University Press.

Rhodes, Richard. (2002) 2004. *Masters of Death*. Reprint, New York: Rosetta Books. ePub.

Seierstad, Asne. 2016. *One of Us*. New York: Farrar, Straus and Giroux.

Shirer, William L. (1961) 2011. *The Rise and Fall of the Third Reich*. Reprint, New York: Rosetta Books. ePub.

Sluka, Jeffrey A. 2008. "Terrorism and Taboo: An Anthropological Perspective on Political Violence against Civilians." *Critical Studies on Terrorism* 1 (2): 167–183. http://dx.doi.org/10.1080/17539150802184579.

———. 2009. "The Contribution of Anthropology to Critical Terrorism Studies." In *Critical Terrorism Studies: A New Research Agenda*, edited by R. Jackson, J. Gunning, and M. Breen Smyth, 138–155. Abingdon: Routledge.

Speer, Albert. 1970. *Inside the Third Reich*. London: Macmillan.

Suzuki, D. T. (1938) 1959. *Zen and Japanese Culture*. Reprint, Princeton, N.J.: Princeton University Press.

Tarrant, Brenton. 2019. *The Great Replacement*. N.p.

Victoria, Brian. 2002. *Zen War Stories*. New York: Routledge.

———. 2006. *Zen at War*. 2nd ed. Oxford: Rowman & Littlefield.

———. 2013a. "D. T. Suzuki, Zen and the Nazis." *Asia-Pacific Journal* 11, issue 43 (no. 4): 1–21.

———. 2013b. "Zen as a Cult of Death in the Wartime Writings of D. T. Suzuki." *Asia-Pacific Journal* 11, issue 30 (no. 5): 1–32.

———. 2014. "A Zen Nazi in Wartime Japan: Count Dürkheim, and His Sources—D. T. Suzuki, Yasutani Haku'un and Eugen Herrigel." *Asia-Pacific Journal* 12, issue 3 (no. 2): 1–52.

Weiss, Sheila Faith. 1987. "The Race Hygiene Movement in Germany." *Osiris* 3 (1): 193–236. http://www.jstor.org/stable/301759.

Wilhelmsen, Fredrik. 2022. "When the Medium Is Not the Message." *Fascism* 11 (1): 109–138. https://doi.org/10.1163/22116257-bja10025.

Žižek, Slavoj. 2003. *The Puppet and the Dwarf: The Perverse Core of Christianity*. Cambridge, Mass.: MIT Press.

PART III GENDERED BODIES AND THERAPEUTIC INTERVENTIONS

6 · BEAUTIFUL, MORAL, FUNCTIONAL
Bodily Self-Alteration in an Italian Center for Eating Disorders

GISELLA ORSINI

Only in the twentieth century, especially since the 1960s, has the slender body replaced other concepts of female beauty in the West (Hesse-Biber 1996). Many streams of feminism initially supported this new aesthetic ideal of the thin woman, seeing in thinness a powerful and symbolic way to express a rebellion against domesticity and patriarchy (Brown and Jasper 1993). Paradoxically, however, rather than a statement of freedom, the pursuit of slenderness soon became a straitjacket for women. It is not surprising, therefore, that popular contemporary understandings and representations of eating disorders, particularly anorexia nervosa, often associate such conditions with an obsessive and self-oppressive quest for thinness.

Nevertheless, it is misleading to equate the altering processes undertaken by people with eating disorders as the result simply of their pursuit of the beauty ideal as such. In this chapter, I argue that within the Italian context, eating disorders can equally be considered the result of a moral self-altering process where control over hunger and bodily needs is a core value and in which the body symbolically expresses and materializes such self-alteration.[1] This self-altering process reflects a strong Cartesian view of oneself, whereby the body's needs and pleasure are perceived as threatening to an idealized mind-self.

Here I focus, then, on the symbolism of anorexic bodies: in the perceptions of my informants, emaciated bodies are not primarily aesthetically beautiful but rather powerfully expressive of a higher level of morality, purity, and mental strength. It is true that during the past decades, anthropologists have highlighted the relevance of understanding bodily experiences—hence, the body as a subject—and questioned the limits of discussing the body as a text/object

(Csordas 1990, 1994). The following analysis aims to combine both approaches, since the meanings expressed through the body will be analyzed by considering my informants' perceptions of embodied presence. In this sense, while focusing "on the body *per se*," I acknowledge "that it can be construed *both* as a source of representations *and* as a ground of being-in-the-world" (Csordas 1999, 184).

My discussion is based on four months of participant observation at an Italian treatment center for eating disorders in 2012. I spent every day at the facility and participated in all the group sessions and activities together with the patients. I also conducted semistructured and structured interviews with twenty patients (nineteen women and one man) aged between sixteen and thirty-eight and semistructured interviews with fifteen staff members.[2]

While I spent most of my time with patients, I also had the opportunity to take part in staff meetings and to speak with patients' relatives during their visits. Hence, the collected data allowed me to understand not only patients' perspectives on and relations between food and their bodies but also the views and practices of institutional professionals regarding eating disorders.

In this chapter, I focus on the analysis of the narratives of nineteen women diagnosed with different eating disorders and residing at the center. I assume that narrative and self are inseparable entities, since humans make sense of their own experiences and lives, as well as of themselves, through narration. The biographies of my informants are characterized by moments of extreme negative "self-awareness" that led them to alter themselves through the adoption of new values and behaviors.

Although the dominant biomedical model defines eating disorders as mental disorders, the accounts of my informants cannot be understood as illness narratives. In fact, while illness narratives tell of a self-transformation "imposed" by the disease, my informants manifest a strong sense of agency, narrating accounts of an activist self-alteration that then leads to "objective" medical diagnoses claiming they suffer from a medical condition.

This process of self-alteration is therefore characterized by experiences of reflexivity, self-awareness, and choice, while driven by specific life events and interactions with others. On the other hand, it is also important to note that the perception that women can morally improve themselves by negating their primary bodily needs resonates with cultural dispositions associated with womanhood in Italy. In this sense, this process of self-alteration is culturally informed.

Equally important, it is crucial to notice that the therapeutic approach proposed at the treatment center entails a contrary type of self-alteration that is imposed on patients. The center's activities aim to transform patients into docile bodies by modifying patients' behaviors that are considered pathological and abnormal. In this sense, the power exerted there can be understood as a creative process too, generative rather than merely repressive (Foucault 1980): "deviant" bodies are sought to be altered into healthy, productive, and functional bodies, in line with a rival set of normative social expectations.

EATING DISORDERS AND CONTEXTS OF CARE IN ITALY

Eating disorders in Italy have been considered a health emergency for the past few decades. In 2011, it was estimated that two million people suffered from an eating disorder (Dalla Ragione, Vicini, and Ciarrocchi 2011). In 1998, a commission of the Italian Ministry of Health published a set of guidelines for the treatment of eating disorders, indicating the need to provide different health-care services (ambulatory services, day-hospital services, hospitalization, and residential rehabilitation) depending on the severity of each case (Ministero della Sanità 1998). The commission also recognized the relevance of having different health-care specialists involved in the treatment of eating disorders and hence encouraged the cooperation of such professionals.

The Italian national health-care system (Servizio Sanitario Nazionale, SSN) provides universal health coverage mostly free of charge, and it is managed and administered regionally. While the Ministry of Health sets the main national goals and strategies, funds are allocated to the regions that are responsible for delivering and organizing health-care provision (Ferré et al. 2014). Considering that the twenty Italian regions vary greatly (in terms of demographic patterns and economic development, just to mention a few factors), it should not be surprising that there are evident regional disparities in the level of services provided.

The first national census on the number of public ambulatories and semiresidential and residential services was conducted in 2021. Forty-eight institutions providing treatment for eating disorders (almost 53 percent) are in the north of Italy, while fourteen (15 percent) are in the center, and twenty-nine (32 percent) are in the south and on the islands (Mastrobattista and Pacifici 2021).

The public residential center where I conducted fieldwork provides residential care for people with eating disorders and, in line with the guidelines set by the SSN in 1998, offers an integrated approach to treatment.[3] This is to say that in addition to psychological, psychiatric, and nutritional care and support, patients attend various therapeutic sessions and activities, such as pet therapy and music therapy. The facility can accommodate up to twenty patients for a period of five months, and all the costs are covered by the Italian health system. The center's approach relies on the idea that eating disorders are complex and challenging conditions to treat, which require a holistic approach to patient care.

RECONCEPTUALIZING NARRATIVE AND SELF

The medical category of "feeding and eating disorders" classifies a number of illnesses, including anorexia nervosa, bulimia nervosa, and binge eating disorder, each characterized by "a persistent disturbance of eating or eating-related behaviour that results in the altered consumption or absorption of food and that significantly impairs physical health or psychosocial functioning" (APA 2013, 329). As such, the biomedical and psychological discourses on eating disorders perceive the adoption of specific behaviors toward food and the body as the result of serious mental conditions that require treatment (Treasure, Duarte, and Schmidt 2020).

From my perspective, however, my informants' behavior can be understood as the outcome of attempting to alter oneself in moral terms rather than as a symptom of a mental problem. As I discuss in the following pages, the idealization and pursuit of extreme thinness reveal the perception of control over bodily pleasures, needs, and hunger as a fundamental moral value.

It is important to point out that all my informants, regardless of their diagnosis, shared the values symbolically expressed through thinness. However, in the case of people diagnosed with bulimia nervosa and binge eating disorder, their behaviors may not be aligned with such values. I therefore consider different eating disorders within the Italian context as consequences of differential achievements in the quest for an ideal moral selfhood (Orsini 2017).

The process of self-alteration at the heart of eating disorders becomes evident when focusing on the symbolism expressed through extreme thinness. It is important, however, to consider the body of a person with an eating disorder as the product of a speaking subject rather than as the mute object of interpretation. This is the reason why the discussion that follows is based on my informants' narratives and views on their embodied experiences.

Narratives have a crucial role in the construction of the self. Having rejected the idea that narratives merely describe and represent facts, social scientists have pointed out the relevance of narratives in identity formation processes—to the extent that some of them have referred to identities in terms of purely narrative matter (Somers 1994; Ochs and Capps 1996; Polkinghorne 1991).

The cognitive and linguistic process through which narratives are produced has the merit of giving coherence to people's lives by linking in a meaningful way past and present events. This fact not only helps individuals imagine and plan their own future, but it also provides meaning and sense to human existence (Polkinghorne 1991). It follows that people speak of themselves through certain narratives. Along these lines, Margaret R. Somers (1994) speaks of narrative identities, claiming that through certain stories (defined as ontological narratives), people make sense of their own life.

In medical anthropology, narrative analysis has been unequivocally defined as the most appropriate way to understand ill people's experiences in different sociocultural contexts (Kleinman 1988). Becoming ill (especially in the case of chronic or acute disease) is certainly a critical event in the human experience (Pearce 2008). The appearance of a disease entails a disruption in the biography as well as in the life project of the person. As Arthur W. Frank notes, "Disease happens in a life that already has a story, and this story goes on, changed by illness but also affecting how the illness story is formed" (1995, 54). Disease leads not only to changes in the performance of common everyday activities but also to a redefinition of the ill person's telos. In addition to this, one's self-perception becomes problematic. In this sense, "illness is a potentially self-changing event as it disconnects the self from both the former self and the commonly shared life world" (Levy 2005, 18).

It follows that by narrating their stories, ill people try to regain a coherent and unitary self-perception. Through our bodies, "we experience, comprehend and act upon the world" (Good 1994, 124). The ill person undergoes a transformation in the experience of their embodied self that can be understood and reflected upon precisely through narration. In the analysis of illness narratives, attention is drawn to the fact that the body of the sick person is experienced as a passive victim of the disease itself. However, this experience is radically different from that which emerges in the narratives of my informants. Indeed, while illness narratives tell of an alteration caused by the insurgence of a disease, my informants narrate a chosen self-alteration that is later reinterpreted as a medical condition. In other words, while through illness narratives people attempt to *regain* an active role in their own biography, my informants' stories cannot be understood as a loss of agency.

During one of the therapeutic group sessions I attended at the residential center, the therapist asked all the attendants to explain if they had an active or passive role in the onset and development of their eating disorder. Each participant claimed to have had an active role. Valentina (twenty years old, diagnosed with bulimia nervosa and having a past history of anorexia nervosa) explained her point of view in the following terms: "The disorder starts if you eat or don't eat. You decide it. No one obliges you to do so." Similarly, Sara (nineteen years old, diagnosed with bulimia nervosa) claimed, "You are definitely active. You decide what to do. Also, in a second phase, when it seems impossible to change habits again, no one is forcing you to persist. You are always deciding what to do."

Therefore, while both narratives of illness and accounts of eating disorders can be understood as narratives of self-alteration, in standard illness narratives, people speak of a change in telos dictated by their new condition. On the other hand, the narratives of my informants tell of a self-directed alteration, which is best understood in moral terms.

MORAL SELF-ALTERATION

One of the common features of my informants' accounts is a self-perception as outsiders in relation to their environment. This self-perception often resulted from a moment of "self-awareness" in their life, a turning point when they felt "not good enough" in the performance of their gendered social roles. This moment of self-awareness was followed by a change in behavior toward food (Orsini 2017).

Although for some people this turning point was easily recalled as a single transformative event, others explained this to me as a growing sense of inadequacy that led them to redefine themselves. While different reasons brought the women involved in my study to make such a claim, all of them presented a negative self-perception as a consequence of feeling "unloved." Some of them referred to specific life events that led them to see themselves as purely sexual objects. Among my informants, five of them (25 percent) claimed to have been sexually abused in the past, while most of them recalled several moments in their lives when they were morally judged or humiliated in relation to their sexuality, as in the case of Valentina.

She used to be a professional dancer, and all clinicians saw her career as the main reason for her eating disorder. Valentina, however, disagreed with the professionals. She explained to me that actually, her problem with food started long before she became a professional dancer. She recalled a specific episode in her past: at the age of fourteen, without any discernible reason, her close friends suddenly changed their attitude toward her. She said, "I still cannot understand why, but they started to call me 'slut,' 'b-tch.' Not only my male friends, but also girls. I remember my cousin as well went to tell my mother that I was a slut! I still remember, that day I thought, 'I am going to show them. I am going to be so skinny and perfect that they will just regret all this.' Since that day, I quit eating. And I always used to love to eat before!" Although Valentina was not able to explain to me the reasons why she changed her perspective toward food specifically to become "perfect," she recalled the specific aforementioned episode as the moment in which she decided to change herself.

As I discuss elsewhere (Orsini 2017), many scholars have described how ascetic women in the Middle Ages adopted specific bodily practices (including self-starvation) in order to enhance their sense of moral worth (Bell 1998; Bynum 1987; Corrington 1986). In this sense, the negation of primary bodily needs as a way to alter oneself in moral terms is a well-documented practice. Anthropologists have also highlighted the sense of moral worth that may characterize the embodied experiences of anorexics. As discussed by Sigal Gooldin in her study on anorexic women in Israel, "Anorexia is about actively using corporeal experiences to construct a sense of heroic selfhood" (2008, 290). Anorexia, in Gooldin's view, is perceived as a process of becoming, a profound alteration of oneself that embraces "masculine" notions of heroic morality (such as strength, dealing with danger, and overcoming hurdles).

Through the analysis of in-depth interviews conducted in Tennessee and Toronto with twenty-two men and women who had recovered from anorexia nervosa, Richard A. O'Connor and Penny Van Esterik (2008, 2015) also refer to anorexia as the outcome of an obsession over virtue rather than beauty. From their perspective, anorexia should be interpreted as an activity rather than a pathology, an ascetic practice whereby bodily control and virtuous eating are perceived as moral achievements. Somewhat differently, while not focusing exclusively on the morality of eating disorders, Rebecca J. Lester (2019) describes a common sense of shame regarding one's needs characterizing the experience of people with an eating disorder. It follows that "hunger, like other kinds of bodily discomfort, can become moralized as evidence that one is 'doing good' by denying oneself what one 'clearly' does not deserve" (75–76).

Unlike Gooldin (2008), however, I argue that the moral self-alteration characterizing my informants entails the adoption of moral values associated with femininity in Italy (self-sacrifice, the negation of bodily needs and pleasure, devotion to the family; Orsini 2022) rather than masculinity. It follows that in contrast with O'Connor and Esterik's (2008, 2015) views, gender plays a crucial role when understanding the narratives of my informants.

The relevance of understanding eating disorders by considering cultural ideas of womanhood in Italy is also discussed by Ann M. Cheney, Steve Sullivan, and Kathleen Grubbs (2018). Through the analysis of the embodied morality of eating disorders and recovery among Italian women in the south of Italy, the authors highlight how the embodied ascetic practices adopted by eating-disordered people are "embedded in a complex cultural and religious framework that constructs moral images of womanhood as self-sacrificial" (453).

When considering the narratives of my informants, self-sacrifice and devotion to others are certainly important elements in their quest for a superior moral self (Orsini 2022). In addition to this, the dualistic view of the self, shared by my informants, is a crucial factor leading them to admire extreme thinness and hence change their behaviors toward food.[4] In other words, it is the perception of a clear distinction between mind and body, as well as a hierarchy between the two, that led the women involved in this study to morally alter themselves by negating the materiality of their embodied selves.

I had the chance to analyze and discuss this aspect during one of the therapeutic group sessions at the residential center. The therapist started the session by asking all the participants to think about three characteristics that they wish to have in order to be a better person. Lara's response in this session clearly exemplifies this particular relationship to the body. While she was admitted to the residential treatment center with the diagnosis of bulimia nervosa, during the past ten years, she has alternated between periods of bulimia nervosa and periods of anorexia nervosa. Her body has been constantly changing over the last decade to the point that it is now fully covered with stretch marks. She started her account in the following way:

> I wish I was more self-confident. I think I am not worthy. I am always taking care more of my mind rather than of my body. For me, mind and body are two very different and distinct things; they are not a whole entity in my perspective. I now accept my body due to the functions it has.[5] Thinking rationally, I do know that I need my body. However, in the past, when I was speaking, I did not have the impression that I was the one speaking. Just to tell you how much I was perceiving the split between my mind and my body, I could not recognize from which mouth that voice was going out. Was it my mouth? Was it my voice? I was wondering from where that sound was coming. Now I accept the fact that I have a body. I have to. However, I still have to learn how to take care of it in a healthy way.

This separation between body and mind was also expressed by Roberta, an eighteen-year-old patient diagnosed with binge eating disorder, who claimed to think about herself only as mind. As a consequence, the therapist asked Roberta to present herself to the group in two different ways: first, as a mind-self and, after, as a body-self. Roberta stood up and moved to the center of the room, while all the participants were sitting around her. After a few minutes of reflection, she introduced her mind-self: "I can do whatever I want. I keep aside all the things I don't like; even if I have emotions, I keep those in a closed box so that no one can see them, not even myself." She then presented her body-self in the following terms: "I am compressed; the mind is not giving me any space. However, I do not oppose any resistance to the mind because I am not worthy."

While the mind is idealized to the point that many of the informants identify their total self as "mind-selves," the body is perceived as alien to the mind-self (Malson 1998, 118), as well as threatening. Therefore, while Roberta claimed that she thought of herself only as a mind-self, Paola, twenty-two years old and diagnosed with an eating disorder not otherwise specified, intervened, claiming that she used to feel like she was "dragging the body." She continued by affirming that despite the fact that now she has accepted ownership of her body, she still feels uncomfortable about it. The idea of a dominant mind-self was expressed by all the participants in the group who frequently devalued their own bodies, expressing a wish to control biological needs.

MORAL BODIES

At the treatment center where I conducted research, patients are not allowed to speak about their eating habits and their appearance. During my fieldwork, I was asked on a couple of occasions about my impression of my informants' physical appearance. I was told by staff that any answer to such questions will only have an adverse effect. People with eating disorders who are told that they look good or are in good shape will often interpret such statements as a failure in their journey. They are in fact aware that an extremely thin body is commonly perceived as sick, rather than good or beautiful, by people without an eating disorder (Lintott 2003).

Elena (seventeen years old) told me during our first meeting that she has been suffering from anorexia nervosa for one year. She continued by telling me that she never transgressed her rules unless she was forced to do so by her parents. As a consequence, she rapidly lost weight. Other people were worried about her appearance. Such apprehension, however, made her feel satisfied with herself rather than worried: "I remember it was June last year. I saw different people whom I hadn't seen for a while. All of them used to tell me, 'Is that you?' They couldn't even recognize me! And the more you hear those kinds of comments, the more you feel *strong* [my emphasis]. It means that you are doing well, that you are actually losing weight. It means that you are really slim! It wasn't enough; I mean, it was always extremely important to know what others thought about my appearance. It was even more important than my own judgment."

Becoming thin is a personal choice that shows, through the changed body, the mental strength to control hunger and pleasure and thus the moral triumph of mind over body. My informants experienced positive moral sentiments, such as a sense of purity, when avoiding eating. This was clearly explained by Erika (thirty-one years old, diagnosed with anorexia nervosa): "I felt stronger. Empty but stronger. The fact of introducing something inside my body felt like I was really polluting it. I used to feel so pure when my stomach was completely empty! I remember that during one period I was also avoiding water. Even a glass of water was not making me feel that empty and pure. I felt great being that empty. That's why when people were telling me that I was risking collapsing, I was just thinking that they didn't understand anything. I couldn't feel better than that!"

The fear of contamination and pollution in people with eating disorders, however, "is not a threat on the self from 'outside' but operates within the self" (Macsween 1995, 209). What people with eating disorders consider dangerous and polluting is the appetite and, as a consequence, the body itself. This should not surprise us considering that for centuries women's biological needs and their own bodies have been considered sinful and shameful, to the point that it is very common for women to feel "a sense of shame and despair" (Chernin 1981, 52) about their own appetites—something quite pronounced among all my informants, regardless of the disorder they were diagnosed with. Viviana (sixteen years old, diagnosed with bulimia nervosa and having a past history of anorexia nervosa) clearly explained to me such sentiments when recalling her bulimic period: "I remember, during that period, I started to feel hungry again. It was awful. It is like I used to feel ashamed about my body's sensations. Feelings of hunger, fullness, . . . I didn't feel them before, when I was anorexic. I was ashamed precisely because of that." Hence, thinness for the people involved in my research represented the annihilation of all physical threats to the idealized mind-self rather than the pursuit of a conventional ideal of beauty. While my informants often used moral terms when speaking about their bodies, they hardly ever used a language of aesthetics, and when such a language was applied, it was infused with moral value. They mostly attributed positive moral values to thinness, while fat bodies were perceived as symbols of moral failure. All my bulimic and anorexic informants who gained weight during their self-transformative process that led them to be diagnosed with an eating disorder avoided meeting other people. In situations in which they were obliged to do so, they used to hide their bodies with large clothes. This fact shows, in my opinion, how people perceived extra kilos as a physical representation of their moral failure, something to hide from others.

Since thinness symbolizes the ideal moral goal for my informants, it should not surprise us that they constantly compared their bodies with others' bodies in order to evaluate their progress and thereby to ascertain their moral superiority (or inferiority). Marianna (twenty-six years old, diagnosed with anorexia nervosa) was admitted to the treatment center a few weeks after my arrival in Italy.

The very same day she was admitted, Elisa (twenty-eight years old, diagnosed with anorexia nervosa) seemed extremely distressed and anxious. At the end of the day, Elisa asked me if we could talk. She then explained that she had a breakdown due to the arrival of the new girl (Marianna). She was too skinny. Skinnier than her. She continued by telling me, proudly, *that she used to be even "worse" than her*.[6] It is interesting to notice that Elisa felt the need to tell me that she used to be skinnier than her in order to restore a sort of moral supremacy, now not expressed anymore through her body.

Pamela (twenty-two years old, diagnosed with bulimia nervosa) recalled Elisa's distress when explaining to me her perception of anorexics:

> Anorexics are extremely competitive. They are lethal! Just think, you remember when Carola arrived? You could easily see her bones, how skinny she is. The first time she was eating with us, all the anorexics were looking at and admiring her. They were feeling bad because they don't have that body anymore. There is an extreme competition about thinness. They always observe if there is anyone thinner than them.... You know what Elisa told me after having seen Marianna for the first time? She told me, "I am sorry; this is a shocking moment for me. She is so skinny, and I am so fat." This is the reason, in my opinion, why she didn't get close with any other anorexics. She prefers to spend time with people fatter than her.

While being thin is, for my informants, a powerful and visible sign of their successful moral self-alteration, anorexic bodies are perceived by the biomedical and psychological establishment as sick bodies, the physical result of a mental condition and hence in need of medical and psychological care.

FUNCTIONAL BODIES

The residential center where I conducted fieldwork is a clear example of the ways in which biopower (Foucault 1990) functions to manage and discipline individuals in contemporary Western societies. As a matter of fact, patients' healing processes can be understood as a veritable reeducational one. All the proposed therapies and activities contribute to transforming deviancy into normality.

The center aims to educate deviant bodies and minds, transforming patients into docile bodies by adopting different interventions, including disciplinary regulation of the body, such as the nutritional approach and mirror therapy. These techniques are based on a medical and psychological knowledge of eating disorders and gain their legitimacy through their authoritative status. By labeling specific behaviors as pathological, staff members aim to discipline patients' bodies (their eating habits, their physical state, and their self-evaluation) by altering patients' attitudes.

While all my informants, regardless of their diagnosis, found the center's regulations to be oppressive, they were particularly troubled by the therapy room (as the dining room was called), the weight checks, and mirror therapy. Interestingly, those are the therapeutic approaches that aim not only to modify in a direct and practical way patients' behaviors toward food and their self-perception but also to monitor patients' compliance with the center's approach. It is therefore exactly through such activities that perceived pathological bodies are trained and modified into healthy, "normal" bodies.

During nutritional therapy (meals), patients are not only assisted to finish their "therapy" (food); they are also educated to eat in specific ways.[7] On the other hand, the mirror therapy sessions aim to help patients reacquire a "normal" self-perception.[8] This therapy relies on the idea that people with an eating disorder, particularly anorexics, have a distorted body image, a "disturbance in the way in which one's body weight or shape is experienced" (APA 2013, 339). In other words, people diagnosed with eating disorders are thought to have a wrong perception of their own bodies. Such a feature is also considered to be one of the main causes of relapses after recovery (Keel et al. 2005).

However, as pointed out by Arthur H. Crisp (1980), while anorexics may overestimate their body size, this is not any different from many adolescent girls who consider themselves overweight, although they are not, strictly speaking, overweight as such. In addition to this, medical body weight classification (underweight, normal weight, overweight, and obesity) based on body mass index does not necessarily reflect one's self-perception and the social ideas of thinness/normal weight.

I had the chance to discuss this aspect with Viviana during one of our meetings. She explained to me her reaction when she was told that she has a "distorted body image":

> I used to tell them that I wanted to lose weight, but they [the staff] were all telling me that I had a normal weight and that therefore I didn't have to. I don't know; I wish to lose a few kilos. The psychologist keeps telling me that I have a greatly distorted body image. But I don't see it like this. However, I cannot see myself as being of a normal weight. At the beginning, they used to tell me, "You are not as you see yourself." And I was thinking, "How do I look then?" It was so strange. They told me I have an illness that prevents me from seeing myself as I *really* am. And I was thinking, "So what do I look like actually?" Especially in the beginning it was hard to understand and to accept. I mean, if I see myself in this way, what can I do? In the end, I see myself in this way, and I think I am like this.

During mirror therapy, patients are asked to stand in front of a full-length mirror and to describe each part of their own body by focusing on its functions rather than judging or evaluating it from an aesthetic perspective. Patients are educated to observe their own bodies from a purely mechanical/biological perspective.

Such an approach should not surprise us considering that biomedicine tends to consider and treat the body as a machine (Nettleton 2021) and since within the capitalist discourse, the body is in very real terms a production machine (Scheper-Hughes and Lock 1987). During the first session, patients are fully dressed. Session by session, they are asked to expose more of their body until the last session, in which they are standing in front of the mirror wearing only their underwear. Patients are then asked to rate their anxiety toward each body part described, selecting a number between zero and ten. The psychologists claimed that in most cases, the level of anxiety heavily decreases toward the end of the seven sessions.[9]

While a few of my informants claimed to have started to consider their own body without aesthetical judgments, others confessed the extreme difficulty they encountered in altering the way they view their own body through such therapy. Some felt demeaned and insulted by such an approach.

One of my informants expressed her doubts regarding mirror therapy in the following terms:

> I understand and I know that it is due to my legs that I can walk, and I am thankful for this. However, in my opinion, those are still like chicken legs. I know perfectly well how my body functions, and again, I am thankful for this, but still . . . I do believe it is too simplistic. I don't think this is enough to start to love my body. I think it is insufficient. When you look at yourself in the mirror, you look at yourself. To love yourself, you have to start to love your own body for what it looks like, not because of its functions. Let's stop bullshitting.

While the treatment center focuses on patients' bodies in order to normalize them, the disciplinary power exerted over patients "is concerned not with repressing, but with creating" (Armstrong 1994, 23). However, the process of self-alteration imposed at the center obscures the symbolic and ethical language of the body, hence overlooking the self-altering process undertaken by my informants in their quest for an ideal moral selfhood.

It is therefore not surprising that people diagnosed with anorexia nervosa tend to resist treatment (Nordbø et al. 2012) and that only one of the eight informants diagnosed with anorexia nervosa has sought professional help without having been forced to do so by other people. While among my informants an emaciated body is the result of a successful moral self-alteration, the healthy body promoted and imposed by the biomedical establishment entails a self-alteration that would go against the moral values associated with thinness. This is evident when considering one of the drawings made by Elisa during one of the art therapy sessions (see figure 6.1).

Elisa drew herself divided into two parts: the left side of her body represents herself without anorexia nervosa, while the right part represents herself with the disorder. Her hair is down only on her left side. This is due to the fact that during the entire period she had her disorder, she did not let her hair down. She drew a pair of scissors instead of her right hand to symbolize the self-harm induced while not eating.[10] The most relevant aspect of such a drawing is the question mark

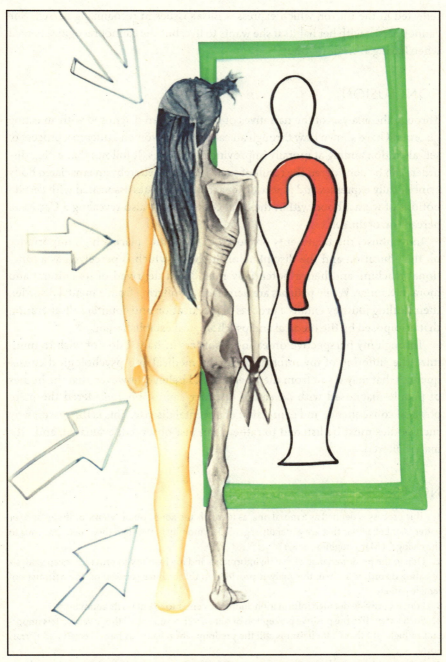

FIGURE 6.1. Drawing made by Elisa during one of the art therapy sessions in which patients were asked to portray themselves. Source: Author, courtesy of Elisa.

reflected in the mirror, which expresses Elisa's issues in recognizing herself. She cannot persist with her habits if she wants to live, but she cannot recognize herself when having a "healthy" body.

CONCLUSION

Through the analysis of the narratives of Italian women diagnosed with an eating disorder, I have shown how through an eating order, women undergo a process of self-alteration aiming at morally improving themselves. It follows that eating disorders can be considered the result of such a process, whereby an emaciated body symbolically expresses and physically enacts moral values associated with certain notions of womanhood within the local context while also revealing a Cartesian perception of the self.

In response, the treatments proposed at the center place a high importance on the education and the discipline of the body, which is perceived as a functional machine and hence potentially muted and deprived of its cultural and moral meanings. While patients are perceived as suffering from a mental disorder, their healing journey entails a process of reeducation and counter self-alteration that is imposed by the medical and psychological establishment.

Through my perspective on eating disorders in Italy, I do not wish to minimize the suffering of my informants or the medical and psychological consequences that may result from their behaviors. I believe, however, that the bodies of people diagnosed with an eating disorder cannot be considered the mere physical consequence and expression of a mental disease. This is the reason why such bodies must be listened to rather than just observed, evaluated, and ultimately altered.

NOTES

1. This process is defined as a moral one, as it entails the adoption of "views, attitudes and/or patterns of behaviour that are generally regarded as morally better than those held previous to the change" (Mac Laughlin 2008, 1).
2. Due to the predominance of female informants and my inability to provide a deep analysis of eating disorders in men, the analysis provided in this chapter is based on the narratives of female patients.
3. I do not provide detailed information about the center to maintain its anonymity.
4. Such a view, like the positive perception of self-sacrifice, reflects Catholic values. It is important to highlight that Catholicism is still the predominant religion in Italy (Ferrari and Ferrari 2015).
5. I discuss this view, which reflects the approach of the center toward the body, below.
6. She used the word *worse*, meaning that she used to be thinner than Marianna. It is also important to highlight that the word *worse*, used by Elisa, actually meant *better*.
7. See Orsini (2022) for more details about the nutritional approach.
8. After the first month spent at the center, each patient attends seven individual mirror therapy sessions.

9. Different scholars (Key et al. 2002; Luethcke, McDaniel, and Becker 2011) have doubts about the effectiveness of such an approach for people diagnosed with an eating disorder.
10. Elisa decided to be admitted to the center after being hospitalized due to the severe health consequences of her eating behaviors.

REFERENCES

APA (American Psychiatric Association). 2013. *Diagnostic and Statistical Manual of Mental Disorders*. 5th ed. Washington, D.C.: APA.

Armstrong, David. 1994. "Bodies of Knowledge / Knowledge of Bodies." In *Reassessing Foucault: Power, Medicine and the Body*, edited by Jones Colin, 17–27. London: Routledge.

Bell, Rudolph M. 1998. *La Santa anoressia: Digiuno e misticismo dal medioevo a oggi*. Rome: Editori Laterza.

Brown, Catrina, and Karin Jasper, eds. 1993. *Consuming Passions: Feminist Approaches to Weight Preoccupation and Eating Disorders*. Toronto: Second Story.

Bynum, Caroline W. 1987. *Holy Feast and Holy Fast: The Religious Significance of Food to Medieval Women*. Berkeley: University of California Press.

Cheney, Ann M., Steve Sullivan, and Kathleen Grubbs. 2018. "The Morality of Disordered Eating and Recovery in Southern Italy." *Medical Anthropology Quarterly* 32 (3): 443–457. https://doi.org/10.1111/maq.12429.

Chernin, Kim. 1981. *The Obsession: Reflections on the Tyranny of Slenderness*. New York: Harper & Row.

Corrington, Gail. 1986. "Anorexia, Asceticism, and Autonomy: Self-Control as Liberation and Transcendence." *Journal of Feminist Studies in Religion* 2 (2): 51–61.

Crisp, Arthur H. 1980. *Anorexia Nervosa: Let Me Be Me*. New York: Grune & Stratton.

Csordas, Thomas J. 1990. "Embodiment as a Paradigm for Anthropology." *Ethos* 18 (1): 5–47.

———, ed. 1994. *Embodiment and Experience: The Existential Ground of Culture and Self*. Cambridge: Cambridge University Press.

———. 1999. "The Body's Career in Anthropology." In *Anthropological Theory Today*, edited by Henrietta L. Moore, 172–205. Cambridge: Polity.

Dalla Ragione, Laura, Maria Vicini, and Alessandro Ciarrocchi. 2011. "I Disturbi del Comportamento Alimentare." In *Pianeta Galileo 2011*, edited by Alberto Peruzzi, 157–163. Florence: Consiglio regionale della Toscana.

Ferrari, Alessandro, and Silvio Ferrari. 2015. "Religion and the Secular State: The Italian Case." In *Religion and the Secular State: National Reports*, edited by Donlu D. Thayer, 431–448. Madrid: Servicio de Publicaciones de la Facultad de Derecho de la Universidad Complutense.

Ferré, Francesca, Antonio Giulio de Belvis, Luca Valerio, Silvia Longhi, Agnese Lazzari, Giovanni Fattore, Walter Ricciardi, and Anna Maresso. 2014. "Italy: Health System Review." *Health Systems in Transition* 16 (4): 1–168.

Foucault, Michel. 1980. *Power/Knowledge: Selected Interviews and Other Writings 1972–1977*. London: Harvester.

———. 1990. *The History of Sexuality*. Vol. 1, *An Introduction*. London: Penguin.

Frank, Arthur W. 1995. *The Wounded Storyteller: Body, Illness, and Ethics*. Chicago: University of Chicago Press.

Good, Byron J. 1994. *Medicine, Rationality and Experience: An Anthropological Perspective*. Cambridge: Cambridge University Press.

Gooldin, Sigal. 2008. "Being Anorexic: Hunger, Subjectivity, and Embodied Morality." *Medical Anthropology Quarterly* 22 (3): 274–296. https://doi.org/10.1111/j.1548-1387.2008.00026.x.

Hesse-Biber, Sharlene. 1996. *Am I Thin Enough Yet? The Cult of Thinness and the Commercialization of Identity*. Oxford: Oxford University Press.
Keel, Pamela K., David J. Dorer, Debra L. Franko, Safia C. Jackson, and David B. Herzog. 2005. "Postremission Predictors of Relapse in Women with Eating Disorders." *American Journal of Psychiatry* 162 (12): 2263–2268. https://doi.org/10.1176/appi.ajp.162.12.2263.
Key, Adrienne, C. Louise George, Desley Beattie, Kate Stammers, Hubert Lacey, and Glenn Waller. 2002. "Body Image Treatment within an Inpatient Programme for Anorexia Nervosa: The Role of Mirror Exposure in the Desensitization Process." *International Journal of Eating Disorders* 31 (2): 185–190. https://doi.org/10.1002/eat.10027.
Kleinman, Arthur. 1988. *The Illness Narratives: Suffering, Healing, and the Human Condition*. New York: Basic Books.
Lester, Rebecca J. 2019. *Famished: Eating Disorders and Failed Care in America*. Berkeley: University of California Press.
Levy, Jennifer M. 2005. "Narrative and Experience: Telling Stories of Illness." *Nexus* 18 (1): 8–33. https://doi.org/10.15173/nexus.v18i1.194.
Lintott, Sheila. 2003. "Sublime Hunger: A Consideration of Eating Disorders beyond Beauty." *Hypatia* 18 (4): 65–86. https://doi.org/10.1111/j.1527-2001.2003.tb01413.x.
Luethcke, Cynthia A., Leda McDaniel, and Carolyn Black Becker. 2011. "A Comparison of Mindfulness, Nonjudgmental, and Cognitive Dissonance-Based Approaches to Mirror Exposure." *Body Image* 8 (3): 251–258. https://doi.org/10.1016/j.bodyim.2011.03.006.
Mac Laughlin, Alfredo. 2008. "Narratives of Hope: A Philosophical Study of Moral Conversion. Dissertation." PhD diss., Loyola University.
Macsween, Morag. 1995. *Anorexic Bodies: A Feminist and Sociological Perspective on Anorexia Nervosa*. London: Routledge.
Malson, Helen. 1998. *The Thin Woman: Feminism, Post-structuralism and the Social Psychology of Anorexia Nervosa*. London: Routledge.
Mastrobattista, Luisa, and Roberta Pacifici, eds. 2021. *Guida ai servizi territoriali per la cura dei disturbi della nutrizione e dell'alimentazione*. Rome: Istituto Superiore di Sanità.
Ministero della Sanità. 1998. "Commissione di studio per l'assistenza ai pazienti affetti da Anoressia e Bulimia Nervosa." *Annali della Sanità Pubblica (Nuova Serie)* III, (1, 2, 3): 9–20.
Nettleton, Sarah. 2021. *The Sociology of Health and Illness*. Cambridge: Polity.
Nordbø, Ragnfrid H. S., Ester M. S. Espeset, Kjersti S. Gulliksen, Finn Skårderud, Josie Geller, and Arne Holte. 2012. "Reluctance to Recover in Anorexia Nervosa." *European Eating Disorders Review* 20 (1): 60–67. https://doi.org/10.1002/erv.1097.
Ochs, Elinor, and Lisa Capps. 1996. "Narrating the Self." *Annual Review of Anthropology* 25:19–43. https://doi.org/10.1146/annurev.anthro.25.1.19.
O'Connor, Richard A., and Penny Van Esterik. 2008. "De-medicalizing Anorexia: A New Cultural Brokering." *Anthropology Today* 24 (5): 6–9. https://doi.org/10.1111/j.1467-8322.2008.00611.x.
———. 2015. *From Virtue to Vice: Negotiating Anorexia*. Oxford: Berghahn.
Orsini, Gisella. 2017. "'Hunger Hurts, but Starving Works': The Moral Conversion to Eating Disorders." *Culture, Medicine, and Psychiatry* 41 (1): 111–141. https://doi.org/10.1007/s11013-016-9507-6.
———. 2022. "Compliance and Resistance to Treatment in an Italian Residential Centre for Eating Disorders." *Anthropology & Medicine* 29 (2): 193–207. https://doi.org/10.1080/13648470.2021.1994333.
Pearce, Caroline. 2008. "World Interrupted: An Autoethnographic Exploration into the Rupture of Self and Family Narratives following the Onset of Chronic Illness and the Death of a Mother." *Qualitative Sociology Review* 4 (1): 131–149.

Polkinghorne, Donald E. 1991. "Narrative and Self-Concept." *Journal of Narrative and Life History* 1 (2–3): 135–153. https://doi.org/10.1075/jnlh.1.2-3.04nar.

Scheper-Hughes, Nancy, and Margaret M. Lock. 1987. "The Mindful Body: A Prolegomenon to Future Work in Medical Anthropology." *Medical Anthropology Quarterly* 1 (1): 6–41. https://doi.org/10.1525/maq.1987.1.1.02a00020.

Somers, Margaret R. 1994. "The Narrative Constitution of Identity: A Relational and Network Approach." *Theory & Society* 23 (5): 605–649. https://doi.org/10.1007/BF00992905.

Treasure, Janet, Tiago Antunes Duarte, and Ulrike Schmidt. 2020. "Eating Disorders." *Lancet* (London, England) 395 (10227): 899–911. https://doi.org/10.1016/S0140-6736(20)30059-3.

7 • POROUS INDIVIDUALITY AS SELF-ALTERATION

Commercial Self-Improvement in Urban China

GIL HIZI

Under global capitalism, people around the world find ready opportunities to cultivate themselves through designated pedagogical and therapeutic practices. These practices are fueled by ideologies that promote the ethos of self-improvement, the commercialization of relevant psychological expertise, and the pluralization and sequestration of social spheres, which enables people to accommodate such practices within their ongoing multiple commitments. The practices at play include those that are oriented explicitly toward market-driven success by fostering employment and business skills, those that prioritize mindful and spiritual experiences in compensation for the stress of everyday life, and those that guide people's emotional management and expression as the key condition for well-being. Scholars and practitioners from behavioral and economic fields who are not critical of postindustrial capitalism tend to endorse the proactive and emotional aspects of these practices, while critics of capitalism diagnose the seemingly superficial or fraudulent character of many such practices, pointing out the ways in which they buttress exploitative structural conditions (e.g., Illouz 2007; Rose 1998; Wilce and Fenigsen 2016).

How do we account for people's transformative experiences via these practices without disavowing the structural problem at issue?

This chapter looks at the properties of self-alteration in market-driven self-improvement programs in urban China, specifically pedagogical practices inspired by positive psychology. I treat positive psychology as a set of principles that promote individual autonomy, proactive behavioral transformations, heightened emotional expression, and the pursuit of happiness, evident in the field championed by Martin E. P. Seligman (2002). The application of positive psychology in

China shows how contemporary therapeutic doctrines are co-constituted with capitalist ideologies and their models of the individualized and entrepreneurial person. Intriguingly, in pedagogical practice itself, positive psychology is also premised on intersubjective experiences, where individuals are encouraged to let go of their habitual behavior and self-image and instead become mutually shaped by the presence of supportive others. As this chapter describes, here is a process of *self-alteration* that is characterized by temporary and space-bounded subject positions within everyday life. This is rarely a (long-term) disciplined process of *self-transformation* but rather a dynamic that emanates through the affordances of distinct practices and the energetic interactions that they induce.

Self-alteration is a term that I apply as a general description of these processes. It gestures to the apparently temporary nature of self-change experienced through these programs. Instructors and participants themselves more commonly use the words *self-improvement*, *self-realization*, and *self-transformation* to denote their actions. *Self-improvement* in this chapter refers to a genre of practices where people "work on themselves." *Self-realization* and *self-transformation* refer to objectives and accomplishments within the category of self-improvement. These are moments when people identify and perform their individuality, perceiving themselves to be singular beings who transcend their everyday obligations or social roles. Despite the clear semantic difference between the verbs *realization* and *transformation*, in the workshops I attended, they were often expressed interchangeably (through the terms *gaibian ziji*, *biaoda zhenzheng de ziwo*, and *ziwo tisheng*), since both instructors and participants regarded the process of "realizing" or accentuating the individualized self as synonymous with the potential for becoming a different—happier, confident, resilient—person.

Urban China offers a unique case study to investigate the expansion of market-driven self-improvement via positive psychology, as well as to illuminate the lived meanings of relevant expertise. The pedagogical practices I describe in this essay develop within the nexus of economic reforms, desires for modernity, and concerns about individual autonomy. People in China navigate among different ethical prescriptions in their social worlds, including familial values, state requirements for good citizenship, social networks of exchange, workplace hierarchies, and self-enterprising labor. Many people in China, educators and therapists most specifically, identify this navigation as a challenge confronting people in their managing of these multiple demands, involving both the establishing of coherent moral practices and the achieving of a continuous individual self across these transitions. The "individual" is positively construed here as a desired ontological reality informed by modernist ideologies in China that associate individualization with social development and well-being (e.g., Liu 1996).

At the same time, it is also regarded as inhibited by local interpersonal norms. Self-improvement via globalized therapeutic expertise is hence oriented toward elevating and enacting the individualized self, notwithstanding the group-oriented practices and intersubjective dynamics at play. Juxtaposing these complex ethical frameworks and conditions in urban China with positive psychology, in this chapter, I identify not only how the latter gains appeal and is culturally translated but also how its pedagogical principles accentuate and instantiate people's desires for self-realization through modal shifts within the sequences of everyday life.

I conclude that this form of self-alteration neither accommodates dominant structures—namely, the market economy and widespread cultural norms—nor enables resistance to them. Rather, through the seemingly nonordinary realm of self-improvement, it reinforces and reconfigures contradictions such as self versus relationality or the autonomous versus the "porous" individual (Taylor 2007). These tensions and frictions produce moments of liminality and modal change, which although fleeting are also charged with stimulating potential for self-making, in practice becoming bounded opportunities within people's paths and social engagements.

SETTING

The practices of self-alteration described below take place in pedagogical programs intended to enhance interpersonal skills. These activities draw on diverse sources, but they have a shared affinity with positive psychology that manifests in market-driven self-improvement and that seeks to maximize people's value and well-being rather than mitigate suffering per se. These activities merge a model of entrepreneurial individuality with affective interactions in intersubjective settings that are designed to destabilize the boundary between the self and the social environment.

I introduce in this chapter two programs in which I conducted participant observation in 2015 (with shorter participation in 2016 and 2017). I participated in workshops in both Heart's Secret and Champion Training, where early suspicion or enthusiasm about my presence was gradually replaced with familiarity and cooperation. In addition, I conducted semistructured interviews with seventeen participants and three instructors of Heart's Secret and thirteen participants and four instructors in Champion Training. With approximately one-third of them, I developed more friendly relationships due to repeated conversations. The two sites differed in their pedagogical frameworks and participants' profiles, yet some of their drills and logic overlapped. In particular, this involved their shared emphasis on interpersonal "soft" skills as capacities that are understood, unlike technical skills or intellectual knowledge as integral to the self, able to be applied by individuals resourcefully in different settings, transcending specific interpersonal commitments or localized wisdom. These convictions tie self-improvement to a vision of entrepreneurial behavior, whereby individual competency is rewarded by the impartial market society and in which mobility and risk-taking are necessary attributes.[1]

Champion Training was a very lively program run by a group of twelve to fourteen students on a big university campus in the city of Jinan. They ran their meetings and activities in a business incubation hub sponsored by the university and several private companies as part of the wider support of business pursuits among students and graduates by the Ministry of Education and the Ministry of Human Resources and Social Security. These students followed the guidance of a charismatic student named Li Chen, who had attended various workshops across the country and identified the importance of bolstering students' *individuality* in contrast to apparently more disciplinary and conformist classroom learning.[2]

Champion Training's main product was a one-week camp that invited students from across the province to shed their inhibitions and transform themselves. The long days of the camp included sessions of public speaking, physical exercises that fostered group trust, selling items to pedestrians, expressing gratitude to parents, promoting imaginary brands, and "crazy dancing" (*kuangwu*). The instructors coordinated these activities with motivational messages and by scolding participants who were supposedly too restrained or lacked independent will. They connected these requirements to the demands and possibilities of the private job market, although they themselves, being undergraduate students, provided little practical advice about future employment. Participants in these camps were usually actively immersed in these interactive exercises but were more ambiguous in their reflections afterward. In my ongoing meetings with former participants, few of them identified any significant change in their behaviors (more extrovert, confident, independent), and some expressed skepticism about applying their learning. They focused instead on the interesting people and new friends they met during the camps.

The second program I attended, Heart's Secret, had a wider variety of activities as well as more possibilities for continuous practice. This was a privately run center focusing on psychology, including lectures, workshops of several hours to several days, and training sessions for licensed counselors. Heart's Secret operated both as a members' club, with annual membership for access to activities, and as an open space for newcomers, with fees that were reasonable for the urban middle class. The center had fifty to sixty members in 2015, most of whom were in their thirties and forties, a majority being women. In the shorter activities, they composed about 30–40 percent of participants, while in courses and counselor training, they were a majority.

From 2002 to 2017, China launched a national exam that licensed millions of counselors following training periods that often did not exceed six months (Huang 2013). Most licensed counselors did not turn to counseling as their main profession or source of income, but this examination system still bolstered psychological services, self-help methods, and the popularization of expertise via various media. Although most counselors I met acknowledged the risk of compromising one's professional level due to the short length of training, and hence emphasized the need for ongoing counselor training after obtaining their license, practitioners also welcomed the expansion of expertise as a driver of social progress. My research focused on activities that included nonpracticing counselors and novices and that, in general, emphasized instantaneous transitions in people's attitudes and emotional expressions rather than promoting direct counseling.

In the workshops, instructors (who were also licensed counselors) drew on various inputs, including concepts by Carl Rogers, Abraham H. Maslow, Virginia Satir, and Irvin Yalom, as well as briefer references to psychoanalytical schools. In addition, they emphasized the importance of active participation in workshops, whereby learning is achieved not through knowledge but by emotional attunement and the associated tropes of "self-containment" (*jiena*) and "self-overcoming" (*tupo*), along with frequent evocations of "happiness" (*xingfu*) and "dreams" (*mengxiang*). Thus, in everyday encounters, good and effective interactions, according to the teaching, combined the elevation of an affective social medium with the assertion of participants' individuality. This logic, while pedagogically produced in a partial vacuum from everyday life, was also discussed in activities in relation to participants' supposed insufficient individual autonomy in their roles as mothers, siblings, children, or employees. The workshop space, accordingly, enabled renewed connection with one's "authentic" desires and recognition of one's singular self.

The wider setting for this project is the city of Jinan, the capital of Shandong Province in the northeastern part of China, south of Beijing. Jinan is a local hub that concentrates governmental offices, educational institutions, and private enterprises, though it is relatively less affluent compared to the category of first-tier cities in China, as well as to two to three metropolises in coastal Shandong. For most residents, Jinan is valued as a historical city due to the roots of settlements that go back four millennia, as well as its proximity to the origins of Confucian thinkers from the sixth century BCE. At the same time, many residents identify this heritage with conservative tendencies that limit social development, in particular the realization of more person-centered ideologies and norms. People propose that the importance of filial piety, exam-driven educational success, and saving "face" (*mianzi*) are elements that potentially undermine one's self-realization in everyday life. This perception extends modernist critique from the late nineteenth century onward that has identified longstanding Chinese culture as an obstacle to individualization and social progress (see Liu 1996, 177–180). These now normative ideas assist in shaping pedagogical spaces for interpersonal skills as sites with unique affordances for self-expression and social interaction.

INDIVIDUAL AUTONOMY VIA GROUP IDENTITY

We near the end of the second day of a workshop on "communication" held in Heart's Secret, but there is one more thrill. Teacher Jiao asks us to push all the tables and chairs toward the walls and open the classroom for movement. As in previous exercises, Jiao provides little detail in advance, incorporating our surprise into the drill itself. We are literally blind, required to sit with closed eyes. Soft instrumental music is played while everyone keeps quiet. Jiao's assistant, a woman in her thirties, takes participants one at a time with her hand and places them in pairs, one facing the other. She directs each of us to touch our partner with our fingertips while remaining silent. Without talking, we are asked to decide who is "A" and who is "B," which we do by pointing at each other's hands. Then we dance, "A" leading for a few minutes, then "B" taking control. This sequence repeats with different musical styles, as the playlist becomes increasingly upbeat. Giggling takes over the room but without disclosing each other's identities. Twenty minutes into the dance party, we open our eyes and reveal ourselves. Most pairs are laughing, smiling, and recounting to each other the memorable moments and their hunches about their partner's identity. By this stage of the workshop, everyone is familiar with others' names, even as instructors seemed to pair up people with some chemistry between them.

Later we divide into small groups where we talk about our experiences, before turning to a larger class discussion. We share moments of embarrassment, curiosity, and surprising bodily cooperation where we feel less conscious of or concerned about our movement. Jiao emphasizes that we need such activities in life to "create fine flavor" (*chuangzao meihao de weidao*) and that this has little to do with romance. Although all dancing pairs were heterosexual and Jiao even makes comments on the romantic potential of two nonmarried individuals in their midtwenties, his pedagogical analysis transcends the gender issue. Jiao explains that the combination of closed eyes and bodily coordination is ideal for exercising issues of control and for developing synchronization with our interlocutors. Through bodily movement, we were supposedly attuned in high resolution to our own as well as to our partner's state of being, even if, clearly, we were also excited due to the specific proceedings coordinated by Jiao.

This exercise, along with other activities in Heart's Secret, is loosely tied to specific knowledge disseminated through the circulation of affective group practices across different pedagogical settings and locations. Jiao emulates drills that he had participated in as a trainee in workshops in Beijing by teachers from China, Japan, Taiwan, and Europe. At the same time, these activities enact a commitment to liberate the potentials of individuals and prompt behavioral transformations, or at least to produce moments when transformations seem plausible. The interactive dynamic and affective intensity of these settings make them experientially distinct from more mundane social engagements. In societies where people perceive the force of long-standing and commanding past traditions through their imprinting upon social interactions, the gap between the mundane and the experimental carries strong cultural interpretations. Pedagogical spaces for self-improvement—and moreover, pedagogies that are valorized as imparting "Western expertise"—are associated with people's individualization in tandem with the telos of social progress.

Yet how is the perception of individualization fostered through the joint activities of a group where participants closely cohere with one another and follow the whims of an instructor? And how do participants assert their "individual self" in exercises that herald self-overcoming via intersubjective experiences?

Part of the answer resides in the symbolic associations among self-improvement, psychological expertise, individualism, capitalism, and social progress, in which a fine line distinguishes identity informed by group practice from individuality. Although participants occasionally reflect upon and problematize this conflation, during practice, engagement is celebrated as a form of immediate self-realization. In the Republican Era (1912–1949), Chinese intellectuals and political reformers, inspired by political philosophies and scientific texts from Japan and the West, correlated the "underdevelopment" of the Chinese nation with Confucian and feudal practices that bound people to households and lineages and de facto inhibited their individuality (Lee 2006). Although new collective identities in the form of the nation and the working class have dominated political discourse since the 1920s, culminating in Maoism (1949–1976), this perceived antagonism between "traditional" affiliations and individuals' self-realization extends to pedagogies of self-improvement in China today.

A related factor of the experience of "individualization" in the workshop practice is its unfolding in the company of insignificant others rather than with family members, colleagues, or close friends. Social interdependence and self-inhibition in China are strongly associated with hierarchies, demanding social networks, and familial obligations. In the mid–twentieth century, anthropologist Fei Xiaotong (1992, 62, 80) discerned a contrast between the Chinese "differential mode of association" (*chaxugeju*) and the Western "organizational mode of association" (*tuanti geju*), in which the former is characterized by milieus that surround the individual like the circles created by a stone that drops on a water surface. Fei's point was that for Chinese individuals, relationships and social roles are experienced via the family, lineage, village, region, and so on, whereby the wider circles contain the smaller (closer) ones. This is apparently different from individuals in the "West," who partake in voluntary associations such as religious communities. Today, Fei's definition is clearly less relevant in China, where people participate in various group settings, extracurricular workshops included, not to mention online platforms. However, my interlocutors' discernments of local norms often echoed Fei's argument, particularly in relation to the family.

The absence of significant others in self-improvement activities affords the experimental enactment of personae, enlivening the possibilities for self-alteration. The workshops that I attended, while producing new forms of interaction, also reinforced the perception of self-inhibiting norms that characterized the wider society. Instructors rarely invited participants to explicitly reflect upon the importance of their familial or workplace obligations and often buttressed gender roles by presuming that women cannot reduce their responsibilities as mothers or wives (see Hizi 2021a). Notably, the family is evoked here among people who are outside to and unfamiliar with its particular individuals. Most workshop participants never attend workshops in the company of friends and relatives. Although friendships occasionally evolved through repeated participation, these ties, from my observations, were usually kept separate from participants' households or old friends. In Champion

Training, moreover, participants often interacted with peers who all resided and studied in other cities. Zhang Li (2018) identifies a dynamic of "disentanglement and re-embedding" in psychology workshops in southern China, where participants identify and understand themselves outside their everyday responsibilities through workshops and isolated individual activities, before returning mindfully to their engagements (see Pagis 2016 for a related phenomenon in life coaching in Israel). The blind-dancing exercise demonstrates this "disentanglement" while also showing how its pedagogical coordination is directed at producing affects that may not necessarily be in sync with the discursive prescription for ongoing self-transformation. While Jiao provided a pedagogical logic for the exercise—the fostering of communication skills—and this explanation was accepted by most participants, this logic was probably less central to the practice than the thrill of this specific exercise in its own terms.

POROUS INDIVIDUALIZATION

How can we conceptualize this form of self-alteration in relation to the ontology of the person? Is this a "false consciousness" of individualization or, alternatively, an updated version of it via psychological expertise?

I suggest that the activities I have described induce "porosity" while deploying individualism as a symbol. My position is not that group interaction is secondary to the ideology of individualism or that there are no meaningful contradictions in the discourse of individualism at play here. Clearly, China demonstrates to some degree the growing importance of individualism as a modern condition of individuals' disembedding from long-standing social structures and a subsequent crisis of identity (Beck, Giddens, and Lash 1994; see Yan 2010 for this condition in China).

In China in the last decades, this has been most evident in the dissolution of state work units and rural communes. In contrast to views that equate individualism with social alienation, Paul Heelas (2006) suggests that values of individualism can inform social spheres as a shared culture. Heelas studied spiritual therapeutic practices in the United Kingdom, where participants exercised values such as self-growth, authenticity, and egalitarianism via groups. It is the experimental and processual nature of these engagements that for Heelas enables the merging of individuality and sociality. Similarly, Julienne Obadia (2020), in a study of an alternative intentional community in the United States, shows that when individualism is construed through ethical *values* rather than via self-centered *attitudes*, it can guide relationships, even if some tension between the individual and community tends to persist.

Heelas and Obadia show the deployment of individualism through values that sustain its promise in dynamic settings. Furthermore, it is also possible that people experience their enhanced individual expression in moments when they override others' expressions rather than assuming that everyone is "self-realizing" simultaneously (see Hizi 2021b). Thus, it is not so much that individual autonomy and relationality are in synergy but more that they are in frictional dialogue, where each is projected as a moral force for the other: individualized people are cast as building blocks for a moral and advanced social order, and at the same, workshops provide positive feedback on individualized expression. The tension generates a fine line for people between reinforcing the social structure (in encouraging market-driven values or heteronormative priorities) and reconfiguring it (in fostering the potential for more moral, sincere, and meritocratic interpersonal realms).

When pursuing individualism as a goal, participants of this group practice experience their porosity. The "porous self" is famously coined by Charles Taylor (2007) to describe the premodern subject who is ethically and existentially constituted through fusion with other human and nonhuman entities. This is particularly evident in religious practices where meaning is derived through unity with transcendental forces, although it may also occur in other settings where meaning making is produced through interpersonal and collective affiliations. In modernity, in tandem with Max Weber's concept of "disenchantment," Taylor argues that the "porous self" is replaced by a "buffered self," which means that people maintain an ethical boundary between their existence and external influences. They may resist influences or adopt them while perceiving them as emanating from their autonomous will, in both cases conceiving the primacy of their interiority in defining who they are. In Taylor's words, "all thought, feeling and purpose, all the features we normally can ascribe to agents, must be in minds, which are distinct from the 'outer' world" (540). Rational thinking that abstracts specific interpersonal contexts, the atheistic celebration of personal choice, and the psychoanalytical attention to one's emotional formation as a condition for well-being all exemplify this trajectory.

This trajectory captures the historical emergence of dominant new self-understandings and experiences (in the West), yet Taylor underestimates porosity as a lived condition in social practice today. As Karl Smith (2012) contends, porosity is the ontological condition that enables socialization, through which people learn models of personhood, including that of the individualized self. This process may or may not entail the merging with spiritual entities, yet intersubjective settings nonetheless induce participants' permeability.

In China, as Yan Yunxiang argues, the person has been defined as separated from nonhuman entities, being "relational yet not partible" (Yan 2017, 14). Porosity in social interactions is a matter of degree but remains a fundamental condition for becoming a person today. In workshops for self-improvement, the absence of significant others makes the feedback between participants and their social surroundings much more contingent, hence experienced as a novel form of socialization. Individual autonomy is celebrated as a desired value through this openness to seemingly new inputs and the constructed dichotomy between the so-called interdependent person of everyday social life and the individualized person who pursues self-improvement, even if the latter is in the process of undoing and refashioning her sense of self (see Smith 2012, 56). Porosity is also implicitly prescribed in workshops through demands to participate proactively, express emotions, and cheer on others. The nonmundane pedagogical space, the seemingly unique group identity, and the ability to express oneself in new ways are all desired aspects of self-improvement as a practice that instantiates new forms of behavior and highlights potential for individual and social transformation, even if there is seldom a clear pathway toward particular goals.

ROGERS AND SELIGMAN IN CHINA

How do these pedagogical principles relate to frameworks of positive psychology and their Chinese derivatives?

In China in the twenty-first millennium, the pedagogical practice of psychology enacts doctrines that stretch from existential and humanistic psychology to positive psychology, even as other foreign and Indigenous inputs are constantly interwoven into specific practices. These weavings link to a pedagogical practice, including workshops and self-help techniques, that is relatively central within the therapeutic industry in comparison to one-on-one counseling (Zhang 2020). These practices also relate to a practical orientation to solving circumstantial problems rather than dissecting inner pathologies, which can be motivated both by an intent to achieve a better lifestyle and by a reluctance to expose one's malaise.[3] These therapeutic doctrines both define the goals of well-being and prescribe the treatment. For example, when Abraham H. Maslow's (1954) "hierarchy of needs" is discussed in workshops, many of my interlocutors identify the higher stage of emotional fulfillment with the current stage of China's development, following the industrial revolution and poverty of the past (downplaying the poverty that prevails today). Although state campaigns and psychological services stress that contemporary life rhythms and financial pressures produce new emotional burdens and anxieties, this is still widely couched within a positivist narrative of development and people's enhanced self-realization (Hizi 2017).

The doctrines at play highlight the positive potential of the individual self, with attention to its authentic realization through choices and behavior. According to existential psychology and its influential representative Viktor Frankl (2005), people can enhance their quality of life by attending to its true meaning. The goal of therapy is to unravel such a purpose. In the humanistic school championed by Maslow and Carl Rogers, psychology moves away from the psychoanalytical focus on disorders and the identification of repressed feelings to a project of self-enhancement where the "good" and "happiness" are accessible. While Maslow's "hierarchy of needs" suggests a long therapeutic journey, this is combined with an emphasis on individuals' existing mastery over their life paths. For Rogers (2012), the key task is undoing "masks" of pretense in uncovering the "true self" and its desires. This is again an often elusive and never-ending task, but it also implies immediate access and existing potential.

In the new millennium, Martin E. P. Seligman and his followers extended this focus by highlighting "happiness" as a central objective of both individuals and societies and by making therapy even less dependent on counseling clinics. With the foundational insight that material subsistence and wealth do not equate to life satisfaction (Seligman and Csikszentmihalyi 2000) and that life circumstances determine only 10 percent of "happiness," Seligman (2002) advanced models for contentment based on accentuating people's life purpose, enhancing their proactive engagement in their milieus, and materializing their "signature strengths." In practice, this influential field invites more people to consume and utilize psychology through visions of self-development. On the macro level, positive psychology allows room to decouple the priority of well-being from livelihood. These models also universalize a narrow model of individualism, leading to a distorted assessment of well-being through surveys as well as prescribing narrow definitions for the good life (Pérez-Álvarez 2016).

From my observations in China, the universal individualistic emphasis and symbolism of these doctrines contribute to their appeal, particularly in workshops that seek to counteract common norms. At the same time, this does not preclude their adaptation to local demands. For example, Zhang Li (2020, 76) illustrates that Rogers's "client-centered" therapy, whereby counselors follow the clients' lead, has limited appeal in China and that once within the client-counselor dynamic, clients seek more directive advice.

Furthermore, harmony in familial relationships seems indispensable to therapy and well-being in China. Champion Training, despite its demand that the student participants become independent and not blindly follow parental and peer expectations, ran exercises where participants tearfully recalled parents' sacrifices in one's upbringing and expressed their gratitude. This was a long exercise in darkness and with dramatic instrumental music, where participants were guided to remember different episodes from their childhood with an emphasis on parents' hardships. Then they were asked to initiate a dialogue with their imagined parents, addressing recurring obstacles in their relationship while also offering a more appreciative attitude toward them in the future. Weeping was heard throughout the room as the exercise developed, while the instructor gradually elevated his voice with dramatic tones. The message of this exercise entailed self-responsibility by not *demanding* further care from parents, yet its effectiveness as a moral-emotional alteration of the self was enhanced through the virtue of filiality.

On a more macro level, humanistic and positive psychology fit well in the current period of economic reforms while also intersecting with earlier political influences. In the introduction of psychoanalysis to China early in the twentieth century, textbooks tended to downplay the reality of the unconscious and instead highlighted the cultivation of moral "spirit" (*jingshen*) through educational tools (Larson 2008, 34). After the establishment of the People's Republic of China (1949), this focus became even more prominent, as people were identified as malleable creatures who could foster correct ideological thinking through political pedagogies, new embodied practices, and group pressure. This period invited Pavlovian behaviorist techniques, whereby "polluted" spirits were cast as ideological pathology yet often also as recoverable.[4] Furthermore, both Maoist "thought work" practices and today's positive psychology require people's self-reflection over meaning and purpose in one's actions, even if the former arguably offers less room for maneuver.

Today, "happiness" (*xingfu*) is a key term not only in therapeutic or entertainment realms in China but also in political speeches, at times adding an abstract dimension to development goals and at times explicitly coupled with the elevation of people's material conditions. The globalized tools for evaluating happiness as a "science" have also contributed to the status of positive psychology at different levels of Chinese society (cf. White 2017). Positive psychology has also intersected with the politically charged term *positive energy* (*zheng nengliang*), which both exemplifies the local adaptation of the field in China and illuminates some of its local principles in regard to social interaction, temporal orientation, and the nexus of mind-body-environment.

ZHENG NENGLIANG AND LIMINAL CONTINGENCY

In the last ten years, Chinese politicians, educators, entertainment personae, and online users have used the term *zheng nengliang* in ways that combine an individualized feel-good priority with intersubjective experiences and collective identities. This term has a life of its own that illuminates the dynamic intersections between governance and therapeutic expertise while also revealing the affordances of specific settings.

This term is ascribed in China to a book by British psychologist and self-help author Richard Wiseman (2012) titled *Rip It Up: The Radically New Approach to Changing Your Life*. The starting point for Wiseman is not contemporary gurus but rather the pragmatist psychological thinker William James and his behaviorist message that we are sad because we cry rather than the other way around and so forth. Although numerous therapists have applied similar messages, Wiseman still treats this idea as usefully counterintuitive and as wrongly downplayed in people's worldviews and behaviors. Wiseman argues that people need both more positive thinking and more "positive action," including their fostering of daily rituals and envisioning themselves as happier and more successful.

Most Chinese people who use this term are not familiar with Wiseman's text, but this backdrop still resonates with some of the settings and practices related to zheng nengliang. Its first instance was during the 2012 London Olympics, when online users encouraged one another to "ignite zheng nengliang" (*fachu zheng nengliang*) in support of Chinese athletes. Later, state actors also applied this term in various ways to promote social harmony and proactive citizenship—for example, in moments of crisis such as epidemic eruptions (e.g., *People's Daily* 2022). Zheng nengliang is used both as a descriptor for good deeds and as a title for campaigns that invite people's online or physical support.

Although zheng nengliang is rightly acknowledged by China observers as an antidote to potentially "negative" feelings and actions that can disrupt the social order (Hird 2018; Yang 2015, 7), it is also, in Wiseman's spirit, used as the virtual collective orientation toward desired results (Olympic success, curbing the pandemic). In large online networks of communication, this may have various effects among various spectators (some more cynical than others). In bounded pedagogical spaces, however, it can produce more cohesive experiences. In Chinese educational texts, zheng nengliang is ascribed to interactive teaching that invites students' self-expression and meaningful emotional experience (see Cai 2014). In extracurricular settings, zheng nengliang is further addressed in relation to affective intensity, associated with objectives of self-improvement but constituted as an opening with nonspecific goals.

In the workshops I attended, participants associated zheng nengliang with inspiring speeches, "emotionally touching" (*gandong*) messages, and moments of enhanced enthusiasm and volume, such as the happy blind-dancing exercise in Heart's Secret or the tearful gratitude to parents in Champion Training. It is through bodily attention and new forms of self-expression that desired feelings and traits are enacted, yet often without clear trajectories or even a coherent model. This resonates with Wiseman's (2012, 36–37) "as if principle," whereby expressive action makes the virtual reality real (my terms). Another influential author and teacher, Tal Ben-Shahar (2007, 70) stresses the importance of defining goals and finding purpose while at the same time emphasizing that "striving" is more important than "attainment." This can be critically viewed as a charlatanic seduction of individuals to consume expertise that offers false promises of personality change and social mobility. Nonetheless, both novice and experienced participants in the workshops I attended found value in these bounded moments, often without making any correlation with demands or commitments to transform their lives.

In these workshops for self-improvement, what does self-alteration entail? Here self-alteration is a liminal experience that both accommodates and rejects what participants identify as dominant norms and structures. Workshops respond and conform to the dominant forces of global capitalism, identifying the individualized person and the inner psyche as a universally valid teleology, as well as frequently promoting entrepreneurship. Furthermore, the workshop practice is cast as enhancing self-knowledge and mindfulness, thereby approximating participants to their so-called authentic attributes and the true nature of social interaction.

At the same time, workshop performances construe and produce a "gap" between common social practice and widespread interpersonal norms, which has both critical and escapist features. Overall, these are not practices that negate the social structure, but they do nonetheless produce affordances for immediate and minor behavioral change and for rethinking one's relationship to the social order. These workshops demonstrate the repeated production of liminality within the temporality of everyday life, corresponding with arguments by Nigel Rapport and Randall Collins. For Rapport (2010, 92–94), globalization increases the moments and affordances for liminality in social life, as people adopt roles beyond the norms of their local place and its dominant classifications. Rapport sees these experiences as largely agentic and individually initiated, hence demonstrating not the fragmentation of social actors but rather their creative usage of diverse cultural resources.

Unlike Rapport, Collins (2014) directs our attention not to the contemporary human condition per se but to the continuous and universal prevalence of liminality, which he identifies as originating in the energetic effect of everyday rituals. According to Collins's hybridization of Durkheim and Goffman, every moment of enacted shared values through communicational gestures may produce a combination of moral conviction and enthusiasm that people carry onward into other social engagements. For example, "training" is not solely about learning but also about synchronizing one's identity with a group through shared values (91).

In China, self-improvement via positive psychology illustrates this proliferation of liminality even as courses also carefully manage liminality in ways that make it seem nonordinary and in tension with the normal state of affairs. Liminality is experienced as palpable shifts in people's behavior and personality, away from their central social circles while staying close to shore in terms of commitments to these circles. Plural values and globalized expertise fuel these experiences in the seam between the abstract individualized self and the intersubjective and momentary reality.

CONCLUSION

The theme of self-alteration allows anthropologists to describe the dynamics of a range of pedagogical and therapeutic practices. This theme assists in unraveling the new social meanings and experiential crescendos without presuming dramatic outcomes or reducing these practices to passive reflections of existing structures. In this chapter, I showed how self-improvement informed by positive psychology involves the generation of affectively intensive moments through a pedagogical enterprise with distinct experiential properties. The "buffered" autonomous individual is weakened, then co-constituted and reconstructed in a practice that seeks, paradoxically, to socialize individuality through group interactions. It is a practice that both responds to and sequestrates itself from the dominant structures and norms of the wider social world. This contradiction, which arguably characterizes self-improvement under global capitalism, produces moments of opportunity. These liminal moments become the experiential trademark of self-improvement and what I identify as self-alteration, a transient yet valuable experience within and contra the course of everyday life.

Against a more functionalist and teleological perspective—the perspective valued by many practitioners and policymakers as the process by which new individualized persons are produced to be the building blocks of the Chinese society and economy—the practices I describe here have limited success.

Nevertheless, in China and elsewhere, part of the global capitalist human condition involves living with contradictions and attending to moments of speculative, virtual, and fleeting value making (see Feher 2009; Thrift 2005, 147). While the literal objective of achieving self-transformation that characterizes much of the self-improvement industry is often misleading and used as a marketing technique rather than facilitating long-term procedures, this "false" promise also operates affectively within designated settings, inviting individuals (along with the more specific pedagogical techniques) to be open to new forms of relationality with their environment and to appreciate this dynamic as an end in itself. It is precisely within the risks of social alienation or heightened self-interest under postindustrial capitalism that intersubjective experiences become, albeit paradoxically, ever more central to people's perception of their self-realization.

NOTES

1. This idea is captured well in Nikolas Rose's (1992) concept of the "enterprising self." Maurizio Lazzarato (1996) further points out the importance of immaterial cognitive and emotional capacities in this ceaseless process of entrepreneurial self-making in postindustrial economies.
2. I apply pseudonyms throughout this chapter.
3. Today, social interactions and self-reflections in China accommodate emotional problems much more than in the past, when Arthur Kleinman (1982) identified a cultural tendency to discern emotional distress through bodily symptoms. Nevertheless, many patients in mental health centers still prefer to minimize the exposure of their emotional problems.
4. Practitioners of cognitive-behavioral techniques in China today identify links between their methods and these revolutionary techniques (Zhang 2020, 54–55).

REFERENCES

Beck, Ulrich, Anthony Giddens, and Scott Lash. 1994. *Reflexive Modernization: Politics, Tradition and Aesthetics in the Modern Social Order*. Stanford, Calif.: Stanford University Press.
Ben-Shahar, Tal. 2007. *Happier: Learn the Secrets to Daily Joy and Lasting Fulfillment*. Vol. 1. New York: McGraw-Hill.
Cai, Wenjuan. 2014. "Spread Zheng Nengliang (chuandi zheng nengliang)." *New Course: Primary School (xin kecheng: xiaoxue)* 3:156–157.
Collins, Randall. 2014. *Interaction Ritual Chains*. Princeton, N.J.: Princeton University Press.
Feher, Michel. 2009. "Self-Appreciation; or, the Aspirations of Human Capital." *Public Culture* 21 (1): 21–41.
Fei, Xiaotong. 1992. *From the Soil: The Foundation of Chinese Society*. Translated by Gary G. Hamilton and Wang Zheng. Berkeley: University of California Press.
Frankl, Viktor. 2005. *On the Theory and Therapy of Mental Disorders: An Introduction to Logotherapy and Existential Analysis*. New York: Routledge.
Heelas, Paul. 2006. "The Infirmity Debate: On the Viability of New Age Spiritualities of Life." *Journal of Contemporary Religion* 21 (2): 223–240.
Hird, Derek. 2018. "Smile Yourself Happy: Zheng Nengliang and the Discursive Construction of Happy Subjects." In *Chinese Discourses on Happiness*, edited by Gerda Wielander and Derek Hird, 106–128. Hong Kong: Hong Kong University Press.

Hizi, Gil. 2017. "'Developmental' Therapy for a 'Modernised' Society: The Sociopolitical Meanings of Psychology in Urban China." *China: An International Journal* 15 (2): 98–119.

———. 2021a. "Against Three 'Cultural' Characters Speaks Self-Improvement: Social Critique and Desires for 'Modernity' in Pedagogies of Soft Skills in Contemporary China." *Anthropology & Education Quarterly* 52 (3): 237–253.

———. 2021b. "Becoming Role Models: Pedagogies of Soft Skills and Affordances of Person-Making in Contemporary China." *Ethos* 49 (2): 135–151.

Huang, Hsuan-ying. 2013. "Psycho-Boom: The Rise of Psychotherapy in Contemporary Urban China." PhD diss., Harvard University.

Illouz, Eva. 2007. *Cold Intimacies: The Making of Emotional Capitalism.* Cambridge: Polity.

Kleinman, Arthur. 1982. "Neurasthenia and Depression: A Study of Somatization and Culture in China." *Culture, Medicine, and Psychiatry* 6 (2): 117–190.

Larson, Wendy. 2008. *From Ah Q to Lei Feng: Freud and Revolutionary Spirit in 20th Century China.* Stanford, Calif.: Stanford University Press.

Lazzarato, Maurizio. 1996. "Immaterial Labor." In *Radical Thought in Italy: A Potential Politics*, edited by Paolo Virno and Michael Hardt, 133–147. Minneapolis: University of Minnesota Press.

Lee, Haiyan. 2006. *Revolution of the Heart: A Genealogy of Love in China, 1900–1950.* Stanford, Calif.: Stanford University Press.

Liu, Lydia H. 1996. *Translingual Practice: The Discourse of Individualism between China and the West.* Minneapolis: University of Minnesota Press.

Maslow, Abraham H. 1954. *Motivation and Personality.* New York: Harper & Brothers.

Obadia, Julienne. 2020. "Assembly by Aggregation: Making Individuals in the Face of Others in an American Intentional Community." *Anthropological Quarterly* 93 (1): 1387–1420.

Pagis, Michal. 2016. "Fashioning Futures: Life Coaching and the Self-Made Identity Paradox." *Sociological Forum* 31 (4): 1083–1103.

People's Daily. 2022. "Xiaoxiao Fanyi Zhiyuanzhe Chuandi Yiqing Fangkong Zheng Nengliang" [Epidemic Prevention Volunteers Transmit Positive Energy for Epidemic Control]. May 12, 2022. http://sd.people.com.cn/n2/2022/0512/c386903-35265311.html.

Pérez-Álvarez, Marino. 2016. "The Science of Happiness: As Felicitous as It Is Fallacious." *Journal of Theoretical and Philosophical Psychology* 36 (1): 1–19.

Rapport, Nigel. 2010. "Apprehending Anyone: The Non-indexical, Post-cultural, and Cosmopolitan Human Actor." *Journal of the Royal Anthropological Institute* 16 (1): 84–101.

Rogers, Carl. 2012. *On Becoming a Person: A Therapist's View of Psychotherapy.* Boston: Houghton Mifflin Harcourt.

Rose, Nikolas. 1992. "Governing the Enterprising Self." In *The Values of the Enterprise Culture: The Moral Debate*, edited by Paul Heelas and Paul Morris, 141–164. New York: Routledge.

———. 1998. *Inventing Our Selves: Psychology, Power, and Personhood.* Cambridge: Cambridge University Press.

Seligman, Martin E. P. 2002. *Authentic Happiness: Using the New Positive Psychology to Realize Your Potential for Lasting Fulfillment.* New York: Simon & Schuster.

Seligman, Martin E. P., and Mihaly Csikszentmihalyi. 2000. "Positive Psychology: An Introduction." *American Psychologist* 55 (1): 5–14.

Smith, Karl. 2012. "From Dividual and Individual Selves to Porous Subjects." *Australian Journal of Anthropology* 23 (1): 50–64.

Taylor, Charles. 2007. *A Secular Age.* Cambridge, Mass.: Harvard University Press.

Thrift, Nigel. 2005. *Knowing Capitalism.* London: Sage.

White, Sarah C. 2017. "Relational Wellbeing: Re-centring the Politics of Happiness, Policy and the Self." *Policy & Politics* 45 (2): 121–136.

Wilce, James M., and Janina Fenigsen. 2016. "Emotion Pedagogies: What Are They, and Why Do They Matter?" *Ethos* 44 (2): 81–95.

Wiseman, Richard. 2012. *Rip It Up: The Radically New Approach to Changing Your Life*. London: Macmillan.

Yan, Yunxiang. 2010. "The Chinese Path to Individualization." *British Journal of Sociology* 61 (3): 489–512.

———. 2017. "Doing Personhood in Chinese Culture: The Desiring Individual, Moralist Self and Relational Person." *Cambridge Journal of Anthropology* 35 (2): 1–17.

Yang, Jie. 2015. *Unknotting the Heart: Unemployment and Therapeutic Governance in China*. Ithaca, N.Y.: Cornell University Press.

Zhang Li. 2018. "Cultivating the Therapeutic Self in China." *Medical Anthropology* 37 (1): 45–58.

———. 2020. *Anxious China: Inner Revolution and Politics of Psychotherapy*. Berkeley: University of California Press.

8 · HOW IS PSYCHOANALYSIS A MODE OF SELF-ALTERATION?
Anthropological Interrogations

JEAN-PAUL BALDACCHINO

> Sometimes I think the notion of self (like that of culture) should be abandoned, or at least accepted for what it is: a native category. I would prefer if we took the self as a moment in an ongoing dialogue, exchange, or conversation—a moment in which it is rhetorically, politically, constituted and reified. We might then recognize the way in which our theories of the self—our psychologies—support certain of these constituting moments and maneuvers.... It's less the alienation, the splitting, that interests me today than the way we tell it, the folly of trying to resolve it, of believing in unity and continuity, as somehow natural rather than as cultural artifices.
> —Vincent Crapanzano (Molino 2006)

AN ANTHROPOLOGY OF PSYCHOANALYSIS

Anthropology has a long history of engagement with psychoanalysis, going back to Bronislaw Malinowski and Franz Boas themselves (Stocking 1986; Groark 2019). A number of notable anthropologists have also pursued psychoanalytic training (Alfred Kroeber, Abram Kardiner, Melford Spiro, George Devereux, and Geza Roheim, among others) and contributed to the founding of psychoanalytic anthropology as a specialization in its own right. It is equally true, however, that just as many anthropologists have not been particularly receptive to psychoanalysis. Indeed, "many, the majority perhaps, have rejected its utility for anthropology" (Crapanzano 1992, 137). This ambivalence notwithstanding, anthropologists have drawn on insights in psychoanalysis to discuss a variety of phenomena particularly in the study of kinship, dreams, ritual, symbol formation, and religion more broadly.

There is, however, a remarkable dearth of anthropological studies *of* psychoanalysis per se (*pace* Gellner 2003) and almost none that have approached psychoanalysis based on participant observation (but see Lakoff 2003 for an exception). When studying psychoanalysis itself (rather than using its insights or methods as a tool), the approach has tended to focus on psychoanalysis sociologically conceived (Gellner 2003) or else a concern for its interpretative framework (Levi-Strauss 1977; Crapanzano 1992; Obeyesekere 1990). There are, of course, some practical limitations to conducting a conventional "participant observation" of psychoanalysis. Most importantly, psychoanalysis is premised upon an encounter between an analyst and a patient within the intimate and confidential setting of the clinic, making conventional participant observation of the actual practice of psychoanalysis almost impossible unless one assumes the role of analyst or patient.

In this essay, I discuss the ways in which psychoanalysis is a mode of self-alteration and how its techniques may make it so. Sited within the domain of "health," psychoanalysis is a therapeutic modality based on a particular sort of speech as its technique (Foucault 1988, 18). By and large, it is also a voluntary undertaking, with some caveats, as we shall discuss further. While originating in Europe, it has spread to other parts of the world. Here I propose two ways of approaching the subject. First, we need to look at what analysts themselves actually aim to do with their work, alongside what clients simultaneously expect or demand from the analyst. Do clients in a clinic aim for self-alteration, and is this the aim of psychoanalysis per se? Second, we must explore what *actually* takes place during the course of analysis. My focus in this essay is on the phenomenological and experiential dimensions of psychoanalysis, but one must also recognize that the possibilities of self-transformation are always conditioned by the historical and political circumstances within which they emerge as meaningful possibilities. Thus, first, we must try to locate psychoanalysis within broader structural contexts of "care."

THE DIFFUSION OF PSYCHOANALYSIS AND THE CONTEXTS OF CARE

Psychoanalysis has often been singled out as unique among the various therapeutic traditions of the twentieth century. Paul Ricoeur notes that compared to other works in psychiatry, "it is Freud's work that exercises the greatest influence on contemporary culture at the popular as well as scientific level of discussion" (2012, 118). Even outside the domain of mental health, the "Freudian outlook" has become a "pervasive and popular language seized and endlessly recycled by the commodified realm of the mass media" (Illouz 2008, 22). Its language has permeated popular understandings of the self in the West: "There has been nothing like this since the spread of the potato and of maize, and this diffusion was even faster and may have deeper implications" (Gellner 2003, 9).

I very much doubt that psychoanalysis itself does indeed still enjoy the status that has been accorded it by its critics. At the very least, I would question whether outside the "West," it has taken root in the same manner. In Japan, psychoanalysis has been present since the 1910s; however, it has never taken hold as a mode of treatment. Writing in 1984, Emiko Ohnuki-Tierney noted that psychoanalysis was viewed with suspicion and that even the members of the Japanese Psychoanalytical Association had not received any training in psychoanalysis. While there has been an increase in the number of clinical psychologists, psychoanalysis has remained marginal at best. However, it is important to note that Japanese encounters with psychoanalysis have been "historically laden with tensions, struggles, and creative re-makings of psychoanalytical theories" (Kitanaka 2003, 245). One of the oft-cited reasons for the lack of interest in psychoanalysis has been the idea that Japanese conceptions of the self are fundamentally different. The Japanese (and East Asian) self has been described as being allocentric (other-oriented) and situational, which is seen to be fundamentally incompatible with the sort of self-examination and introspection required in Western psychoanalysis (Horiguchi 2014, 521n). By contrast, therapeutic alternatives developed in the early twentieth century such as Morita therapy, with its clear influences from Buddhism, are seen to be more in tune with Japanese understandings of the self.

Even within the West, one can question the position of psychoanalysis today. Psychoanalysis, once considered a "culture-bound syndrome" of French society in its own right, is in a fierce controversy with cognitive behavior therapy (CBT) even though the latter is less pervasive than in other high-income countries in Europe and elsewhere (Botbol and Gourbil 2018, 3). In other countries, like Australia, psychoanalysis has not been integrated within state health-care systems. When practitioners offer psychoanalytic care through Medicare, it is only because they are warranted practitioners in other state-approved professions—psychologists or social workers, for example. Psychoanalysis is otherwise relegated to the private sector. The situation is similar in Japan, where even clinical psychology was not a warranted profession by the state until 2018. Psychotherapists in Japan are underpaid and without any official licensing.

There are some notable exceptions. In Argentina, psychoanalysis had long dominated psychiatry.[1] In his fieldwork in a psychiatric women's ward in a public hospital in Buenos Aries, Andrew Lakoff describes a situation where patients were treated by analyst-physicians who had to navigate their role as medics and as analysts combining psychoanalytically informed care with psychopharmaceutical interventions. In Argentina, psychoanalysts came to be appointed to some of the highest positions in public mental health administration, and Lacanian psychoanalysis became mainstream, with Argentina becoming "one of the world leaders in Lacanian practice" (Ben Plotkin 2001, 226).

The fate of the practice of psychoanalysis in Argentina (and elsewhere) needs to be read against the political climate of the times. Within different systems, psychoanalysis has evolved either as a form of specialist training in medicine and psychiatry or else as part of a separate formation that does not require previous medical training—what Freud (1926) calls "lay analysis." The foregoing discussion highlights the importance of considering psychoanalysis within the particular national contexts within which it is practiced. The context is important for understanding not only the *kind* of psychoanalysis practiced (Jungian, Lacanian, etc.) and the way it adapts and integrates with the local cultural context but also what psychoanalysis "stands for" and how the local actors conceive of the sort of self-transformation that is understood to take place through it.

Malta, where I draw my case studies from for this chapter, has a population of just over half a million. There are various therapeutic modalities available to people—namely, CBT, family therapy, and gestalt therapy. There is as yet, however, no training available for psychoanalysts. In 2007, the Malta Depth Psychology Association was founded to disseminate knowledge about "analytical psychology." Jungian "analytical psychology," however, is not quite psychoanalysis. It is interesting that in Malta there seems to be an affinity to Jungian depth psychology (just as in Japan [Kitanaka 2003]). This may be due to the fact that Jungian analysis is more "welcoming" of Christian spirituality and religion more broadly, and Malta is a country that is Catholic in many significant ways (Baldacchino 2011; Deguara 2020). The Facebook page of the Malta Depth Psychology Association frequently features posts on Christian iconography and symbols as inspirational messages. Jungian analytical psychology is, however, still far from the mainstream or readily accessible to clients in the public system.

In 2018, through the promulgation of the Psychotherapy Profession Act, psychotherapy became subject to a state-warranting system. Psychoanalysis in Malta tends to be subsumed under the broader umbrella term *psychotherapy*. In Malta, there are only a handful of analysts, mostly Jungian (6), and I am the only Lacanian analyst. For the past seven years, I have been practicing within the mental health sector offering outpatient care. I am also, however, an anthropologist and have worked on various topics in the Mediterranean and in East Asia.

My "ethnographic data" in this chapter is drawn from my clinical experience and my own analysis. As such, I presume the usefulness of what Rapport has described as "methodological individualism" (1997, 25). First, a caveat: most of the patients I see do not come seeking psychoanalytic treatment per se. This is partly due to the relative absence of psychoanalysis in Malta. For many clients, the undifferentiated term *doctor* is used to refer in a generic sense to any person with medical authority. Clients are often simply "assigned" a therapist in a system that is strained, with three-to-five-month waiting lists being the norm.

THE CLIENT'S DEMAND AND THE AIMS OF PSYCHOANALYSIS

I started my own analysis, in part, motivated by my own desire to become an analyst after having completed my doctoral fieldwork in South Korea. To become an analyst, one has to undergo a "training analysis," although Lacan often said that there are no differences between a "training analysis" and analysis itself. Perhaps the only difference is that on a practical level, as you lie on the couch, you cannot help but think of the known diagnostic categories and concepts you have learned from studying the canon.

In my own sessions, sometimes I sought confirmation from the analyst: "I suppose this is quite obsessional" or "I wonder if this is what is meant when . . ." Was this a failure on my part to adhere to the "golden rule" of free association? Free association is ostensibly one of psychoanalysis's simplest instructions—speak without restriction.

In some ways, this imperative comes to feel like a restriction in and of itself. I found myself trying to pay attention to any inadvertent attempt on my part to censor my speech or to somehow move my own subjectivity to a more "academic" debate on psychoanalysis per se. I focused on the analyst: Is he listening to me? I was tempted to propose to my analyst, "You must find this so boring," and yet I also felt engaging him in that manner would not be the "proper" way to behave as a "good" analysand. To engage in this manner is to engage along an imaginary line that projects onto the analyst one's own insecurities. Psychoanalysts would call this "resistance"—that which detracts from putting my own subjectivity on the line. But perhaps this very sort of resistance merely confirms the neurotic tendencies of the obsessional—lost as he is in a world of thought.

During the time and space of my sessions, I found that I entered a mode of being characterized by a different order of speech. Psychoanalysis is a "talking cure" but by no means the only kind. On entering the clinic, the analysand is enjoined to speak without censorship. Through the speech of the client, the analyst will trace the contours of the subject's unconscious, trying to get at what cannot be said through what is said. Clients react to the analytical context differently: some are visibly nervous, wringing their hands and anxiously looking at different parts of the room. Many people feel daunted speaking about things that are intimate and private in front of a total stranger. Eventually, however, many start to find it liberating for this very reason.

The space and the structure of interaction in the consulting rooms are designed to engender an interactional space that is different from that of customary social engagement. Many psychoanalysts in private practice devote considerable care to the setup of their rooms, choosing soothing yet somber surroundings often adorned by works of art meant to evoke associations with the master and his work. (There is an anthropological study to be made here.) Most orthodox analysts have some sort of couch in their rooms situated in such a way that the analyst sits out of the line of sight of the analysand. While placing the analysand in a comfortable state—some would insist it is a malleable state (Schachter and Kächele 2010, 448)—the analysand is forced to engage with a disembodied voice. This act of speaking in someone's presence without looking at them already serves to destabilize ordinary language conventions. Being looked at but not being able to see the face of the other is at first an unsettling experience. Nowadays in this world of teaching through Zoom, we have all had similar experiences of talking without knowing the measure of our words as we face blacked-out screens.

Many clients speak positively about the freedom of speaking in a space where they do not feel they are being judged by conventional moral standards. I remember a young female client who felt relieved telling me how she enjoys "hurting" her partner by snubbing him, not providing him with emotional reassurance and not displaying any emotional attachment to him or telling him she loves him. She both cultivates this attitude and relishes it: a fact she attributes to a sort of repayment for the ways in which as a younger woman she herself felt totally at the mercy of a previous partner, the father of her child—a drug dealer who had multiple lovers and treated her like a disposable object. I have often had clients tell me that after their previous session, they felt much better, feeling "lighter." Many indeed feel that the therapeutic effect is the result of speaking and unburdening oneself: "*Taqla li jkollok minn fuq l-istonku*" (Expel what's in your stomach), as one client put it.

Foucault famously criticized psychoanalysis for carrying into the present forms of "inquisitorial confession" (Sangren 2004, 113). Deriving the term from the context of pastoral power/care, Foucault defines the confession as

> a ritual of discourse in which the speaking subject is also the subject of the statement; it is also a ritual that unfolds within a power relationship, for one does not confess without the presence (or virtual presence) of a partner who is not simply the interlocutor but the authority that requires the confession, prescribes and appreciates it, and intervenes in order to judge, punish, forgive, console, and reconcile; a ritual in which the truth is corroborated by the obstacles and resistances it has to surmount in order to be formulated; and finally, a ritual in which the expression alone, independently of its external consequences, produces intrinsic modifications in the person who articulates it: it exonerates, redeems, and purifies him, it unburdens him of his wrongs, liberates him, and promises him salvation. (Foucault 1998, 61–62)

In the sense identified by Foucault, it is true that there are interesting analogues to confession. Clients feel unburdened, and for some, the therapeutic effect is limited precisely to this sense of cathartic release. It also resembles the confessional insofar as clients come seeking some sort of moral reassurance from the therapist. There is, however, a fundamental difference with what takes place in confession, as the analyst does not "judge, punish, or console," and neither does analysis purify or "save" the individual. When asked whether psychoanalysis resembles confession, Lacan answered very directly: "Absolutely not! They are not at all alike. In analysis, we begin by explaining to people that they are not there in order to confess. It is the first step in the art. They are there to talk—to talk about anything" (2013, 63). For many clients, the simple opportunity to speak is enough to make them "feel better." This is not because psychoanalysis creates a "confessional redemption" but because an aspect of what these clients are looking for is a recognition of their own suffering and of the moral complexities of their life and relationships. The very act of listening to the client's speech provides the structural context for its—and therefore of the subject's—recognition. Yet this is not enough to achieve self-alteration. At most, this provides a sense of reassurance and relief, which can lead to a measure of dependence on the analysis without resulting in transformation per se.

If you were to ask any therapist what the aim of therapy is, from behavioralists to hypnotherapists, you would find that most would describe it as some kind of "self-transformation." In psychoanalysis, this is generally expressed as a version of "enlightenment." The British psychoanalyst Roger Money-Kyrle, also an anthropologist, defines the aim of psychoanalysis as follows: "To help the patient understand, and so overcome, emotional impediments to his discovering what he innately already knows" (1971, 103). This knowledge is in turn meant to transform the subject in fundamental ways. The situation is rendered more complex, however, since the client might not necessarily seek that which the analyst aims to provide. The question of what a client wants is not simple to answer.

In Malta, Foucault's reference to pastoral modes of power/domination is particularly prescient. Many clients come to therapy after having sought the advice of their parish priest. Sandra is a married woman in her fifties who came to therapy complaining of feeling trapped in an abusive marriage. Prior to coming to me, Sandra had sought help from different quarters, including the state support service for victims of abuse, the local parish priest, and the church-run marriage counseling organization. In the course of treatment, she frequently put me in the position of someone who could confirm that she is indeed a "good person." "I don't think I am doing something wrong, am I?" was something she would repeat often as she contemplated her separation from her husband. Sandra had already seen at least three different figures who were far more qualified than me to speak about her moral standing—a priest, a social worker, and a marriage counselor—and yet in spite of the reassurance they gave her, she was still looking for "moral" surety. Her demand was indeed for some sort of confirmation and recognition as a "good person." This demand, of course, runs counter to the aims of psychoanalysis—analysts are not in the business of trafficking in moral goods.[2] In my work with Sandra, I made it clear that analysts cannot provide an answer to her moral question. What almost all patients have in common, however, is that they come to the analyst with demands that place the analyst in a position of a "subject-supposed-to-know." The demand comes in the form of the client's suffering and is often articulated through a set of symptoms, although it is not always recognized as such.

Claire is a forty-eight-year-old health-care professional whom I have been seeing weekly for a year. Her main symptomatic presentations were chronic and acute urinary retention and constipation leading to a dramatic swelling of her abdomen. When she started therapy, her main cause of suffering was her daughter. She is at a loss with how to deal with her daughter, who is in her midtwenties, still living at home, friendless, and unemployed. The mother feels she can't cope anymore: "*Mulej aħfirli, ma niflaħiex iktar, għajjejt*" (God forgive me, I can't take it anymore, I'm tired), she repeatedly told me during our sessions. After long and demanding shifts, the daughter expects her mother to go out with her or to listen to her while the mother is tired and needs to attend to house chores, and yet she feels she has to keep her daughter company, since no one else will. As analysis would reveal, there was an intimate relation between her somatic symptoms and her own psychological state.

To be sure, one does encounter clients who come to therapy simply to satisfy the demand of an other—a partner threatening to leave the client if they do not go to therapy, for example, or children being taken to therapy by concerned parents. It is hardly surprising that in the former case, clients do not normally last long in therapy. This is because one of the fundamental requirements for psychoanalytic treatment is that a rapport is formed between the analyst and the client.

In the first session, I always ask patients what they hope to achieve from the work we will be doing together. The answers are varied and range from "I want to be happy" or "I want to not feel this way anymore" to "I want to control my feelings better." As Lacan writes, "In the first place, is it the end of analysis that is demanded of us? What is demanded can be expressed in a simple word, *bonheur* or 'happiness' as they say in English" (1997, 292). It is a curious feature that in spite of the stated intent to change something about themselves, many clients seem to focus much of their time on the other. A specific other or set of others is often seen to be the cause of the clients' suffering, although in cases of psychoses, this "other" can often be more generalized and diffuse.

The "other" is seen to have wronged them in some way, and clients spend many sessions rehearsing the multiple ways in which the other has become intolerable. Most often this "other" is a lover, a spouse, or a parent; however, this is not always the case. Paul is twenty-four years old. After many years apart, Paul started living with his father as a teenager. However, his father would steal from him, shout at him, and be generally "unloving" while doting on certain strangers and neighbors. Most of the time in his sessions, Paul was trying to understand why his father, a sixty-year-old abusive alcoholic, would treat him like that. He kept asking me, "Why would he behave this way?" "Why does he treat me like this?" "This is not normal though, is it?" These were questions that Paul kept returning to—he just could not make sense of his father's actions. At one level, for clients like these, the problem is very clear—it is the *other* who causes them suffering. Therapy, if unchecked, can easily become a space for clients to express their hostility and disappointment toward the other. What many patients *really* seem to want, therefore, is for the other to change or else to find some way to understand the other and not necessarily to alter oneself.

In some cases, psychoanalysis is simply used to confirm what the subject already knows. I only saw Philip very briefly for a few months. He worked as a handyman and was very proud of the fact that he was not too macho to come seek help. He suffered from anxiety, used to get very concerned about his health, and had paranoid tendencies particularly exacerbated after three enforced quarantines. However, what most aggrieved him was that his wife could not understand what he was going through. She had told him that she was "feeling like a single mum," and this phrase really wounded my client. His wife, he said, does not understand mental issues and does not see the scope of therapy. He was concerned that she might be starting to develop romantic interests with someone at work, since she recently bought three bottles of perfume and was putting more effort into the way she dressed for work. By the fifth session, he told me he was feeling much better. He came in with sunglasses, walked with a swagger, and sat with legs open wide.

He said that even his wife told him, "You are back on track." His sex life had improved greatly, and he had trouble finding time and space for it. He told me that he had spoken to his wife about the issue with the perfume, and she told him, "I did it to draw your attention." She then told him that she was sorry for being insensitive and started crying and apologizing, to which he told her, "What's important is that we go back on track; we have three kids, and we know we need to raise them." It seems that what he needed was for his wife to apologize to him and to admit that she was at fault. He needed things to be "back on track," whatever that signifier meant for him, and his wife's apology was pivotal for that. He then offered his own assessment of his wife's problem: "She is too focused on the children, on being a mum; this hampers the flame between the couple.... As soon as a problem comes, then it's too much." According to my client, his wife agreed with his assessment and agreed to his suggestion to leave the children with their grandparents so they could go on a date night.

I couldn't say that Philip was ever really in analysis, since he had his own firm convictions about what the scope of therapy would entail.

This is, therefore, the first paradoxical aspect of self-alteration in psychoanalytic treatment. Patients come in with the stated goal of changing something about who they are and how they behave, but oftentimes, sessions evolve into a litany of complaints against the other who has wounded them. It is, then, the analyst's task to reorient the speech of the client. Lacan (2006, 500) reserved the term *subjective rectification* to this process whereby the analyst directs the client to the recognition of their own position in their symptomatic constellation. To go back to the previous example, in the case of Sandra, I suggested to her that she had already seen a string of people who could tell her she was a good person, and yet this had not been enough—might it be that behind her conscious wish for affirmation, there was another perhaps contradictory one? Perhaps she was waiting for someone to tell her that she was indeed a bad person. Then the question could become, *How was she a bad person?*

EVENT AND TRANSFORMATION IN PSYCHOANALYSIS

In the preceding section, I have discussed people's motivations, stated or otherwise, for seeking therapy and the position that the analyst assumes in directing the treatment toward the question of desire. After contrasting what the client wants with what the analyst provides, let me now turn to the question of the actual self-alterations that take place in analysis.

The question remains to what extent is an alteration achieved through analysis, notwithstanding or indeed despite the demands of the client? What sort of change results from the psychoanalytic encounter? Is this change something that radically transforms the self? Is it experienced as something that is sudden and closer to the experience of total and illuminating conversion rather than gradual and incremental like learning the *ney* under the guidance of a master (see Şenay this volume)?

Philosophy has been a useful source of inspiration for anthropologists who seek to engage with the "self." In deconstructionist versions of philosophy, the term *event* is often used for experiences of radical transformation. Caroline Humphrey draws on Badiou's notion of the event—that "extraordinary happening that brings about a rupture of previous knowledge(s)" (Humphrey 2008, 360). The event is not objectively framed. In the place of already constituted knowledge, the event interposes a "new truth" whose "singular innovations . . . persist by means of conscious acts of witness by individuals who constitute themselves as immortal subjects by their fidelity to its truth" (360). The religious overtones of this notion of the "event" are hard to miss. Indeed, the example that Badiou brings is that of St. Paul, an example that one might think would be of relevance for Catholic Malta. Similarly, John D. Caputo, a student of Derrida, proposes a postmodern "theology of the event" (2006). Caputo notes that the event is situated not in chronological time but rather in *kairological* time. It cannot be considered according to day-to-day chronometrics, but rather it has to do with "a transforming moment that releases us from the grip of the present and opens up the future in a way that makes possible a new birth, a new beginning, a new invention of ourselves, even as it awakens dangerous memories" (6). Seen in this light, there certainly could be evental qualities to the transformations brought about in analysis.

However, looking back at my own experience, I do not feel that there has been any singular transformative moment of revelation for myself. I have been in analysis for roughly seven years, and I find that self-alteration in psychoanalysis has worked in a much more uneven manner. "Revelation" or even new knowledge in this sense is neither absolute nor final even though it is always illuminating in the same way that it is singular and nonuniversalizable. The *moment* in this sense does not subsist in its chronological properties. Perhaps much like the transference that develops in analysis, it is more accurate to think of self-alteration as "a series of temporally concise moments within a broader dialectical and intersubjective movement" (Cauwe and Vanheule 2018, 703).

TRANSFORMATION 1: INTERPRETATIVE FRAMEWORKS

Nevertheless, as a result of analysis, the world somehow feels different to me. Analysis provides a different or new interpretative framework within which one can locate the self and the Other primarily premised on the notion of desire and lack. Psychoanalysis displaces visions of the cohesive self (the ego) in favor of a metapsychology premised on the notion of a desiring subject, a desire that is born out of a foundational lack that keeps the subject engaged with the world around it. This desire is embodied and implicates the drives, but it is also existential, acting as a knotting point for the subject's existence. Through the clinical encounter but also perhaps more fundamentally through the process of becoming an analyst, this "framework" becomes part and parcel of new ways in which the self and the other are *experienced*. This, however, is not necessarily lived as an act of conscious reflection so much as it is *transformative, habituated*, and *enduring*.

Rather than unitary persons endowed with self-identity, will, and autonomy, I see humans as divided subjects struggling to maintain coherency and consistency. This struggle is slow and patchily enacted: it is in moments where this altered vision rubs up against a different worldview that its effects come to be seen. I have a friend who has been struggling in his relationship with his estranged father, whom he sees as being aggressive and "hateful." However, what I saw was a friend's aggression in the face of a humiliated father. For my friend, his father had to be monstrous, humiliating, and disgusting. Whereas I could not bring myself to support my friend in his demonization of the father. At the same time, I did not want to address my friend as an analyst. I was not able to simply "switch off" the way of seeing the world enacted through the self-transformation of being an analyst. As a result, I tried to disengage from the topic even though this was constantly at the forefront of my friend's concerns. This has regrettably led to the loss of a close friendship. Friendship establishes enduring bonds based on empathy and loyalty, while in the end, the analyst's willed fate is to be discarded. Perhaps, however, this is more commonly experienced by those who are undergoing analytical training and not necessarily for clients in analysis per se.

TRANSFORMATION 2: REFLEXIVITY

A second kind of alteration caused by psychoanalysis is more likely to be shared by nonanalysts and analysts alike. Analysis leads to a sort of *reflexivity*. One's own actions, even outside the clinic, become the subject of an inner interrogation. Analysis becomes an opportunity to work through whatever has happened or is happening, and in doing so, it becomes part of one's everyday life. Daily encounters and experiences are formed and informed by the backdrop of the analysis and the so-called transference relation established with the analyst. Clients often come to the session clearly wanting to work through something that has happened during the time between sessions.

Michael is a young man in his twenties whom I have been seeing for about six months. One session, he came in and expressed his exasperation: "It is so frustrating that during the week, I kept thinking, 'Oh, I must tell this to you,' but then once I come here, I can't remember anything." Analysts use the term *transference* to describe the effects of the situational context of analysis. In turn, such moments of "forgetting," as those experienced by Michael, become fertile ground for speaking about the actual relationship to the analysis itself. After several years of analysis and seeing clients in the clinic, this reflexivity is not confined to the time of the clinic. Analysis often leads subjects to assume a disposition to reflexive interrogation where one's own experiences, wishes, and desires are no longer taken at face value.

In sum, analysis gradually provides a new way of seeing and interpreting the world. It also provides a different relation to one's own behavior and feelings through a reflexive self-examination that is at first made possible through the "dummy" person of the analyst even as the latter is fated to be discarded. That being said, there might be more "forms" of self-alteration enacted through analysis, or rather more aspects to the modes of alteration that reorient different aspects of an individual's life, including their sexual relations, their familial relations, and perhaps their own "spiritual" lives. The ways in which this self-alteration is lived and the impact it has on different dimensions of our being-in-the-world can be as varied as they are far-reaching. As an analyst, it is often quite surprising, and indeed satisfying, to see when this oftentimes unpredictable self-transformation does indeed lead to a reorientation in a client's subjectivity.

THE QUESTION OF TRUTH AND THE ETHICS OF ANALYSIS AND ANTHROPOLOGY

Michael was in weekly analysis for almost a year. He started analysis when a colleague in his workplace committed suicide. In our first session, I asked Michael why he came to therapy. He never knew this colleague, but he figured that this was a good opportunity to make use of a service that was being provided for free and that his father had always taught him never to pass on an opportunity. In one of our later sessions, he asked me about the goal of analysis. At this point, he told me that actually he originally wanted to come to therapy to know if he was suffering from depression, but he didn't want to tell me this so as not to "put it in my head."[3] That question had by now faded into insignificance; what he really wanted to know was "What do I want from my work?" and "What do I want from my relationships?" For a long time he was afraid of these questions because they provoked anxiety in him, which he used to obliterate by smoking marijuana. In that session, I advised Michael that perhaps he had already done some important steps in terms of self-transformation in analytical terms.

Michael started analysis ostensibly in the absence of any "suffering," wanting to "test" the therapist to see if he would offer him a diagnosis. In reposing the question to the analyst as a matter of his own desire, there was a shift in the way in which he perceived his own subjectivity. The demand to the analyst became articulated as a question of his own desire addressed to the Other. Lacan's famous aphorism "Desire is the Desire of the Other" has been the subject of endless discussion. This is not the place to enter into that discussion, but it suffices to note at this point that psychoanalysis aims not at the "good" but rather at "truth."

Michael Lambek proposes an approach to ethics that emerges out of "the attempts in everyday practice and thought to inhabit and persevere in light of uncertainty, suffering, injustice, incompleteness, inconsistency, the unsayable, the unforgivable, the irresolvable, and the limits of voice and reason" (2010, 4). The clinical encounter in psychoanalysis opens up an important space for the study of "ordinary ethics," when we face a "suffering" that emerges from the unsayable and the incoherence that results from it. One of the critiques of Freudian analysis is that it is "moralistic" in that it proposes a "will to knowledge" based on an ethics of veracity, itself a legacy of enlightenment ethics of the fin de siècle Vienna, from where it was born (see discussion in Ricoeur 2012, 78).

I suspect that Lacanian psychoanalysts would not object to this characterization, with perhaps some qualifications. Truth, as understood in psychoanalysis, does not correspond to ontological categories of the order of reality (Lacan 2001). Truth, psychoanalytic truth, is always emergent in language in the analytical encounter. The idea that there is an intimate connection between ethics and language is not unique to psychoanalysis. In outlining the features of an ordinary ethics, Lambek draws attention to the centrality of language in ethical constructs: "We may find the well-spring of ethical insight deeply embedded in the categories and functions of language and ways of speaking" (2010, 2). Psychoanalysis—in terms of its clinical practice—is a form of speech that aims at truth just as it produces it through its dialogic encounter in the transference. As one philosopher aptly puts it, truth in psychoanalysis enjoys "a peculiar status, being what one might call an emergent property of a relational process" (Brigati 2015, 1). This truth, the truth of psychoanalysis, comes with a certain disestablishment of the "I think" of the Cartesian ego—what Lacan termed as the de-being (*desêtre*) of the subject. This event is singular, heralding the reconfiguration of the subject in its dialectical encounter with the Other in analysis.[4]

Humphrey notes that anthropological studies of the self have been characterized by a "long-running onslaught on the sovereign individual" (2008, 359). Psychoanalysis takes as its starting point not the sovereign individual but the disunity of the subject. Within Lacanian analysis, the disunity of the subject, the split nature of the self is the bedrock of its foundation, for as Crapanzano notes, "Lacan does not give us any illusions about the unity of the self" (Molino 2006).[5] A notion of the "dividual self" (Strathern 1988) therefore lies at the core of psychoanalysis and indeed could be seen at the nodal point of the self-alteration brought about through its dialogic encounter. It is perhaps this subjective realization of the disunity of the self that constitutes the most meaningful dimension of self-alteration in psychoanalysis immanent in its dialogic form.

ANTHROPOLOGY AS SELF-TRANSFORMATION

In *Hermes' Dilemma*, Crapanzano faces a similar challenge to the one confronting me here—namely, "How does an anthropologist talk about psychoanalysis?" (1992, 141). Is it possible, he asks, "to talk about psychoanalysis without talking psychoanalysis?" He argues that insofar as we use the same language as psychoanalysis uses in its own practice, we are trapped in a "hermeneutic circle": "We can achieve distance but not a fully external perspective" (141). As Crapanzano notes, it is questionable whether we can ever truly achieve a full external perspective on anything.

By way of conclusion, I would like to bring the question back to anthropology itself. While anthropology does not really *aim* at self-alteration (of the student), this is oftentimes an unintended effect of fieldwork and anthropological research. Students often describe learning anthropology as transformative. What was previously taken for granted—emotions, sexuality, nationality, values, all or any of which may have been core elements of one's identity—becomes the subject of critical reflection. Their naturalness and "givenness" can no longer be assumed. In certain crucial ways, students are no longer who they were before "becoming anthropologists." The effect is perhaps best described as a kind of "self-alienation." I would argue that both anthropology and psychoanalysis therefore produce a subjective destitution and engender their own kinds of reflexivity through an encounter with the Other.

Nevertheless, a more fundamental difference lies in the aim of analysis itself. The analyst faces a demand for happiness that is potentially replaced with a recognition of truth. This is at the core of the ethics of psychoanalysis. It has to be said that the ethics of anthropology are sometimes far less clear. Questioning the ethics of anthropology could start by addressing the demands and desires of the anthropologist—desires and demands that he or she addresses to the Other. These could oftentimes bear greater interrogation.

NOTES

1. As Andrew Lakoff notes, "The most striking feature of the Buenos Aires *mundu-psi* in the late 1990s was the prominence within it of Lacanian psychoanalysis, especially in the city's public hospitals and counselling centers" (2003, 85).
2. "The direction of conscience, in the sense of the moral guidance a faithful Catholic might find in it, is radically excluded here. If psychoanalysis raises problems for moral theology, they are not those of the direction of conscience—which let me remind you also raises problems" (Lacan 2006, 490).
3. Depression, incidentally, is not part of the psychoanalytical nosological canon, and indeed, many Lacanians would be particularly resistant to the diagnostic label, which they would consider to be more of "a construction of pharmaceutical companies than a precise and particularly useful concept in psychotherapy" (Hook 2017, 2).
4. "The analyst must therefore know that, far from being the measure of reality, he only clears a path for the subject to his truth by offering himself up as a support for this de-being, thanks to which this subject subsists in an alienated reality, without being for all that incapable of

conceiving of himself as divided, something for which properly speaking the analyst is the cause" (Lacan 2001, 359).

5. Lacan famously considered the subject to be fundamentally "alienated" in a number of ways—through his specular relation to the ego as well as a function of having an unconscious and subject to language.

REFERENCES

Baldacchino, Jean-Paul. 2011. "Miracles in the Waiting Room of Modernity: The Canonisation of Dun Gorg of Malta." *Australian Journal of Anthropology* 22 (1): 104–124.
Ben Plotkin, Mariano. 2001. *Freud in the Pampas: The Emergence and Development of a Psychoanalytic Culture in Argentina*. Stanford, Calif.: Stanford University Press.
Botbol, Michel, and Adeline Gourbil. 2018. "The Place of Psychoanalysis in French Psychiatry." *BJPsych International* 15 (1): 3–5.
Brigati, Roberto. 2015. "Staging the Truth: Psychoanalysis and Pragmatism." *European Journal of Pragmatism and American Philosophy* 7 (1). https://journals.openedition.org/ejpap/381.
Caputo, John D. 2006. *The Weakness of God: A Theology of the Event*. Bloomington: Indiana University Press.
Cauwe, Joachim, and Stijn Vanheule. 2018. "On Beginning the Treatment: Lacanian Perspectives." *Psychoanalytic Quarterly* 87 (4): 695–727.
Crapanzano, Vincent. 1992. *Hermes' Dilemma and Hamlet's Desire: On the Epistemology of Interpretation*. Cambridge, Mass.: Harvard University Press.
Deguara, Angele. 2020. "Secularisation and Intimate Relationships in a Catholic Community: Is Malta a Resistant Niche?" *Social Compass* 67 (3): 372–388.
Foucault, Michel. 1988. *Technologies of the Self: A Seminar with Michel Foucault*. Edited by Patrick H. Hutton, Luther H. Martin, and Huck Gutman. Amherst: University of Massachusetts Press.
———. 1998. *The History of Sexuality*. London: Penguin.
Freud, Sigmund. 1926. "The Question of Lay Analysis." In *The Standard Edition of the Complete Psychological Works of Sigmund Freud*, 177–258. Vol. 20. London: Vintage Books.
Gellner, Ernest. 2003. *The Psychoanalytic Movement: The Cunning of Unreason*. Oxford: Blackwell.
Groark, Kevin. 2019. "Freud among the Boasians: Psychoanalytic Influence and Ambivalence in Anthropology." *Current Anthropology* 60 (4): 559–588.
Hook, Derek. 2017. "The Failings of Depression: A Review of Lacanian Psychoanalytic Critiques." *Acta Psychopathologica* 3:55. https://doi.org/10.4172/2469-6676.100127.
Horiguchi, Sachiko. 2014. "Mental Health and Therapy in Japan: Conceptions, Practices and Challenges." In *Critical Issues in Contemporary Japan*, edited by Jeff Kingston, 500–528. Oxford: Routledge.
Humphrey, Caroline. 2008. "Reassembling Individual Subjects: Events and Decisions in Troubled Times." *Anthropological Theory* 8 (4): 357–380. https://doi.org/10.1177/1463499608096644.
Illouz, Eva. 2008. *Saving the Modern Soul: Therapy, Emotions, and the Culture of Self-Help*. Berkeley: University of California Press.
Kitanaka, Junko. 2003. "Jungians and the Rise of Psychotherapy in Japan: A Brief Historical Note." *Transcult Psychiatry* 40 (2): 239–247.
Lacan, Jacques. 1997. *The Seminar of Jacques Lacan VII: The Ethics of Psychoanalysis 1959–1960*. Translated by Dennis Porter. New York: W. W. Norton.
———. 2001. "De la psychanalyse dans se rapports avec la réalité." Translated by S. Savaiano. In *Autres écrits*, 351–361. Lonrai, France: Seuil.
———. 2006. "The Direction of the Treatment and the Principles of Its Power." In *Écrits*, translated by Bruce Fink, 489–542. New York: W. W. Norton.

———. 2013. *The Triumph of Religion Preceded by Discourse to Catholics*. Translated by Bruce Fink. Cambridge: Polity.
Lakoff, Andrew. 2003. "The Lacan Ward: Pharmacology and Subjectivity in Buenos Aires." *Social Analysis* 47 (2): 82–101.
Lambek, Michael. 2010. *Ordinary Ethics: Anthropology, Language, and Action*. New York: Fordham University Press.
Levi-Strauss, Claude. 1977. "The Effectiveness of Symbols." In *Structural Anthropology*, 181–201. Harmondsworth: Penguin.
Molino, Anthony. 2006. "Moments of the Self in Psychoanalysis and Anthropology a Conversation with Vincent Crapanzano." *European Journal of Psychoanalysis* 23 (2). https://www.journal-psychoanalysis.eu/articles/moments-of-the-self-in-psychoanalysis-and-anthropology-a-conversation-with-vincent-crapanzano-1/.
Money-Kyrle, Roger. 1971. "The Aim of Psychoanalysis." *International Journal of Psychoanalysis* 53:103–106.
Obeyesekere, Gananath. 1990. *The Work of Culture: Symbolic Transformation in Psychoanalysis and Anthropology*. Chicago: University of Chicago Press.
Ohnuki-Tierney, Emiko. 1984. *Illness and Culture in Contemporary Japan: An Anthropological View*. Cambridge: Cambridge University Press.
Rapport, Nigel. 1997. *Transcendent Individual: Towards a Literary and Liberal Anthropology*. London: Routledge.
Ricoeur, Paul. 2012. *On Psychoanalysis*. Cambridge: Polity.
Sangren, P. Steven. 2004. "Psychoanalysis and Its Resistances in Michel Foucault's 'The History of Sexuality': Lessons for Anthropology." *Ethos* 32 (1): 110–122.
Schachter, Joseph, and Horst Kächele. 2010. "The Couch in Psychoanalysis." *Contemporary Psychoanalysis* 46 (3): 439–459.
Stocking, George W., Jr. 1986. "Anthropology and the Science of the Irrational: Malinowski's Encounter with Freudian Analysis." In *Malinowski, Rivers, Benedict, and Others: Essays on Culture and Personality*, edited by George W. Stocking Jr., 13–49. Madison: University of Wisconsin Press.
Strathern, Marilyn. 1988. *The Gender of the Gift: Problems with Women and Problems with Society in Melanesia*. Berkeley: University of California Press.

PART IV SELF-ALTERATION, THE HUMAN, AND THE MORE-THAN-HUMAN

PART IV

9 · MUTUALISTIC SELF-ALTERATION
Human-Pigeon Assemblages in Rural Pakistan

MUHAMMAD A. KAVESH

In late November 2014, a pigeon flying friend informed me about a *khokha* (coop) competition held in a nearby village. As we arrived there on a motorbike, the competition was already in progress. Five coops, each filled with about seventy colorful pigeons, were placed almost four hundred meters away from one another in a cotton field, their keepers completely absorbed in flying their cherished birds with gusto. Each man used multipitched whistles to send his birds the farthest away and mingle with opponents' flocks and then artfully made them return to their coop with soft sounds of *aao, aao* (come, come). The competition was staged on the endeavor to lure as many opponents' pigeons to one's coop as possible and then return them at the end of the competition to their owner for an amount of three hundred rupees (about three U.S. dollars at that time) for each pigeon. The person who captured the most pigeons at the end of this two-hour-long competition accumulated not only economic but also social capital—pride, honor, dignity—all essential ingredients of masculinity in rural Pakistan.

The season for khokha competitions starts in late November or early December and lasts until the end of winter, around mid-February. Because this was an early season competition, the flyers knew that their more-than-human companions were not in their best condition and errors were possible. Yet there was a sense of mutual trust between humans and pigeons that structured the aura of this competition. The flyers trusted that their birds would recognize them through the color of their clothes and the sound of their whistles and believed that the sight of a tin can that contained pigeons' feed and the unique shape and color of their coop would help them find their home. And the pigeons, it appeared, knew that they would receive a nourishing environment with their keeper, a feed prepared with care, protection from predatory animals (cats, mongooses, hawks), and an opportunity to reconnect with their mating pair. While this interspecies mutualism was formed on an intersubjective, relational association between pigeons and humans, it also led each of them to alter themselves and attain a sense of co-sociality in a world otherwise influenced by (post)colonial divisions between nature and culture, wild and domesticated, controlling and sharing.

In this chapter, I argue that the mutualistic human-pigeon relationship enables many rural Pakistani men to spend hours on their rooftops, away from other societal bonds, and to cultivate an enthusiasm for "living" with pigeons. This relationship is mutualistic because both pigeons and humans actively contribute to its continuity and nurturance and co-live with each other, offering a critique of the neoliberal understanding of relationships. As I explore this noncolonial form of coexistence—something that existed within Indian society before colonialism and that was marginalized during the colonial era and postcolonial era—I ask why it is reciprocally beneficial to interspecies relatedness. To put it differently, I contend that precolonial modes of relating with more-than-human others guide toward interspecies coexistence and, in the process, help reconstitute the project of mutualistic self-alteration—humans altering themselves in the company of pigeons and pigeons altering themselves in the company of humans.

A burgeoning scholarship in multispecies studies shows how mutualistic interdependence between species leads to an alteration of the self and transformation of the material world. Colin Jerolmack's (2013, 132) fascinating ethnography of Turkish pigeon flyers in Berlin demonstrates how the bird enables these immigrant men to undergo an inner (self-)alteration to form a nostalgic association with Turkish culture and heritage while residing in Germany. Similarly, Radhika Govindrajan's (2018, 64–66) discussion of Jersey cows in Uttarakhand, India, explores how people compare the divine power (*shakti*) of local Pahari cows with imported cattle, which are believed to lack any spiritual merit, and how this alters people's perception of the self as well as more-than-human relatedness, spirituality, and religious activism. Garry Marvin's (2007, 347–348) discussion on the ritualized practice of hunting foxes in England explicates how the 2005 British Parliament ban altered not only people's mode of co-living with foxes but also their notions of rural life, belonging, and connecting with the countryside. In a similar vein, Rebecca Cassidy's (2002, 31–48) analysis of horse racing in England critically describes how racing is commonly perceived to be "in the blood"—both for horses and for specific elite racing families—thus allowing the human racing class to alter their perceptions, social capital, and worldviews through their conceptualization of pedigree. In all these instances, animals (pigeons, cows, foxes, horses) emerge as active subjects, actors, and agents, directly or indirectly altering human's understanding of the self and the surrounding world.

Sport has often been categorized by anthropologists, among others, as an important mode to achieve or to understand the project of self-alteration. In traditional and emerging discussions within the anthropology of sport, the self is understood as existing in between the constant fluxes of alteration and therefore shapes lived experiences of participants, spectators, and organizers. In his famous study with Indian wrestlers, Joseph S. Alter (1992) eloquently shows how the dwindling practice of rural wrestling becomes a critical medium through which the wrestlers and the audience think about themselves and alter their perception of living a moral life. Loïc J. Wacquant's (1995, 2004) boxers, as his ethnography in Chicago demonstrates, also embark on a project of self-alteration not only within the moral boundary of the ring but also in their everyday societal dealings: "Fighting is not simply something they *do*, an instrumental activity, a pastime and a side job separable from their persona. Because it demands and effects a far-reaching restructuring of the self as well as an integral colonization of one's life-world, boxing is what they *are*: it defines at once their innermost identity, their practical attachments, and everyday doings, and their access to and place in the public realm" (1995, 507; emphasis in the original). A distinct embodied transformation of athletes is achieved as they follow strict training regimens, become completely devoted to attaining excellence, and cultivate a new persona that is ambitious and practical, succeeds and fails, and trumps and receives constant feedback from the opponent (Besnier 2012; Rial 2012; Esson 2013; Guinness 2018). The role of reflexivity in self-alteration remains crucial, as it actively enables athletes to not only become successful but also strive to transform themselves into virtuous human beings who are courteous, kind, and role models in the larger society. For example, when Michael Vick, once a star quarterback in American football, pleaded guilty to dogfighting, his relationship with animals shaped his public image and his sporting career. After spending twenty-one months in federal prison, Vick struggled to revive his past glory, not because of his sporting form but rather due to the altered public perception of his treatment of animals (Weaver 2013, 695–696). His ultimate success was tied to his virtuous self-alteration associated with his new compassionate treatment of all living beings.

Pigeon flying, as an expression of more-than-human relatedness and as a sporting practice, dynamically alters Pakistani rural flyers' understanding of the inner self as well as their public persona. Staying on the rooftops and structuring co-sociality with their companion birds is a meaningful avocation for many rural flyers belonging to the lower and lower-middle classes. Their affective modes of relating with nonhuman companions assist them to keep, breed, and fly colorful birds; decorate their ankles with beads and rings; mate them; and witness their life from egg to their death. However, to the wider community, pigeon flying remains an intoxication (*nasha*), a sort of obsession that turns responsible men into indolent enthusiasts. So what does this *romance of flying pigeons* mean for those who are castigated by society? Why is the *seduction* of keeping and raising pigeons essential to them when the economic benefits from this sporting practice fall woefully short of its expenses? Below, I untangle such questions, suggesting that humans and pigeons form an intertwined relatedness that, despite being shaped through colonial and postcolonial modes of relating with nonhuman others, survives through interspecies mutualistic associations. Its decolonization reveals how self-alteration is attained in connection to others.

DECOLONIZING THE MODES OF MORE-THAN-HUMAN (MUTUALISTIC) SELF-ALTERATION

Many historians of South Asia have explored modes of human-animal relatedness within the wild sphere through conservation writing and hunting narratives (Shresth 2009; Hussain 2010, 2019; Jalais 2010; Pandian 2001; Storey 1991). However, the subject of more-than-human relationality within the domestic sphere is less well known. The gap has been most effectively filled out by postcolonial resistance writings that interpret modes of decolonization by recapturing the social, historical, and political contexts in which domestic animals played agentive roles and actively shaped human lifeworlds. One such work is the Indian Urdu short story *Taos Chaman ki Myna* (*The Myna from Peacock Garden*), which led its author, Naiyer Masud, to not only receive wider scholarly acclaim but also win several prestigious awards from the Indian government, including the Sahitya Akademi Award (2001) and Saraswati Samman (2007).[1]

The story (Masud 1997) is set in the 1850s in the region of Oudh and reflects upon values of coexistence with more-than-human Others and mutualistic processes of self-alteration. Masud begins the story with the innocent request of Falak Ara to her widowed father, Kale Khan, for a pet hill myna. Kale Khan works at the Royal Peacock Garden of the sultan of Oudh, Wajid Ali Shah, and spends most of his meager salary paying off debts to moneylenders. Even though his little girl is everything to him after the recent death of his wife, he cannot afford to buy her a hill myna. A few days later, when the sultan visits the Peacock Garden, forty royal hill mynas are released in a newly placed giant Wondrous Cage, which is decorated with star-shaped mirrors and made with the finest artistry by the leading jewelers of Oudh. Kale Khan is appointed as the caretaker of this cage and soon develops an affection for one particular myna. After careful planning, he succeeds in stealing the royal bird, hiding her in the inner pocket of his long kurta, and bringing her home as a gift to his daughter. No one in the garden notices a missing myna. Taking an exact count of mynas is almost impossible in this giant cage—some are always hiding out of sight, while others continuously fly from one branch to another—and no one in the garden, even the caretakers, notices a difference between thirty-nine and forty birds. His daughter spends her days with the royal myna, talking to her, feeding her, and caring for her.

One day, the sultan revisits the garden on an unannounced notice and checks on the well-being of the animals in his menagerie. He chats with the caretakers and asks about his elephants and tigers. He looks at the mynas of the Wondrous Cage and affectionately praises their beauty. Soon, he notices the missing myna and asks one of the servants about her. Everyone is stunned by the king's careful regard for more-than-human life and assures him that she must be hiding somewhere in the giant cage. Standing obediently among the servants, Kale Khan is confused, surprised, and petrified. As the sultan leaves, Kale Khan runs home, lies to his daughter that the myna is sick and needs to see a doctor, and brings the royal myna back to the Wondrous Cage.

Hill mynas are famous for imitating human sounds, and a famous trainer of Lucknow is given the duty to train the birds in imitation. When the sultan visits the garden again accompanied by his ministers, courtiers, and English officers from the Residency, the mynas collectively greet the sultan and royal guests by imitating the masculine human sound. Everyone was enjoying this remarkable occasion until one myna started intoning in a childish voice, imitating Kale Khan's daughter, Falak Ara.

Everyone, including the sultan, realized that this had something to do with the caretaker of the Wondrous Cage, Kale Khan. He is fired from his job, with a potential fine and exile from Oudh looming over him. Convincing a decent petition writer, he sends his appeal to the sultan for mercy, explaining all his sufferings and how his daughter begged him for a hill myna. The sultan is impressed by the mutualistic relatedness between Kale Khan's daughter and the myna and not only pardons him but also gifts the bird along with a golden cage to his daughter.

The story continues to include a discussion of political turmoil in the twilight years of Oudh, the annexation of Lucknow, the removal and imprisonment of the sultan from the throne by the British, the arrest of Kale Khan on some other fabricated charges, the destruction of the royal gardens, and the killing of animals by the colonial government. However, for our analysis of mutualistic forms of interspecies coexistence aiding projects of self-alteration, I end the story where the royal myna and Falak Ara are reunited. This allows us to emphasize two key questions. First, how does coexistence between humans and animals (or between the sultan / Falak Ara and the royal myna) facilitate the project of self-alteration? And second, what forms of interspecies intimacy prevailed in precolonial South Asia? This could allow us to imagine how an alternative decolonization requires thinking beyond the modernistic postcolonial boundaries that dominate contemporary India and Pakistan to comprehend mutualistic coexistence between humans and animals in the domestic sphere.

Masud's story effectively depicts the persona of precolonial rulers—in this case, the sultan Wajid Ali Shah—as someone who despite being preoccupied with everyday matters of governing the state has serious regard for life, both human and more-than-human. Although in much colonial literature the sultan is presented as an Oriental despot, Masud's story offers us another side of his personality: a ruler who is attentive to everyone in his kingdom, including mynas, and who takes them as distinct beings with individual traits, attributes, and characteristics. When Kale Khan steals the royal myna and the sultan visits the Peacock Garden after a long time, he realizes that one of his mynas, a "being" of his kingdom, is missing. The sultan's regard for more-than-human connectedness becomes further crucial when he pardons Kale Khan for stealing and even presents the royal myna to his daughter in a golden cage. In conventional colonial representations, acts of forgiveness or the practice of gift giving to lower classes is not usually associated with kings and rulers of South Asia. However, Masud's narration demonstrates how the myna, as an active agent and *actant*, alters the self of the sultan and transforms his authoritative behavior into a benevolent demeanor. I will elaborate on this connection between the myna's agentive role and the possible emergence of mutualistic self-alteration later in the chapter; however, it is vital to note here that the union, separation, and reunion between the royal myna and the sultan / Falak Ara in this story tell the tale of coexistence in a time of political chaos, distrust, and confusion.

In an interview with Sagaree Sengupta (1998), Masud notes how the plot of the story is heavily inspired by historical accounts. He says the myna theft, the Peacock Garden, the Wondrous Cage, the increasing influence of the British in Oudh and its subsequent annexation, and the sultan's menagerie all are real (Masud and Sengupta 1998, 124). The fictitious account of true events portrayed through a bird, Masud insists, inspires us to consider differences between precolonial and colonial systems, including in the spheres of ethics and values of life, modes of relating with others, and between the self and others. For example, in colonial archives, Wajid Ali Shah has been described as an effeminate and indolent ruler. He is presented as drowned in enfeebling debauchery so that his understandings were "emasculated" (see, for example, the description by Joseph Frayer [1900, 94–95], an assistant resident in Lucknow around the 1850s).

Yet the literature produced by authors from the subcontinent—such as Mirza Ali Azhar's (1982) *King Wajid Ali Shah of Awadh*, Abdul Halim Sharar's (1975) *Lucknow: The Last Phase of an Oriental Culture*, and others—demonstrates the illusory truth effect of the colonial literature. Facts were stated without understanding the cultural systems, and conclusions were drawn and redrawn through a systematic production of knowledge that Edward W. Said (1978) has famously called "Orientalism." For example, most of the activities (fighting animals, bestowing gifts, poetry, flying kits or pigeons) described in colonial accounts of the court were culturally meaningful and a symbol of precolonial elite masculinity (Nandy 1983). They depicted the high culture, authoritative demeanor, and economic prosperity of the king. However, as many of these activities did not comply with Anglo-Protestant masculinity, colonial administrators described them as indolent, effeminate, and extravagant pursuits.

The myna story, similarly, emerges as one of the postcolonial resistance writings that, as Masud states, not only "offer[s] a corrective to the bad reputation" the sultan had acquired but also transforms his character from an Oriental despot to a responsible ruler with "amazing powers of memory" (Masud and Sengupta 1998, 123, 144), a sultan who is fond of gardens and animals (125) and who remains attentive to all beings. However, how does an account of fiction, such as Masud's *The Myna from Peacock Garden*, counter historical misappropriations and inadequacies? To this end, I agree with many South Asian art historians and literary critics who suggest that Masud's writings provide a *language* to capture those subtle lived experiences that are often ignored in historical accounts. For B. Venkat Mani (2008, 23), Masud's fictional symbiosis between aesthetics and politics aptly captures conflicts between "the critical and the sentimental, the interrogative and the affirmative, the irreconcilable and the reconcilable" and thus challenges the reader to reconsider historical formulations. Similarly, Sengupta (1998, 82) suggests that Masud's oeuvre is imbued with "evocations of memory and time" and explores layers of history as it unfolds in the popular imagination. In *The Myna from Peacock Garden*, John Muse (2006, 4–5) argues, Masud specifically brings a social and historical lens into conversation with themes of decay and deterioration and frustrates "conventional dualities like clarity and obfuscation, earnestness and dissimulation, realism and modernism, memory and forgetting." Masud's fictional accounts such as the myna story can offer nuanced descriptions of multispecies mutualism in colonial India. That is, when we carefully analyze "meaning" in Masud's writing, as Jane A. Shum (2006, 90) argues, we find that interspecies connectedness does not restrict people from "caring" and that multispecies associations dismantle rather than create a dichotomy between nature and culture.

PIGEONS AND HUMANS LIVING WITH EACH OTHER

Pigeons, like Masud's royal myna, actively alter the self and values of those who relate closely with them in present-day rural Pakistan. They not only shape the flyers' public presence and societal status but also structure their inner transformations. Like the royal myna who is distinct from the other thirty-nine mynas of the Peacock Garden, domesticated and trained pigeons are different from wild pigeons. They take on an ambivalent status—belonging to nature but distinct from other birds of the same species, domesticated but also agents who are active and mutualistic in this relationship, not only transforming themselves in the company of humans but also enabling humans to alter themselves while living with them.

Anthropologist Anna Tsing argues that to broaden our understanding of mutually living with more-than-human Others, we must consider three steps seriously: "birds watching humans, birds and humans watching each other, and humans watching birds" (2022, 18). Tsing's emphasis, based on the observations of Indigenous and Euro-American bird-watchers in West Papua, helps me explore how humans' everyday interconnection with pigeons creates multiple possibilities of mutualistic coexistence. Building on Tsing's three steps, in this section, I explore the possibilities of self-alteration emerging through the experiences of pigeons living with humans, humans living with pigeons, and pigeons and humans living through a mutualistic co-relation. This approach helps me take seriously how pigeons, while living interdependently with rural Pakistani pigeon flyers, remain active agents, as well as how both men and pigeons shape each other's lifeworlds.

The khokha pigeon flying competition with which I started this chapter is specific to rural areas of South Punjab, in central Pakistan. Since the 1970s, it has been held informally among many pigeon flyers, who bring their coops filled with colorful pigeons to a neutral ground for competition. In the past, many old-timers told me, people would come from other provinces and even from neighboring countries such as India to witness the joy of khokha competition in the city of Multan. However, with the recent popularity of the *asmani* tippler pigeon competition and the racing pigeon sport, the khokha competition has lost its pride of place. Nevertheless, today the competition continues to be held on traditional rules where two or multiple coops are placed in front of one another, and a referee oversees the game. The flyers fly their pigeons, the flocks intermingle in the air, and then the men recall their birds with soft-pitched whistles. As soon as the birds land in front of their coop, the flyer instantly identifies the opponent's pigeons in his flock who have misjudged the landing location and leap in with a pigeon-catching net (*dogaza*) to confiscate the bird. At the end of the competition, both flyers count the captured birds and return them to their original keeper in exchange for a preagreed sum of money.

However, this process of play—flying, identifying, capturing, and exchanging pigeons—is not the only thing that inspired people from other provinces and neighboring countries in the past to attend these competitions; rather, it is the vivid display of mutualistic connectedness between men and their birds. During the process of play, when pigeons are constantly flying, mingling with the other flock, and landing, it is their intimate relationality with their flyer that makes them land at their specified coop. After one pigeon flying competition I observed in 2008, I asked Aslam what makes pigeons find their coop amid dust, shouts, whistles, and hundreds of spectators. He replied with a smile, "It is their *pyar* [love] and *aqal* [intelligence] that makes them remember the color of the coop, the smell of the flyer, the sound of the tin can that contained grain mixed with purified butter, diced almonds, and pistachios." Aslam has kept and flown khokha pigeons for more than twenty years, and it was his experience of spending days and nights with his cherished birds that made him arrive at such a conclusion. His views were not different from other khokha pigeon flyers, who also emphasized the multispecies sensory experiences of pigeons that aided them to foster interspecies relationality.

The "love" and "intelligence" of pigeons identified by my pigeon flying interlocutors were dependent on the multisensory experiences of the bird. Unlike humans, they told me, a pigeon utilized the memory of the color of the coop, the aroma of the sweaty flyer, the rhythmic sound of the tin can that was shaken to lure pigeons, and the superior taste of the pigeon diet that the flyer had prepared after hours of toil. This multisensory experience formed pigeons' relatedness, strengthened their *pyar* (love) and *aqal* (intelligence), consolidated their mutualistic association with the flyer, and made them loyal to their coop. This multisensory experience of the bird also, according to Aslam and many other khokha pigeon flyers, formed the basis of khokha competition and enabled pigeons to alter their self. Like the royal myna of Masud's story, these pigeons emerged as active subjects through this relationship of mutualistic interdependence (on multispecies multisensorial relationships, see Fijn and Kavesh 2021; Lemelson and Young 2018; Howes 2019).

However, this mutualistic self-alteration cannot be fully comprehended without accounting for the relatedness of pigeon flyers with their birds. As this enthusiasm enables the flyer to alter his self and form a profound connection and obsessive devotion to this passion, it transforms the men's whole being, refashioning their bodily experiences, emotional aspirations, and sense of well-being. For them, keeping pigeons is more than an activity on which they spend an inordinate amount of time. Their interspecies relatedness alters their complete persona, restructures their self, and changes their way of being.

On the rooftop with his pigeons, where a flyer spends much of his time during the day, he forms a type of "gentle masculinity." As I have argued elsewhere (Kavesh 2021), this type of masculinity can be conceived as almost the opposite of the values of "hegemonic" or "hyper"-masculinity and resides at the bottom of the structure of multiple masculinities in rural Pakistan (cf. Connell 2005). It allows the flyers to express those emotions that men are usually discouraged from portraying in a village setting. For example, the hegemonic values attached to masculinity in rural Pakistan expect a man to be aggressive, competitive, assertive, and enforcing rather than loving, caring, or appreciating. On the rooftop, as these flyers provide "maternal care" (*maa ala pyar*) to pigeons, clean their coops, raise the young birds, or train them with love, the reversal of hypermasculine values sometimes leads them to be categorized as effeminate and incomplete men. Despite such stigma, many spend hours breeding, raising, feeding, training, and flying their pigeons and cherish this enthusiasm (*shauq*).

Pigeon flying demands a flyer follow a strict regimen from dawn to dusk. After starting the day by feeding pigeons, a flyer, on average, spends about two hours of his morning with his birds—checking on them, ensuring the squabs (baby pigeons) get an adequate diet, confirming that the mating pairs are at best health, and allowing the birds to fly and stretch their wings. Then the flyer goes to work, and later in the afternoon when he returns, he spends a couple of hours again with his pigeons, flying and training them. Such a close association allows the flyer to develop the necessary skills to identify his pigeons through their distinct physical traits and bodily patterns and even locate them while flying hundreds of meters away in the air. It is widely believed that a person becomes a true pigeon flyer when he can identify his pigeons in the opponent's flock, the opponent's pigeons in his flock, and a missing pigeon from his flock.

During the khokha competition in the winter months, this knowledge of pigeons' bodies and behavior becomes indispensable. It allows a flyer to select the best-trained pigeons for the competition, fly and familiarize them with their surroundings, and then compete them against the opponent's flock. As both flocks intermingle in the air, it is the pigeon flyer's knowledge of his birds, his mutualistic association with them, and his skills in flying and recalling his pigeons effectively that translate into victory or defeat. During the competition, when pigeons are constantly flying and landing on their flyer's orders, the flyer calls them by their names and signals them with multipitched whistles to land or fly in different formations. This is also the time when the audience observes the flyer's mutualistic association with his birds and carefully scrutinizes how pigeons reciprocate this interspecies association.

The acquisition of knowledge about pigeons' names, their behavior, and their body color and patterns is the way through which a person transforms into a pigeon flyer. Just as a bird learns about his keeper through multiple sensory modes, similarly, a flyer uses his faculties to strengthen this mutualistic association. This interdependence allows the bird and the man to alter their self and reside with each other. It structures their personality, relationships, way of life, and sense of well-being.

The "field" of keeping and flying pigeons, using Bourdieu's (1990) language, is regulated through informal yet organized and collective philosophy that is dependent upon following strict routine, structure, purpose, and meaning. For example, during my fieldwork, I often heard the accusation that pigeon flyers are addicts (*nashai*), having caught this disease (*bemari*) of developing an unthinkable association with pigeons at the cost of their familial and societal relationships. Many pigeon flyers did not deny this, acknowledging their entrenched enthusiasm (*shauq*) for keeping and flying pigeons but suggesting that this passion has brought them to a new universe, one that remains incomprehensible to outsiders. They agreed that the labor their pigeons required on a daily basis absorbed much of their energies to the point that they found it hard to fulfill many of their familial and societal roles. Despite this, most argued that they remained happy with their pigeons and suggested that their love for pigeons turns them into "a better person" all around.

Some pigeon flyers even try to involve their male children in this craft, arguing that, as Rafik once told me, "when you cultivate a love for pigeons, you won't ever develop a taste for any other thing—women, drugs, or crime." The passion for keeping pigeons, Rafik and many others said, keeps a person away from common social vices and criminal tendencies and cultivates a better person within. They argued that the enthusiasm for pigeon flying requires a person to cultivate civility and courteous and respectful behavior while following values of reciprocity, sharing, and exchange. For example, during the heat of the competition, if a flyer develops enmity against his opponent, he is often reminded by his peers of the accepted behavior associated with pigeon flying—the internalization of control, disdain for violence, and obedience to the authority of the referee.

In sum, pigeon flying restructures men's identity, transforms their values of connectedness with their cherished pigeons, motivates them to develop social bonds with other enthusiasts, and reconstitutes their imaginations, emotions, and philosophy of life. Khudla, a pigeon flyer in his early fifties, once related, "A pigeon flyer never gets too old to fly pigeons. The activity becomes a part of his soul [*ruh*]." I also noticed how men might temporarily sell their pigeons or claim to have quit this enthusiasm altogether but after a few years would be training and flying pigeons again, suggesting they are "helpless before this passion" (*shauq dy hatho majboor hain*). On their rooftops, they found solace and companionship that they said they could not find at any other place, and there, while developing a mutualistic association with their birds, they altered their self and achieved a sense of well-being amid everyday economic troubles.

THE MYNA AND THE PIGEON: MODES OF SELF-ALTERATION

Pakistani pigeon flyers develop shared experiences of coexistence with their pigeons, and most of the time, this results in "mutual attunement" (Smuts 2001, 304). As humans and pigeons spend mornings and evenings together for years, they develop a "shared biographical history" (Knight 2012, 344), living as companions rather than as two distinct species separated through domination-subordination relationships. This mutualism is evident in their daily acts of recognizing and trusting each other, understanding and interpreting bodily and behavioral signals, developing a deep loyalty and interdependence, and expecting safety and security in each other's company. Like Masud's myna, these pigeons are aware of their surroundings, remain active while determining the modes and types of companionship, and stay sincere in their fidelity. In fact, there are three interconnected similarities regarding multispecies mutualism in Masud's historical fiction of the human-myna relationship and my ethnography of khokha pigeons in contemporary Pakistan—all emerging through the experience of domestication.

First, both the myna and the pigeon require skillful training that is possible when both partners—humans and birds—are working together and fully dedicate themselves to attain this objective. In Masud's story, Falak Ara provides intimate and affective training to the royal myna, sitting alongside her, chatting to her, and telling her all her stories. This enables the bird to imitate her voice in front of the sultan. The royal myna's imitation is possible through her provision of dedicated attention and regard, as well as unconditional care. The sultan notices this mutualism, recognizes the established more-than-human sociality that he is so familiar with, and therefore decides to "gift" the royal myna to Falak Ara. That gift, like all other gifts, can be interpreted as conforming to Marcel Mauss's ([1925] 2002) three obligations: given, accepted, and reciprocated (Falak Ara's care for the royal myna is reciprocated through the provision of the golden cage). Similarly, for rural Pakistani pigeon flyers, the training of their pigeons not only is achieved by following strict regimens twice a day (*maar*, literally punishing) but also required mutualistic affection for each other (*pyar*, literally love). Because khokha competition is a quintessentially interactive game, understanding the basics—how to fly pigeons, signal them to intermingle with the opponent's flock, determine which pigeon to lead the flock, know when to signal them to land—is only possible when both the flyer and the pigeons form an intimate relationality. As pigeons and the flyer develop interdependence, this helps the flock fly well, integrate and separate from the opponent's flock, stay resilient in unexpected situations, and achieve mastery of technical and tactical aspects (different formations, understanding whistles, remembering the flyer and the coop). While training their flock, flyers understand their pigeons' strengths and weaknesses and adjust their disciplining and caring methods, keeping in view the strengths and weaknesses of the opponent's flock. This is the time when pigeons also learn to recognize their keeper; cultivate a sensory understanding of his body, clothes, and scent; and remember their coop. At the time of the competition, it is the appropriate mix of both, disciplining by the flyer (*maar*) and reciprocal acceptance from the birds (*pyar*), that yields favorable results. If the flyer and pigeons lose this mutualistic balance of *maar-pyar* (strictness and companionship, obedience and free flying, and punishment and acceptance) during the training, pigeons do not fly well and bring dishonor to the flyer in front of the crowd. This right balance between the flyer's training and the pigeons' dedication remains a key to success and structures values of mutualistic companionship.

Second, the interspecies harmony (between the royal myna and Falak Ara / the sultan and between pigeons and the flyer) is achieved through everyday acts of care, ethical regard for the other, and embodied acceptance. In Masud's story, we find that both the sultan and Falak Ara conceive the royal myna as an agentive being who maintains its distinctiveness and individuality. The story carefully specifies that, unlike colonial administrators who saw a clear ascendency of humans over animals and nature, the sultan accepts the uniqueness of even a myna. His noticing of a missing myna in the Wondrous Cage upon his visit displays his careful regard for all life-forms. Falak Ara also finds the royal myna as a distinct being with individual tastes, possessing an ability to listen and interact and the agency to accept or reject various forms of companionship. To the sultan and Falak Ara, this agentivity of the myna demands care and ethical regard equivalent to the one provided to humans.

Pakistani pigeon flyers also form a relationship of interdependence with their pigeons that determines their mutualistic attachment. On a daily basis, many flyers would decorate their birds with bells and anklets, sometimes color their wings, and selectively breed pigeons with different color patterns to get unique squabs. Extensive care is also provided in pigeons' feed, particularly when it is mixed with diced almonds and pistachio, fried in clarified butter, or grounded with rock sugar, cardamom, and cumin seeds. Every ingredient is believed to alter the taste and has numerous benefits that affect birds' flight, stamina, and concentration during the competition. Similarly, while healing a pigeon, a flyer uses the wisdom of experienced flyers and prepares a medicine using local ingredients to cure the ailment without harming the larger body. Unlike biomedical, pharmacy medicines, a cure developed through *Unani* (Greek) medicine is believed to have minimal effects on other parts of the body. All this care is connected with the embodied knowledge of pigeons' physiology, cognition, emotionality, and conative dispositions and allows the flyer to form an ethical acceptance of the more-than-human Other.

Last, the interdependent relationality constituted through everyday acts of care and acceptance between the bird (the myna or the pigeon) and the human (Falak Ara, the sultan, the rural Pakistani pigeon flyer) leads to mutualistic self-alteration. The royal myna alters itself when it actively decides to prioritize Falak Ara's company over the company of thirty-nine other mynas of the Wondrous Cage. Her choice to imitate the childish sound of Falak Ara instead of following the lead of other birds of her species also alters the sultan, who, after some convincing, decides to bestow the bird to young Falak Ara. Falak Ara's father, Kale Khan, also alters his self as he steals and returns the royal bird, and Falak Ara herself is altered as she develops more-than-human companionship with the bird—speaking to the myna, feeding her, telling her stories, and understanding her behavior.

The khokha pigeon competition similarly offers the prospect of visible mutualistic multispecies self-alteration in rural Pakistan. It enables the crowd to experience the possibility of living with others in companionship. That is, unlike other forms of pigeon competitions in Pakistan where the pigeon may not distinctively appear to be playing a highly agentive role, the mutualistic and instantaneous recognition of pigeons by the flyer emerges vividly in the khokha competition. In racing pigeon competition or high-flying tippler pigeon competition, it is usually the *homing* ability of pigeons, their natural navigational skill, that is believed to assist them in finding their loft. In khokha competition, however, as Aslam's quote above suggests, it is pigeons' mutualistic love (*pyar*) and intelligence (*aqal*) that forms their association with the flyer. To generate this, a tangled set of techniques—including dexterity, attention, the certainty of decision, composure, and sharpness—is required from both the bird and the flyer. Such skills are developed through years of training, creating a unique fusion of what Loïc J. Wacquant (1995, 506) calls "body and mind, instinct and strategy, emotion and rationality."

The unlimited hours a flyer spends on his rooftop with his pigeons, the infinite energies he bestows on his birds, and the monetary, mental, and emotional investments he devotes to this enthusiasm make it impossible for him to abandon this practice. This enthusiasm makes many switch jobs that consume too much of their time or conflict with their pigeons' flying routine. Every day on the rooftop, the flyer witnesses the pigeons' embodied acceptance of his corporeal presence, their growing trust in him, their reciprocal affection, and their understanding of his whistles, signs, and gestures. As pigeons alter themselves in the company of the flyer, develop a sensory understanding of his presence, and fly and descend on his signals, the flyer's self becomes braided into the affective and moral universe of the rooftop.

NOTE

1. In 1997, the *Annual of Urdu Studies* (vol. 12) at the University of Wisconsin–Madison devoted a special issue to translating and analyzing the works of Naiyer Masud (see Memon 1997).

REFERENCES

Alter, Joseph S. 1992. *The Wrestler's Body: Identity and Ideology in North India*. Berkeley: University of California Press.

Azhar, Mirza Ali. 1982. *King Wajid Ali Shah of Awadh*. Karachi: Royal Book Company.

Besnier, Niko. 2012. "The Athlete's Body and the Global Condition: Tongan Rugby Players in Japan." *American Ethnologist* 39 (3): 491–510.

Bourdieu, Pierre. 1990. *The Logic of Practice*. Translated by Richard Nice. Cambridge: Polity.

Cassidy, Rebecca. 2002. *The Sport of Kings: Kinship, Class, and Thoroughbred Breeding in Newmarket*. Cambridge: Cambridge University Press.

Connell, Raewyn W. 2005. *Masculinities*. Berkeley: University of California Press.

Esson, James. 2013. "A Body and a Dream at a Vital Conjuncture: Ghanaian Youth, Uncertainty and the Allure of Football." *Geoforum* 47:84–92.

Fijn, Natasha, and Muhammad A. Kavesh. 2021. "A Sensory Approach for Multispecies Anthropology." *Australian Journal of Anthropology* 32 (S1): 6–22.

Frayer, Joseph. 1900. *Recollections of My Life*. Edinburg: William Blackwood & Sons.

Govindrajan, Radhika. 2018. *Animal Intimacies: Interspecies Relatedness in India's Central Himalayas*. Chicago: University of Chicago Press.

Guinness, Daniel. 2018. "Corporal Destinies: Faith, Ethno-nationalism, and Raw Talent in Fijian Professional Rugby Aspirations." *HAU: Journal of Ethnographic Theory* 8 (1–2): 314–328.

Howes, David. 2019. "Multisensory Anthropology." *Annual Review of Anthropology* 48:17–28.

Hussain, Shafqat. 2010. "Sports-Hunting, Fairness and Colonial Identity: Collaboration and Subversion in the Northwestern Frontier Region of the British Indian." *Conservation and Society* 8 (2): 112. https://doi.org/10.4103/0972-4923.68911.

———. 2019. *The Snow Leopard and the Goat: Politics of Conservation in the Western Himalayas*. Seattle: University of Washington Press.

Jalais, Annu. 2010. *Forest of Tigers: People, Politics and Environment in the Sundarbans*. New Delhi: Routledge.

Jerolmack, Colin. 2013. *The Global Pigeon*. Chicago: University of Chicago Press.

Kavesh, Muhammad A. 2021. *Animal Enthusiasms: Life beyond Cage and Leash in Rural Pakistan*. London: Routledge.

Knight, John. 2012. "The Anonymity of the Hunt: A Critique of Hunting as Sharing." *Current Anthropology* 53 (3): 334–355. https://doi.org/10.1086/665535.

Lemelson, Robert, and Briana Young. 2018. "The Balinese Cockfight Reimagined: Tajen: Interactive and the Prospects for a Multimodal Anthropology." *American Anthropologist* 120 (4): 831–843.

Mani, B. Venkat. 2008. "Cages in Search of Birds: Preliminary Reflections on Naiyer Masud." *Annual of Urdu Studies* 23:21–35.

Marvin, Garry. 2007. "English Foxhunting: A Prohibited Practice." *International Journal of Cultural Property* 14 (3): 339–360.

Masud, Naiyer. 1997. "The Myna from Peacock Garden." Translated by Sagaree Sengupta. *Annual of Urdu Studies* 12:155–192.

Masud, Naiyer, and Sagaree Sengupta. 1998. "An Interview with Naiyer Masud." *Annual of Urdu Studies* 13:123–160.

Mauss, Marcel. (1925) 2002. *The Gift: The Form and Functions of Exchange in Archaic Societies*. Translated by W. D. Halls. London: Routledge.

Memon, Muhammad Umar. 1997. "This Issue of the Annual." *Annual of Urdu Studies* 12:1–2. https://minds.wisconsin.edu/handle/1793/11485/browse?rpp=20&offset=88&etal=-1&sort_by=2&type=dateissued&starts_with=2000&order=ASC.

Muse, John Kenneth. 2006. "The Craft of Naiyer Masud." *Annual of Urdu Studies* 21:3–22.

Nandy, Ashis. 1983. *The Intimate Enemy: Loss and Recovery of Self under Colonialism*. Delhi: Oxford University Press.
Pandian, Anand S. 2001. "Predatory Care: The Imperial Hunt in Mughal and British India." *Journal of Historical Sociology* 14 (1): 79–107.
Rial, Carmen. 2012. "Banal Religiosity: Brazilian Athletes as New Missionaries of the Neo-Pentecostal Diaspora." *Vibrant: Virtual Brazilian Anthropology* 9:128–159.
Said, Edward W. 1978. *Orientalism*. London: Penguin.
Sengupta, Sagaree. 1998. "Evocations, Obsessions, and Objects in the Fiction of Naiyer Masud." *Annual of Urdu Studies* 13:81–89.
Sharar, Abdul Halim. 1975. *Lucknow: The Last Phase of an Oriental Culture*. Translated by E. S. Harcourt and Fakhir Hussain. London: Elek.
Shresth, Swati. 2009. "Sahibs and Shikar: Colonial Hunting and Wildlife in British India, 1800–1935." PhD diss., Duke University.
Shum, Jane A. 2006. "Authorial Intention and the Question of Meaning in the Works of Naiyer Masud." *Annual of Urdu Studies* 21:23–100.
Smuts, Barbara. 2001. "Encounters with Animal Minds." *Journal of Consciousness Studies* 8 (5–6): 293–309.
Storey, William K. 1991. "Big Cats and Imperialism: Lion and Tiger Hunting in Kenya and Northern India, 1898–1930." *Journal of World History* 2 (2): 135–173.
Tsing, Anna Lowenhaupt. 2022. "The Sociality of Birds: Reflections on Ontological Edge Effects." In *Kin: Thinking with Deborah Bird Rose*, 24–41. Durham, N.C.: Duke University Press.
Wacquant, Loïc J. 1995. "The Pugilistic Point of View: How Boxers Think and Feel about Their Trade." *Theory & Society* 24 (4): 489–535.
———. 2004. *Body and Soul: Notebooks of an Apprentice Boxer*. New York: Oxford University Press.
Weaver, Harlan. 2013. "'Becoming in Kind': Race, Class, Gender, and Nation in Cultures of Dog Rescue and Dogfighting." *American Quarterly* 65 (3): 689–709.

10 · SELF-ALTERATION AS HUMAN CAPACITY AND AS COSMOPOLITAN RIGHT

NIGEL RAPPORT

Are individuals limited by cultural traditions? Irony, eccentricity, idiosyncrasy, creativity, and revolutionariness as universal markers of human behavior would suggest not. Cultural traditions are more properly appreciated as symbolic fabrications: rhetorical constructs and political claims that do not necessarily correspond with phenomenological reality, to how life is individually lived and experienced. How we relate as individual human beings to a so-called common, shared, or collective cultural tradition is a personal matter.

As I sit writing this in my study in St. Andrews, in Scotland, my daughter sits next door watching a loud American soap opera on TV. On my iTunes app, I listen to Yiddish klezmer music from pre-Holocaust Poland. Glancing up, I see the Israeli flag on a miniature flagpole that I have placed on my windowsill. Beside it are framed photographs of the philosophers John Stuart Mill and Friedrich Nietzsche; next to them is a pebble that I collected on my last visit to Sydney. Not only is this "network" of materials particular to me, but so is the reason for assembling it, the worldview that deems it as having integrity, and the consciousness that reflects on it amid my writing: the consciousness that reckons it to be instantiatory of a way of knowing the world that is personal vis-à-vis any particular culture. My experiential location in a physical and social space is not a collective one or a determinant one. Nor does my location in such a space preclude location in other spaces (Israel, Sydney) and other times (Nietzsche's 1800s, pre-Holocaust Yiddishkeit) as I might construe them.

To be human is to be individual, I say. I come to consciousness in a particular environment of cultural-symbolic systems and a particular material environment, but I *appropriate* these and make sense of them, inhabit them, in personal and self-conscious ways. My membership of a cultural community pertains to symbolic forms deployed publicly in common; but the meaning of those forms and my purpose in exchanging them remain essentially private and idiosyncratic. I am not my St. Andrews neighbors, then; I am not my fellow British citizens; I am not my fellow Jewish sister; and so on. I am myself over and against my particular and plural cultural or communitarian belongings.

PART I: INDIVIDUALITY AND EXISTENTIAL POWER

Let me elaborate on the individuality of human life.

There is a distinctness and discreteness to human embodiment whereby consciousness attaches itself solely to individual bodies that exist as unique and finite organisms. Those organisms possess an interiority that sets them against the otherness of the world around them. Individuality is ontological: the universal reality of a human condition. This ontological reality is distinct from symbolic reality, independent of how cultures and societies may *construe* the nature of social and cultural identities. An aspect of an ontological human nature is the possession of innate capacities for metabolic self-maintenance: for maintaining the homeostasis of a bodily integument and for existing as organisms that regulate the passage of "stuff"—nutrients, information—across the permeable boundary of the skin. Self-maintenance is both conscious and subconscious. Human consciousness is to perceive and interpret: to make sense of selfhood and what lies beyond its bodily integument and to order and make meaningful the otherness of the world. Inhabiting their discrete embodiment—their "bone box" (Golding 1962, 10)— human beings create individual worldviews and life projects for themselves, personal and private in nature. Nietzsche's summary is useful here: "The individual is something quite new which creates new things, something absolute; all his acts are entirely his own. Ultimately, the individual derives the value of his acts from himself; because he has to interpret in a quite individual way even the words he has inherited. His interpretation of a formula at least is personal, even if he does not create a formula: as an interpreter he is still creative" (1968, 767). The practice of interpretation is constant, moreover. The world around the individual is in continuous flux, and maintaining the homeostasis of self means that the individual is in a constant process of making sense, construing and effecting relations between itself and what exists beyond itself, and considering its own identity. Human consciousness is an "ironic" stance, including the self-conscious perspectivism of looking at itself askance, as if from the outside, querying its own intentionality. The individual human being has the innate capacity and—given the changing nature of the world—the proclivity to reflect on itself and to alter itself, to make itself anew (cf. Baldacchino in this volume). Is this how the individual would have itself be: as itself to itself and to otherness?

Since self-alteration is intrinsic to the nature of individual human life and consciousness, the nature of power—and its relation to cultural belonging and social life—becomes a significant issue. Existentially, it can be argued, power should be conceived of as an inherent attribute of individuals as active beings: beings who, through their ongoing, willful activity-in-the-world, create and re-create identities for themselves and the meaningful environments in which their selves live (Rapport, forthcoming). Residing within individuals, and lent to the relations and groupings on which they bestow their allegiance, "existential power" encompasses the force, the will, the energy—in a word, the agency—whereby individuals produce effects in their worlds: effect worlds, in fact (Rapport 2003). Such existential power is at once something metabolic, something pertaining to individuals as embodied physical organisms, and something intelligent pertaining to the capacity to sense and make sense. Individual human beings can be conceived of as discrete centers of energy, as "energy sources" (Bateson 1973, 126). While individuals' bodily boundaries are permeable, and while they are dependent on energy transfers across these borders, inasmuch as they exist, individuals possess an inescapable physical and experiential separateness that differentiates and distinguishes them from the rest of the world.

As discrete centers of energy, individuals begin, from before birth, to become distinctly themselves: to accrete identities and personalities. This takes place through activity-in-the-world, through movement, and through assessment of what the senses relay to be the results of that movement. There exists a "phenomenological subjectivity": a personal, environing "sensorium" in which individual minds dwell, according to James Fernandez (1992, 127, 134–135); Gregory Bateson's portmanteau term for this was the individual "organism-in-its-environment" (1973, 426). Two things are further to be stressed: not only does the energy behind this activity-in-the-world remain individually based, but it is also individually directed. From the moment the individual energy source begins moving in its environment and becoming itself, a unique history of embodiment and of worldly engagement unfolds and grows that compasses its own logics, its own habits, its own ways of doing and being, and its own purposes.

The individual organism-plus-environment is not alone in the world. It is discrete but not alone. It has embarked upon its distinct voyage of activity-in-the-world (-in-*its*-world) and sense making, but it is surrounded by a plurality of other things-in-the-world, inorganic and organic, some engaged in comparable voyages to its own. The consequence of this coming-together, the effects that these individual energetic things-in-the-world have upon one another, is far from a singular or direct or easily generalizable matter. Since each individual center-of-energy is driven by its own metabolism, within its own embodiment, along its own historical course of activity-in-the-world, how each will react to other things is not predeterminable. This is so for three reasons: first, to repeat, because each is set upon its own life course (each is engaged in furthering a lifeworld whose direction and logic has been distinct from the moment "it" began); second, because each engages with others from the position of an outsider (each is dependent on bodily sense-making apparatuses that are discrete and distinctive to itself, which imbue it with its own perspective on the world and no other); and third, because the sense-making procedures of each is characterized by a creativity, a randomness even, which makes their generation of perspectives unpredictable even to themselves (Rapport 2001). The generation of identity (of selfhood) and its alteration and re-creation remain intrinsically individual phenomena, with the "collaboration" of others being unpredictable and "indirect," a matter of purely personal construal.

PART II: ROGER WEIR AT CONSTANCE HOSPITAL

An appropriate way to conceive of human social life, Ralph Waldo Emerson argued, was as a meeting between individuals' "native force" and social conventions: "human life is made up of the two elements, power and form" (1981, 278). Even as they dealt with and employed conventional social-symbolic forms as means and modes of expression and communication, it was individuals' native force that drove them to accrue and maintain senses of themselves and their worlds, to appropriate and inhabit those forms in idiosyncratic ways.

Let me translate the above discussion into an ethnographic register. One field research saw me working as a porter or orderly for a year in a large hospital in eastern Scotland (Rapport 2008). "Easterneuk" is a poor, postindustrial city, with male employment being particularly scarce; hospital porters earned a minimum wage. And yet the capacity to create and re-create the self—in imagination, in verbal expression, and in structural intervention—was far from absent, even among this professionally disadvantaged collective.

Roger Weir was a fellow porter who became a regular interlocutor of mine. We had begun on the same day and undergone the same induction procedure. Roger was some twenty years my junior (in his early twenties), but I would match my assimilation into the institutionalism and hierarchy of the hospital against his: we would often meet at lunchtime, eat our sandwiches together in a quiet corner of the dining room, and compare notes on the day or week, trading accounts of successes and grievances.

"Constance Hospital" had a workforce of thousands, including some 150 porters, employed to ferry patients around the extensive site. Since the work called for physical stamina more than any other attribute or training, and since the hospital rewarded the practice and management of medicine, porters found themselves at the base of a hierarchy of esteem. Only the (female) domestic cleaners could be relied upon to give the (male) porters a confidential and conspiratorial ear. Porters and domestics formed a kind of unholy family of relatively unskilled ancillary laborers, relatively demeaned by the other hospital trades.

He had been a premature baby, Roger told me shortly after we first met. This left him with certain physical difficulties. He had taken up karate to help stretch his tendons, and it became a major pastime: three times per week, consistently, for the past eight years. He still had his dyslexia, but the other great love in his life was music: Black Sabbath and Ozzy Osbourne, to be precise, the epitome of heavy metal. While his disadvantage in achieving karate excellence persisted, in music—enjoying "Sabbath," writing his own songs, and singing them in his band—there were no limits. Ultimately, his life had no limits, Roger would insist with bravado: "Keep on rocking, Nigel!"

While I remained a front-door porter, Roger was stationed in the operating theaters, an assignment he came to hate. It was boring and messy, he complained, and the people working there were officious automatons who didn't know the meaning of the word *fun*. He was forced to clear up after operations without any proper training: bloody floors, bloody clogs and overalls, bits of bodies; he could catch a superbug. He was going to have to start telling his hospital bosses straight what he thought, Roger decided. (It was not as if his job at Constance were the real thing—or anywhere near as significant as his band or having fun!) Roger spoke repeatedly of two specific escapes that he planned. The first was to the annual Black Sabbath Ozzfest in Milton Keynes, near London; the second was a karate tour of Japan, him experiencing firsthand the manners, spirituality, and perfect gentlemanliness of the Japanese masters. Meanwhile, Roger stuck it out at Constance, determined to hold his own. He was, he told me by way of a statement of character and life project, "a wild child with a heart of gold."

An abiding image I have of Roger is of accompanying him down the busy corridors of Constance Hospital en route to a job. We walk side by side, me in my front-door yellow polo shirt (with "N. Rapport, Support Services" stamped on the chest), Roger in his operating-theater greens. While we walk, to the bemusement of passersby, Roger plays loud Black Sabbath riffs on an imaginary air guitar. He also practices his karate kicks, showing off force, speed, and dexterity. He kicks his way through various swing doors, he demolishes signs pinned to official noticeboards that we pass, and he proves himself against the solid walls, undeterred by the impact.

How, then, do I write Roger anthropologically, confront him as a research subject? Roger Weir is not essentially "Scottish," "a porter," "White," or "masculine," I say. These labels, or any such labels purporting to membership of categories and collectivities in a cultural classification and suggesting a profiling of consciousness and identity, are secondary, epiphenomenal. "Embodied subjectivity," the human nature of having a body as an organ of conscious activities, pertains universally over and against "differentiating social maleness or femaleness, specific and inculcated national-ness, and varying class-cultural subjectivities" (Houston 2022, 39). Through Roger Weir, I discern how a human capacity to kick out at the world might be individually substantiated, expressing and effecting particular things. Cultural categories and social classes do not explain this; they are rhetorical or discursive, acts of naming and defining (and confining). The only defining I feel I am warranted to make is a human-natural one: Roger Weir kicks out at the world around him at Constance Hospital as he aspires to an idiosyncratic (martial-cum-musical) formulation of his identity. My anthropological project is to chart how human capacities are substantiated in individual lives; I flesh out a *human* context for Roger over and against the contingent contexts of history, society, and culture that would "fictionalize" his identity in made-up categorial terms. In this way, I may hope better to know the human individual as an ontological reality.

PART III: SUBTLETIES OF SELF-ALTERATION

On the one hand, there is Nietzsche's claim that we all have the Overman (Übermensch) within our grasp, the ability to change ourselves from moment to moment and be masters of our destiny. On the other hand, there is the notion of ontogenesis, of continuous development, whereby each step forward that we take is determined by the steps that we have already taken, each life course a patterned unfolding with no possible beginning again. How should one navigate between the stark phenomenological choice of the Nietzschean against the ontogenetic? More precisely, what does the case of Roger Weir cause me to know of self-alteration as a human proclivity? A conceptual subtlety is necessary.

In considering the place of the individual's consciousness of self in social life, Anthony Cohen counseled anthropologists to make deliberate efforts to "acknowledge the subtleties, inflections and varieties of individual consciousness which are concealed by the categorical masks which we have invented so adeptly. Otherwise, we will continue to deny people the right to be themselves, deny their rights to their own identities" (1994, 180). Cohen was responding to what he saw as a tendency in social science to "colonize" individual consciousness and to deem individual behavior as socially driven rather than self-effected. Individual agency was seen to be overwritten by, if not itself intrinsically a manifestation of, social structure and institutionalism, culture and community, habitus and hegemony, hierarchy and history (Rapport 2003, 56–74). Nevertheless, there are subtleties of feature and of motivation that must be accounted for in the matter of self-alteration. Alongside the differentiation between Nietzschean and ontogenetic development, then, nine further distinctions would seem to require conceptual attention:

1. A *scale* of self-alteration exists, from possibly minor adjustments to major transformations.
2. There is a *direction of travel* in self-alteration, from that which is possibly valued more, or valued positively, to that which is valued less or negatively. Self-alteration might make the individual "better" or "worse" in their own eyes.
3. There is a *temporal dimension* to self-alteration. The changes might take place suddenly or gradually. They might take place immediately or be set for a future date.
4. Self-alteration might represent a *developmental stage* in the life of the individual human being as against a *lifelong practice*. Different kinds of alteration might pertain to each: more major at stage(s) of development followed by more minor over a lifetime—or vice versa.

5. The changes involved in self-alteration might be *teleological*, aimed at a particular end point, or they might be *haphazard* or piecemeal, their "logic" emerging only during the process and over time or not at all.
6. The changes to which the individual subjects himself or herself might be deemed *self-derived* or *socially derived*; individuals might tell themselves the alterations are their own inventions or others'.
7. Relatedly, the individual might construe their self-alterations to be *forced upon them* or to be personally *sought after*. The motivation and desire might be their own or others'.
8. The changes individuals make to themselves (even radical self-alteration) may be publicly *visible* or may remain *secret*, private, known to themselves alone.
9. Finally, self-alteration might take place in *imaginary* terms as against *actual* ones. The individual might come to lead a fantasy life distinct from what they regard as their actual one.

In identifying these conceptual distinctions, my position remains that questions of how individuals find meaning and why they act as they do—why they are as they are and why they alter themselves as they do—should be seen as properties of a personal consciousness. There can be no intersubjective determination of an individual's self-alteration because consciousness is a discrete property of the individual human being: "alone, unique, secret," as Emmanuel Levinas (1996, 76) summed up. The creativity of self-making and self-alteration belongs intrinsically to an individual mind.

In a useful discussion, Alfred Schütz (1972) suggested a distinction between "in order to motives" and "because motives," identifying those actions motivated by the individual's own intentions and objectives as against those determined by others'. But strictly speaking, only "in order to motives" can exist, of which "because motives" are a subset. "Because motives" are how individuals may formulate their decisions *as if* someone or something other than themselves were responsible. All motives are intrinsically "in order to," however, in that they are interpretations of self and other made by individuals in occupation of a discrete consciousness. In wishing to know self-alteration as a human proclivity, my anthropological project is to retain the individual as an agent in their own right and their consciousness a thing-in-itself.

How do I interpret the case of Roger Weir in light of this? Roger sought to alter what he felt to be weaknesses due to his premature birth by practicing karate—altering his body's flexibility, reach, balance, and general sportiness. He was pleased with how far he had come while feeling he would never reach the heights of those grand masters of the art. In his music making, however, the sky was the limit of his transformational potential. It might seem as if his life in Easterneuk and work at Constance Hospital were fundamental realities, but more real was the person he became on stage: singing songs that he had written, with his band behind him. Here was adulation that brought him closer to the celebrity Ozzy Osbourne, while the annual coach trip to Milton Keynes for Ozzfest was a pilgrimage that inspired and energized and emboldened him for the year to come. It also made him imagine that a karate trip to Japan, learning from masters of the art firsthand, might be within his grasp. Music and karate were not only positive and sought-after changes to his life and his body but teleological ends in his becoming. Roger took his cues from social material he found around him—Black Sabbath, heavy metal, and Japanese karate mastery—but he selected these as his personal telos, and he motivated himself to cause them to express his desire. Moreover, he made these expressions visible at work, karate kicking his way down the hospital corridors and playing riffs on his air guitar. He brought in some of the lyrics he had written for his band's songs to show me during our lunch break together, aware of how their powerful mythic dramas of apocalyptic darkness contrasted with his "heart of gold."

But when I left Constance Hospital at the end of my period of fieldwork, Roger remained. The "reality" of his self-alteration—in the image of a rock star and karate master—had not (yet) impacted upon his work realities in Easterneuk to the extent of removing him from them. Whatever his altered images of himself might later effect, most of his time in the present was still spent as a porter. Indeed, it could be construed that Roger's "escapes" worked, contrastingly, to integrate him into portering life at Constance Hospital—albeit on his own terms. Indeed, with his distinctive gait and his music and karate as pastimes, Roger was also a distinctive and recognized figure on the streets and in the housing estates around Constance Hospital. On occasion, dismissive and disparaging depictions circulated among the porters of Roger as "retarded": harmless but mad. But then it was also the case that Roger came to be accepted by the porters in terms of the characteristics he chose for himself.

It was the porters' practice to download sexual content from the internet and post images on the noticeboard in the porter's lodge—the more freakish the better. Roy McMadden was respected as particularly skilled in this regard—somehow linked to his work in the gynecology operating theater—seeking out the most outlandish images, then adding an insulting, localizing graffito and pinning a printout to the lodge wall. Roger confided in me one day, in a hopeful tone, that sooner or later he expected to be the subject of one of Roy's "teases," and when it occurred, he would laugh along with the rest with pleasure. And so it happened. One afternoon, there was Roy in the lodge with a crowd of porters around him, ogling an image of a full-breasted female figure with knickers lowered revealing her penis and with the inscription "Oliver's Bride"—Oliver being a young porter known to have short-lived liaisons. This was coupled with a cartoon image of an oversized dog trying to maneuver a toy car and Roy's inscription "New Hospital Trolley. One careful owner. Contact Roger Weir, ENT Theatre." Everyone laughed—including Roger—while Roy was complimented, him promising copies to those who wanted them. I accompanied Roger back to the ear, nose, and throat theater, still laughing, him teasing me that next time it might be me having this attention paid to them.

Not only did I find Roger gaining a place for himself in the portering community at Constance Hospital—a public persona that, however comic, reflected the self he had made for himself—but his work at self-alteration also seemed to give him the confidence to face outward, beyond the porters, to the wider (hierarchical) institution of the hospital. It would not be appropriate to deem Roger's self-alteration "fantastical," rather than actual, because, at least insofar as I could judge, he actually transformed himself psychologically and physically. It was a common grievance among the porters that they did not garner proper respect from the doctors, nurses, administrators, and clerical workers who worked around them. Contrariwise, the porters concluded, the claims to professionalism of these other trades were themselves not to be trusted; it was the porters who deserved respect, while their coworkers failed often to be as professional, as dedicated, and as knowledgeable. Not only did the porters know that their physical prowess marked them off in the hospital—assured them of a skill and a function that no one else could gainsay—they also knew that they might use their physicality as a route to redress when their institutional rights were particularly under threat. They could threaten to withdraw their physical labor—take industrial action and walk out on strike—and they could turn their physical power directly against the institution's other professions. I took it as a sign of Roger's personal passage from neophyte to established and confident porter, then, when one day he reported to me,

> It's not right what I am made to do in the theater: like clean the doctors' clogs after the operations. Who knows what's on them after an operation. The doctors just leave them and their greens on the floor, and I'm meant to go in and clear up. And clean the floors. But I'm a porter: Why should I do that? I'm gonna write a letter of complaint. They tell me that porters do it because they always have done it. But that's not right! That's just porters not having the guts to stand up and say no. I'm only wearing little rubber gloves and my greens. I could catch anything, any super-bug. And porters aren't properly trained for the work: not told what to do and what to avoid. And the other day this nurse asked me to pop down to the canteen for her and buy her a macaroni and chips. That's not right either! Why couldn't she go for herself? I said OK because I'm a nice guy, but why should I?

I nodded and mumbled in agreement, and Roger continued: "I'm gonna start telling people straight what I think of them. Sod it! . . . You know, Roy McMadden nearly hit a doctor yesterday! 'Come on then! If you want it, come on then!' he said. Aye! [Roger grins] The doctor had been moaning at him all day. . . . In the end, the doctor sent him an apology, but Roy had had enough by then and was going home. But he said if he sees that doctor again today, he's gonna shove a catheter up his arse!"

Knowing Roger Weir for only a year means I cannot know whether self-alteration was a stage only in the development of Roger's personality or whether self-alteration continued to characterize his intellectual and emotional life in the everyday. The imaginary of his alteration could be said to be conventional:

a man in early adulthood imagining himself in relation to masculine physicality, to musical stardom and celebrity, to rebellion, and to girls—those who saw him on stage and those he would tell me he was or would like to be involved with around the hospital. But Roger was also very much his own person. I liked him and was drawn to him and spent time with him—in ways others did not at the hospital—because of what was individual to him. I would consider that Roger's images of self-alteration—how he inhabited them, how he related them to what surrounded him, how he construed them relative to his own life—were his alone.

PART IV: SELF-ALTERATION AND SOCIAL ETHICS

Similar to the way that Ralph Waldo Emerson distinguished between social convention and individuals' native force in his characterization of human social life, Georg Simmel insisted on a dissociation between the individual and the social as being foundational of sociological insight. It is the case that "life is not entirely social," Simmel argued, and "a society is a structure which consists of beings who stand inside and outside it at the same time": a social environment "does not surround all of the individual" (1971, 23; 2005, 13–15). More precisely, a society can be said to exist "where a number of individuals enter into interaction," an interaction that "arises on the basis of certain drives or for the sake of certain purposes" such that the sociological comprehension of this phenomenon is "an exercise of psychological knowledge" (Simmel 1971, 32).

Human life in society comprises an intrinsic "problem," moreover, Simmel elaborated, since members only come to know their fellows by way of distortion: through imposing alien and alienating labels, categories, and taxonomies that traduce the "individual law" of the person (2005, xvi). Social life is a distortion of individual identities when they are ascribed to collective classes, communities, genders, religions, nations, professions, and so on. That individuality exists in conflict with conventional terms amounts to a "tragedy," Simmel concluded (1968, 27), the tragic loss of subjective truth to fictional objectivity.

Might the tragedy be ameliorated? Emerson's prescription for an equable social life was for individuals to practice a kind of self-conscious separation: to keep their *hands* in the social realm but their *heads* in a solitudinous psychological one, keeping to a "diagonal line" between autonomy and sympathy (1981, 394). Another orientation to the problem might be to imagine a form of social inclusion that does not distort along categorial lines, an interactional code that endeavors to accommodate the "law" of individuality. A human being possesses an intrinsic identity by virtue of their distinct and finite embodiment, I have argued. Each inhabits a body that affords a unique perspective on the world, a unique capacity for interpreting the world and making it meaningful—including the creation and re-creation of self-identity—and a unique history and practice in this individual world-making. This is the ontological reality of human individuality as a species-wide phenomenon. An ethical interactional code might be one that seeks to recognize this global reality and give it its proper respect. Here is a linguistic and behavioral style of public engagement—let us name it "cosmopolitan politesse"—that would address the common humanity and the distinct individuality of fellow interactants but classifies them in no more specific fashion. One presumes that in social interaction one is engaging with an individual human Other—with "Anyone"—while refraining from ascribing them membership of a specific class: a "woman," an "Australian," a "Jew," someone in the "working class," "heterosexual," "pious," and so on. One recognizes Anyone as an individual human being entrained on a life course amid worldviews of his or her own determination; one would "emancipate" Anyone from the social "tragedy" of being made subject to the arbitrary constructions, the "fictions," of merely cultural, symbolic classes and categories (Rapport 2012a).

In presuming the individuality of interacting citizens, moreover, such cosmopolitan politesse does not extend to intimacy: it does not claim or expect to know and name an individual other's private self. Rather, here is a linguistic and behavioral medium through which one interacts with Anyone at a respectful distance. One affords another the space necessary to fulfill their personal life projects (to the extent that these do not prejudice the potential fulfillment of anyone else's); a "cosmopolitan" public space is secured where individual human beings engage with one another at a respectful distance. One cares sufficiently about fellow human beings to ensure that they are given the space to come into their own—to engage in processes of self-making and self-alteration—and do not become mere means to others' (classificatory) ends. But one does not wish or presume to know in any detail, or seek to influence in any substantial way, what another individual's "coming into their own" might entail.

In sum, cosmopolitan politesse is an interactional code by virtue of which individual lives may be led whose meanings remain personal. Anyone, any individual human being, is accorded a place, recognized as a potential interlocutor, on the basis of a common humanity rather than any supposed communitarian identity or requisite affiliation. Cosmopolitan politesse endeavors to effect a balance between public respect for the individual Other and their life course of self-creation and self-alteration and public ignorance of that personal process. Restraint and reticence become key virtues.

Cosmopolitan politesse thus accords with what Iris Murdoch would define as the "good society" (2001). "Real compassion is agnosticism," Murdoch advises (1962, 340), and a good society may be conceived of less in terms of aiming to do good to one's fellow members than in refraining from doing them harm. One refrains from visiting one's desires upon others; goodness as a social virtue entails a virtuous abstention from a cultural politics of identity where one identifies the Other through the distorting lens of categories and classes and claims to know their nature and future needs. Goodness entails guaranteeing a space in which a society's members are afforded an optimum of opportunity for self-formation and self-expression as birthright and as mundane practice.

In the good society, one recognizes that even being face-to-face with an individual Other is always "a relationship with a Mystery." This is the formulation of Emmanuel Levinas (1989, 43), once more, whose philosophical insights provide perhaps the most incisive contemporary mediation upon human engagement that is at once ethical and humanistic, individualistic, in its orientation. To "liberate human beings from the categories adapted uniquely for things," Levinas continues, entails accepting that one must enter a conceptual and ethical space where the individual Other "no longer offers itself to our powers" (1996, 8). A conventional, cultural construction of the world, by contrast, is "totalizing" and likely totalitarian, in that through systems of symbolic classification all in the "known" world is assigned a place, defined, and limited. Cultural knowledge imposes a "tyranny of the order of the same," a violent possession that denies the independence and radical otherness of individual being (Levinas 1996, 161–162). An authentically "free" society would be one that supersedes cultural tradition—transcends the idols of place, family, tribe, and nation—so as to "render justice to that secrecy which for each person is his life" (Levinas 1985, 79–81). Founded upon "the secrecy of subjectivity" rather than totalizing concepts of collective samenesses, the free society recognizes that there is a "not-knowing" that is of the essence of human reality and whose accommodation is fundamental to a moral being-in-the-world.

Levinas is assured that individual human beings may "straightforwardly" experience the world around them beyond a cultural habitus, moreover. The exercise of scientific reason achieves this end, as does the intense emotional engagements of love and of suffering. But more mundanely, through the apparently banal acts of civility, hospitality, kindness, and politeness, we may accommodate ourselves to the individuality of life. This is something that human beings can achieve purely on the basis of their common humanity. A "sense of the human," Levinas sums up, "is exhausted neither by the political necessities that hold it bound nor by the sentiments that relax that hold. We believe that what moves outside the order of things can be brought into the general picture without having recourse to any supernatural or miraculous dimension and, demanding an approach irreducible to the established precedents, can authorise proper projects and models to which every mind, that is to say reason, can none the less gain access" (1989, 278). In other words, a "purely human" recognition of another's humanity supervenes phenomenologically upon the established cultural order of things—politics, religion, and so on—so as to give onto the possibility of "properly" moral and rational engagements. The capacity for this kind of experience is universal, and the practice of this kind of engagement is ubiquitous, even mundane, and ethically it is fundamental. "When I really stare, with a straightforwardness devoid of trickery or evasion, into the Other's unguarded, absolutely unprotected eyes," Levinas concludes, a "conscience" is born, a "primordial tenderness for the Other," a "gratuitous goodness" that has nothing to do with cultural values or social institutions but is "an access to external being" that proceeds "from one human uniqueness to another" (1990, 293; 1994, 89).

That the good society of a cosmopolitan politesse might be secured by a mundane moral restraint that admits the mystery of individual human otherness over and against a culture's totalizing claims is further enjoined, finally, by an argument of Luce Irigaray's (2002) in favor of what she terms *loving speech*. An everyday engagement with difference is necessary and is possible, Irigaray claims, such that any human being might be included "lovingly" in social interaction not as categorized or classified persons (gendered, ethnicized, classed, and so on) but as their individual selves. This is true despite the fact that human history has seen us exist as "eunuchs of the heart and the flesh," using tropes—conventional cultural practices and meanings—that violate and cause a vanishing of the individuality of Other and Self both (3). Rather than "dialoguing in difference," we have sought to incorporate otherness in culture's comprehensive order; no culture and no language to date has done more than veil the irreducible core of human being in collective forms that traduce "the initial being of each human" (140).

The path to the Other that Irigaray promotes—the "way of love"—entails practicing a form of interaction that does not simply "seize" and name difference in a conventional, predetermined way, reproducing the same. A "loving speech" involves tentative visual, acoustic, and physical approaches and withdrawals, interactional conjectures and explorings that do not amount to a designating. A different temporality is introduced, neither linear nor repetitive, neither needing nor expecting to conclude in representation. This is, moreover, a constant, ongoing work: loving speech cannot be invented only once. But it is possible, Irigaray is assured, for in our freedom "we live before speaking" (2002, 84–85). We are not prisoners within the horizons of our languages, and we may "transgress" their already learned forms.

For instance, however paradoxical it may seem, we might establish a language of exchange that does justice to the encounter with otherness and its unknown meanings by developing the "negative" linguistic technique of silence. Loving speech can be a silent being-with, characterized by an indirection that has no (cultural) telos. What is fundamental is that no interactant wishes or expects to be master of the movements involved, and none expects to overcome difference and make the Other the same. Loving speech is a process of mutuality where the Other is not reduced to the Ego's object. Nor is assurance sought in any external measure of conventional authenticity concerning what is co-built during an encounter. The relationship is a work of interior blossoming, held by no external standard and assured only by the integrity of the individual human beings who encounter one another.

Through loving speech, Irigaray would offer a vision of human beings moving toward one another in social interaction while acknowledging individual being-in-the-world. In a "community of exceptions" (Finkielkraut 2001, 80), the personal phenomenologies of self-making (and self-altering) are afforded space and respect.

CONCLUSION: SELF-ALTERATION AND THE GLOBAL

In the above discussion, I have wanted to provide guarantees for self-alteration within an ethical social form. Cosmopolitan politesse has been mooted as a linguistic and behavioral code for recognizing Anyone mundanely and also universally. But then the global is a social reality as much as a moral imaginary, our inhabitation of a "globalizing world" that "pits fundamentalism against cosmopolitan tolerance" (Giddens 2002, 4). How does self-alteration fare?

It is a cosmopolitan duty to surmount the "accident" of birth, Martha Nussbaum exhorts: "Any human being might have been born in any nation," and we must "recognize humanity wherever it occurs and give its fundamental ingredients, reason and moral capacity, our first allegiance and respect" (Nussbaum 1996, 7). This might be parsed ethnographically to say that the global context of contemporary human practice no longer makes it legitimate—whether scientifically or ethically—to talk of cultures in essentialist terms, as if fundamentally discrete worlds of traditional and ongoing difference. Notwithstanding, in an era of identity politics, we are witness to vehement and often violent rhetorics of cultural exclusiveness, people defining themselves and others not in terms of a universal humanity and individuality but as collective part-beings: essentially constituted by communitarian histories, traditions, and affiliations. "Cultures are not options," proclaims Bhikhu Parekh (1998, 206, 212), lobbying for a kind of "multiculturalism" that would prescribe demarcations of fundamental and essential kinds between individuals on the basis of communitarian differences: ethnicity, religion, and race. Here is an ideological program that appears happily to revisit a pre-Enlightenment ancien régime of a "society of orders": of different kinds of human being (Amit and Rapport 2002, 2012).

The claim that "cultures are not options" we know, however, to be a falsehood. The idea that personal selfhood is constituted by and forever tied to particular cultural milieus—particular beliefs and practices, particular histories, habits, and discourses—and the related claim that individuals who exit such collectively secured lifeworlds must find themselves ontologically devastated, without social anchor or cognitive guarantee, are refuted by the empirical reality of individual lives at home in movement and transition (Rapport and Dawson 1998). Cultural belonging is always an act of negotiation and contestation, and cultural tradition is always a matter of interpretation, always part of an argument: cultural practice is always a matter of particular and interested application. "A culture" is a process, and only deliberate programs of cultural fundamentalism may endeavor to fix, define, and sanction its fluidity and claim the crystallization of a set of "traditional" givens (Kurzwelly, Rapport, and Spiegel 2020). Anthropology has a particular edificatory and emancipatory role to play here.

"We are all human and should treat each other decently and with respect," Ernest Gellner urges, addressing himself to anthropology and the ethical program of a civil society alike: "Don't take more specific classifications seriously"

(1993a, 3). The symbolic constructions "society," "culture," "nationality," "community," "ethnicity," "religion," and "class" (literally "fictions" in that they are invented and remain dependent on human belief and practice) need have no place in the scientific apprehension of the human condition as an ontology—as natural being, as a set of universal capacities, as an independent truth—and they need have no place in the ideal vision of how human beings should be recognized and respected, included, in a liberal society (Rapport 2012b). Science proved that "knowledge beyond culture" was possible, argues Gellner (1993b, 54), representing, indeed, "*the* fact of our lives." Equally, within the "well-matured" political framework of liberal society, we can work toward "a morality beyond culture" where traditionally prescribed roles and relations are replaced by a "free, individualistic choice of identity" (Gellner 1993a, 3). Such a morality does justice to a species-wide capacity to determine the substance of human lives in individual ways.

To overcome the pernicious consequences of having human beings ascribed to particular cultures—to put culture in its proper place—is for anthropology to insist that individuals are human *not* inasmuch as they inhabit different worlds of culture but *over and against* these symbolic and rhetorical constructs. Self-alteration becomes a human birthright in a society where difference is a manifestation not of collectivist classification but of individuals fulfilling their human capacity for self-making. One commits to Anyone, respecting and recognizing globally the individual capacity and proclivity to create and re-create selfhood.

REFERENCES

Amit, Vered, and Nigel Rapport. 2002. *The Trouble with Community: Anthropological Reflections on Movement, Identity and Collectivity*. London: Pluto.

———. 2012. *Community, Cosmopolitanism and the Problem of Human Commonality*. London: Pluto.

Bateson, Gregory. 1973. *Steps to an Ecology of Mind*. Frogmore: Paladin.

Cohen, Anthony. 1994. *Self Consciousness*. London: Routledge.

Emerson, Ralph Waldo. 1981. *The Portable Emerson*. Edited by C. Bode. Harmondsworth: Penguin.

Fernandez, James. 1992. "What It Is like to Be a Banzie: On Sharing the Experience of an Equatorial Microcosm." In *On Sharing Religious Experience*, edited by Jerald Gort, Hendrik Vroom, Rein Fernhout, and Anton Wessels, 125–135. Grand Rapids: Eerdmans.

Finkielkraut, Alain. 2001. *In the Name of Humanity*. London: Pimlico.

Gellner, Ernest. 1993a. "The Mightier Pen? Edward Said and the Double Standards of Inside-Out Colonialism." *Times Literary Supplement* 4690:3–4.

———. 1993b. *Postmodernism, Reason and Religion*. London: Routledge.

Giddens, Anthony. 2002. *Runaway World*. London: Profile.

Golding, William. 1962. *Free Fall*. London: Harbinger.

Houston, Christopher. 2022. "Why Social Scientists Still Need Phenomenology." *Thesis Eleven* 168 (1): 37–54. https://doi.org/10.1177/07255136211064326.

Irigaray, Luce. 2002. *The Way of Love*. London: Continuum.

Kurzwelly, Jonatan, Nigel Rapport, and Andrew Spiegel. 2020. "Encountering, Explaining and Refuting Essentialism." *Anthropology Southern Africa* 43 (1 & 2): 65–81.

Levinas, Emmanuel. 1985. *Ethics and Infinity*. Translated by R. Cohen. Pittsburgh: Duquesne University Press.
———. 1989. *The Levinas Reader*. Edited by S. Hand. Oxford: Blackwell.
———. 1990. *Difficult Freedom*. Translated by S. Hand. London: Athlone.
———. 1994. *In the Time of the Nations*. Translated by M. Smith. London: Athlone.
———. 1996. *Basic Philosophical Writings*. Edited by A. Peperzak, S. Critchley, and R. Bernasconi. Bloomington: Indiana University Press.
Murdoch, Iris. 1962. *An Unofficial Rose*. London: Chatto & Windus.
———. 2001. *The Sovereignty of Good*. London: Routledge.
Nietzsche, F. 1968. *The Will to Power*. Edited by W. Kaufmann. New York: Random House.
Nussbaum, Martha. 1996. "Patriotism and Cosmopolitanism." In *Love of Country*, edited by Joshua Cohen, 3–120. Boston: Beacon.
Parekh, Bhikhu. 1998. "Cultural Diversity and Liberal Democracy." In *Democracy, Difference and Social Justice*, edited by Gurpreet Mahajan, 202–227. Delhi: Oxford University Press.
Rapport, Nigel. 2001. "Random Mind: Towards an Appreciation of Openness in Individual, Society and Anthropology." *Australian Journal of Anthropology* 12 (2): 190–220.
———. 2003. *I Am Dynamite: An Alternative Anthropology of Power*. London: Routledge.
———. 2008. *Of Orderlies and Men: Hospital Porters Achieving Wellness at Work*. Durham N.C.: Carolina Academic.
———. 2012a. *Anyone, the Cosmopolitan Subject of Anthropology*. Oxford: Berghahn.
———. 2012b. "Emancipatory Cosmopolitanism: A Vision of the Individual Free from Culture, Custom and Community." In *Handbook of Cosmopolitan Studies*, edited by Gerard Delanty, 101–114. London: Routledge.
———. Forthcoming. "Moments of Willing: On the Existential Power to Will Identity and Movement in Self and World." *Ethnos*.
Rapport, Nigel, and Andrew Dawson, eds. 1998. *Migrants of Identity: Perceptions of Home in a World of Movement*. Oxford: Berg.
Schütz, Alfred. 1972. *The Phenomenology of the Social World*. London: Heinemann.
Simmel, Georg. 1968. *The Conflict in Modern Culture and Other Essays*. New York: Teachers College Press.
———. 1971. *On Individuality and Social Forms*. Chicago: University of Chicago Press.
———. 2005. *Rembrandt*. New York: Routledge.

AFTERWORD
MAKING ONESELF
OTHERWISE
Reflections on Natality

MICHAEL JACKSON

> It is in the nature of beginnings that something new is started which cannot be expected from whatever may have happened before. This character of startling unexpectedness is inherent in all beginnings and in all origins.... The new always happens against the overwhelming odds of statistical laws and probability [and] therefore always appears in the guise of a miracle.
> —Arendt 1958, 177–178

So various and fluid are the ways in which people comprehend themselves and their capacities that there may be little point in trying to decide whether selves are individually fashioned or socially constructed, free or fated, singular or several, actors or acted upon, since all these possibilities will, under different circumstances, appear to be true. I therefore follow Christopher Houston's phenomenological approach that assumes change to be a natural condition of human consciousness.[1] I also draw on Hannah Arendt's concept of natality in which birth and labor are ontological metaphors for actions and interactions that, while preserving something of what is already given, initiate something new (1958, 177). Regardless of whether such alterations are accidental or intentional, they are informed by an element of surprise and hopefulness that inspires a sense that we are creators and not simply creatures of circumstance, able to start over, redeem the past, reshape ourselves, and transform the world.

Whether new personal or political beginnings are the result of choices we make or factors and forces beyond our comprehension may be impossible to determine.[2] What remains true, however, is the dynamic interplay between selves and situations, such that what we make of ourselves is irreducible to the world in which we are made. For writers like Bataille, Nietzsche, Sartre, and Winnicott, our capacity to play with reality, reimagining it in fantasies, stories, rituals, and art, suggests that human beings are driven not only by a desire to adapt to and accept their situations in life but by a transgressive drive to expend surplus energy, break with routine, take chances, and experiment with consciousness, thereby living on their own terms, in their own time, and making *the* world *theirs*.

This essay comprises three sections. In the first, I review recent psychoanalytical work on multiple self-states. In the second, I explore situations in which a person feels at odds with the world in which he or she is born and raised. What fascinates me here is how a sense of not belonging may be changed into a sense of being at home in the world. In the third section, I consider voluntary migration, in which individuals alter their place in the world as a way of altering themselves. Was Horace wrong, I ask, when he wrote "They change their sky but not their soul who cross the ocean"? (Horace 1994, 27, I, xi).

MAKING SENSE OF OURSELVES

According to Heraclitus's famous aphorism, "Everything is in flux" (*panta rhei*). One cannot step into the same river twice, for neither the self nor the river stays the same over time. Yet while we change in the course of our lives, we cling to the belief that some things never change. Despite age and infirmity, we claim to be forever young. Though love dies and friendships fail, the fallout of our earliest affections and disaffections is felt for as long as we live. Though we alter in relation to who we are with, what task we are performing, and what language we speak, we want to insist on a core self that, like the polestar, remains constant in the darkness, guiding us home.

Recent psychoanalytical work on the self throws light on this mutability of the self. Rather than postulate a seamless, stable, skin-encapsulated monad (Mitchell 1993), the self is seen as subject to continual change *from within and without*. Like chameleons, we alter ourselves or are altered by our situations, possessing an extraordinary "capacity to feel like oneself while being many" (Bromberg 1993, 186). Indeed, our ability to shape-shift—adjusting our self-states in response to who we are with, what our interests are, and what circumstance demands—is not only adaptive; our lives would be otherwise impossible.[3]

For William James, the critical issue is not whether we *are* constant but why we need to believe we are. Why, he asks, do we find it so difficult to accept the diversity of our lifeworlds and the mutability of ourselves, creating the appearance of social unity and moral consistency through the artifice of singular nouns—the nation-state, ethnic identity, democratic values? James compares this process to a spring roundup when scattered animals are herded together and given a common brand. We are less concerned with whether these animals are all of a kind than with the warm feeling we get from having brought them into the same corral and imposed our will on a hitherto scattered and unruly mob (see also Rapport in this volume). "There is a self-brand, just as there is a herd," James says, and though this branding may satisfy our need to compress multiple forms of life into a single synthetic mold, we may also sometimes feel that this proprietary act does violence to the contingency, discontinuity, and inconstancy of life, including the life we call our own (James 1950, 331–337).

James's insights echo Michel de Montaigne's 1580 essay "On the Inconstancy of Our Actions." "Anyone who turns his prime attention on to himself will hardly find himself in the same state twice," Montaigne observes. "Every sort of contradiction can be found in me, depending on some twist or attribute.... There is nothing I can say about myself as a whole, simply and completely, without intermingling and admixture.... We are fashioned out of oddments put together.... We are entirely made up of bits and pieces, woven together so diversely and so shapelessly that each one of them pulls its own way at every moment. And there is as much difference between us and ourselves as there is between us and other people" (Montaigne 1993, 128–129, 131).

In 1857, Herman Melville wrote in a similar vein against the "fiction" of an independent, unique self that remains stable over time. "A consistent character is a *rara avis*," he says, and he goes on to explain that a work of fiction "where every character can, by reason of its consistency, be comprehended at a glance, either exhibits but sections of character, making them appear for wholes, or else is very untrue to reality; while on the other hand, that author who draws a character, even though to common view incongruous in its parts, as the flying-squirrel, and, at different periods, as much at variance with itself as the caterpillar is with the butterfly into which it changes, may yet, in so doing, be not false but faithful to facts" (Melville 1990, 84–85).

For William James, the inconstancy of the self is a function of its relationship to other selves, its social environment, and the objects with which it identifies. In this intersubjective view, we are not only as several as the significant others who recognize us, but we are the sum of everything we call our own, including our material possessions, our talents, our ancestors, and our professions (James 1950, 291, 294).

In shifting our focus from epistemologies of the self to a phenomenology of self-states, it becomes clear that subtle shadings of mood, emotion, and thought are constantly occurring despite the category words we deploy in creating the illusions of stasis and identity. Something new emerges from every encounter, event, or relationship regardless of how such encounters, events, and relationships are discursively represented.

MYSELF MUST I REMAKE

On New Year's Eve in Denmark, friends and family gather and smash old plates as if to make way for a new beginning in their lives.[4] In Rome, old furniture is thrown into the street in a similar gesture of clearing a space for the new. On St. Anthony's Day in Naples, bonfires are lit and household items are cast into the flames, symbolizing the destruction of the old (as winter comes to an end) and the birth of the new (as spring approaches), and in Northern Sierra Leone, thousands of visitors climb to the summit of an inselberg called Albitaiya on New Year's Day to celebrate the passing of the old year and watch the sun rising on the new. Even the mundane business of spring-cleaning and the making of New Year's resolutions suggest a hope that it is always possible to start anew and even that we can achieve some measure of immortality.

Processes of birth, death, and rebirth are common to all life-forms as well as universal metaphors for the phases of human life. Birth and begetting create genealogical continuity through time and across space. Initiation involves a dramatic metamorphosis in which childhood is exorcised and a neophyte is reborn as an autonomous adult. Marriage marks a transition from youthful freedom to new and binding ties. And mortuary rituals transform a mortal human being into an exemplar of moral virtue. For many people, moreover, death presages a transition to an afterlife or a karmic reincarnation or is imagined, as in the Māori notion of whakapapa, as a process of "laying one thing upon another," with the first foundational layer succeeded by others up to the present time (Ngata 1972, 6).

Nevertheless, just as natality and mortality are not always associated with biological birth and death, so new beginnings are not always institutionalized in rites of passage.

Consider these examples.

After seven years of psychotherapy, the French author Marie Cardinal (1984) wrote a memoir chronicling her experience of escaping insanity and reaching an understanding of what had thrown her off course. Like Dante's account of "the dark, impenetrable place where the straightway was lost," Cardinal speaks of creating a new life for herself, so different from the old that she is moved to dedicate her book "to the doctor who helped [her] be reborn" (1). (But see also Baldacchino in this volume.)

Among the desperate Afghans outside Kabul Airport in late August 2021 were hundreds of individuals who had worked for the Americans and feared for their lives under Taliban rule. Abdul Qader Zaman served as an interpreter in a frontline American unit, and his fate now lay in the hands of a group of activists in the United States and its contact inside the besieged airport. After several days of texting and negotiating, Zaman was given instructions on how to make himself known to the soldiers guarding the terminal building. Zaman carried his five children, one by one, across the putrid canal that separated them from the terminal. Finally, he led his wife to safety. After months in Qatar and Germany, Zaman's family was resettled in Erie, Pennsylvania, where Zaman was interviewed in February 2022. Recalling the harrowing moments when he crossed and recrossed the canal and finally entered the secure space of the terminal, Zaman said, "I just felt that I'm just born."

Surprised by this remark, the interviewer, Hari Sreenivasan, repeated the phrase. "That you were born?"

"Yes," Zaman said, as this was something more than a manner of speaking. It was literally how he had felt. That he and his family had escaped Afghanistan against all odds was nothing short of a miracle (Sreenivasan 2022).

Zaman's remark echoes something that West African friends in London, Amsterdam, and Copenhagen have often told me. Their lives back home had been so impoverished and hopeless that not migrating would have spelled social death, and if they were deported from Europe, where life was also a struggle, though of a different kind, it would be tantamount to a death sentence.

These are dramatic examples of new beginnings. But even in situations where one's life is not on the line, rebirth can appear as a compelling motif. Everyone starts out somewhere with someone, only to start over elsewhere with someone else. We are forever in the process of dying to one life and being reborn to another. As Bob Dylan puts it, "He that is not being born is busy dying" (Dylan 1965). Within a single day, we can be instantly crushed by bad news or boosted by a lucky break, thrown into despair or filled with happiness. Within seconds, our moods shift or our fortunes can change.

In the course of a lifetime, most of us will inevitably separate from our parents, strike out on our own. Some of us will become parents ourselves. Equally inevitable is aging and the loss of those we love. There are instances when we kick over the traces, break engrained habits, and head off in a new direction because we feel that some cosmic error has been made. We have been born to the wrong parents, in the wrong place, or at the wrong time and must discover where we rightfully belong.

A Danish colleague, Birgitte Refslund Sorensen, shared with me an anecdote from her time in Sri Lanka. A small boy walked out on his parents one day and disappeared. When he was finally traced, he was found to be living with a family in another village. He said he belonged there. He had asked the family to take him in, and they had agreed. All this was explained as karmic recognition of a genealogical link in a previous life. The boy was simply correcting an accident of birth by moving from his natal to his karmically authentic home.

In a 2005 interview, Bob Dylan spoke of a sense of having been born far from his true home: "I had ambitions to set out, like an odyssey, going home somewhere. So I set out to find this home I'd left a while back, and I couldn't remember exactly where it was, but I was on my way there and encountering what I encountered on the way was how I envisioned it all."[5]

Bob Dylan's odyssey is not without precedent. The restive longing that Charlotte Brontë attributed to Jane Eyre was undoubtedly born of her own experience. Confined to the house of her employer, Jane climbs to the attic to gaze out "over sequestered field and hill, and along dim sky-line," longing for "a power of vision which might overpass that limit; which might reach the busy world, towns, regions full of life I had heard of but never seen" (Brontë 1864, 113).

Consider, too, the case of Frédéric-Louis Sauser, born in the Swiss town of La Chaux-de-Fonds in 1887. His parents sent him to a German boarding school from which he ran away. He was then enrolled in a school in Neuchâtel but showed no interest in schoolwork. At the age of fifteen, he boarded a train to Basel, traveled to Berlin, and thence went to Russia. In 1907, he arrived in Paris and rented a room in the Hôtel des Étrangers that he thereafter regarded as his true birthplace.

This initiatory birth demanded a complete erasure of the past as well as a new name, Blaise Cendrars, composed of "braise" (embers) and "cendres" (ashes), with overtones of "ars" (art) suggesting a clean break from outmoded literary styles.

Twenty-three years later, Henry Miller arrived in Paris, having cut his ties with America and renounced literature:

> It is now the fall of my second year in Paris. I was sent here for a reason I have not yet been able to fathom.
>
> I have no money, no resources, no hopes. I am the happiest man alive. A year ago, six months ago, I thought that I was an artist. I no longer think about it, *I am*. Everything that was literature has fallen from me. There are no more books to be written, thank God.
>
> This then? This is not a book. This is libel, slander, defamation of character. This is not a book, in the ordinary sense of the word. No, this is a prolonged insult, a gob of spit in the face of Art. (Miller 1934, 1)

As for the birth of a nation, whose very etymology invokes natality, this also involves a symbolic death. The old must be destroyed if a new order is to arise. So declared the Congolese rebel leader, Christopher Gbenye, in 1964 when he ordered the execution of everyone who was literate or had worked for the Belgians, "We must destroy what existed before, we must start again at zero with an ignorant mass" (Jackson 2021, 90). A decade later, Pol Pot's pogroms in Cambodia echoed the same genocidal logic. Highly educated in French lycées, Pol Pot's political extremism was as much an attempt to exorcise the colonial demons in himself as his orchestrated murder of those who were allegedly contaminated by their association with the colonial epoch. Religious and cultural fundamentalism in our own day and age reiterate the same leitmotif of cleansing as a prelude to rebirth.

Personal and political revolutions share a similar aim. They seek to rewrite histories and life stories alike. Thinly veiled in the revolutionaries' hunger for freedom is an impulse to countermand the experience of having been born and raised in a world they did not choose but was visited upon them by others (but see Houston in this volume).

Not everyone feels such desperation for change. Rather than work toward building a brave new world, some prefer a return to a utopian period in the past when life was supposedly simpler and happier. Historically, the idea of creating a self or society that has not existed before is a relatively recent idea. In Hannah Arendt's opinion, far from seeking a new beginning, the premodern worldview regarded history as cyclical, its course as preordained as it was unchangeable (2005, 11). Unfortunately, this view implies that so-called premodern peoples not only live outside history but are solely committed to the perpetuation of ancestral values.

The following story suggests a very different perspective.

In 1950, the Australian anthropologist Kenneth Read was on patrol in an area of the Eastern Highlands of New Guinea where people had never seen a White man. One morning, as Read and his companions were breaking camp, a young boy from the village approached them. Using gestures, he made it clear that he wanted to return with them to the place they had come from. The boy was perhaps thirteen or fourteen. He spoke no language but his own. Yet he was prepared to throw in his lot with these outsiders and undertake a journey, Read notes, "immeasurably greater than the distance involved, virtually a transition from one world to another." Although the terrors of the unknown were mitigated by the Gahuku-Gama belief that true manhood could only be achieved by braving the hazards of the outside world, this "leap through time," Read says, "took a measure of courage and a degree of foresight almost, impossible to comprehend" (Jackson 1995, 3).

Did the boy, Susuro, whose new name was an affectionate diminutive of the name of his adopted village, ever realize his dreams? Thirty years after leaving the high valley, Read went back. Old acquaintances told him that Susuro had remained in Susuroka for several years, growing to manhood there and working from time to time in a nearby township. He then returned home. Of Susuro's subsequent fate, all Read could learn was that he was dead, killed by sorcery among his own people.

THE MAKING OF A MIGRANT

Alterations in self-states are seldom straightforward. To be in transition is to be in doubt and adrift and to experience dissociation—to suddenly discover that one has become a stranger to oneself. As Ibrahim Ouedraego—a friend from Burkina Faso—put it, reflecting on his first bewildered days in Amsterdam, "You cannot do everything you want to do. There are always rules that will stop you crossing borders, stop you going where you want to go, stop you finding an easier path. It's papers that count, not words. No one trusts anything you say. You can't talk to people directly. You've got to have papers. Even if the papers are false, they will count more than your words. There is no more truth in words."

In the course of my research with migrants, I became accustomed to the double binds of leaving a place of "social death" only to suffer the atrophy of one's roots and the melancholy realization that the place in which one hoped for a second birth was also a place of death. For Ibrahim, these metaphors were not mere figures of speech, for he had grown up in the Sahel, where drought and desertification had rendered life unsustainable.

When the American anthropologist Della E. McMillan first visited Ibrahim's natal village of Damesma in 1977, people were suffering the effects of declining crop yields, low income, and impoverished soils, and many were leaving the village to resettle in river basins where "some of the most debilitating diseases known to humanity—malaria, schistosomiasis, sleeping sickness (trypanosomiasis) and river blindness (onchocerciasis)"—had been partially brought under control (McMillan 1995, 1). One of the most arresting comments in McMillan's ethnography concerns the unpredictable effects of migration. Like migrants everywhere, she writes, the "brave families who voluntarily immigrated to the AVV [Autorité des Aménagements des Vallées des Volta] went in pursuit of . . . a better life for themselves and their children" (xxx). But their visions changed. At first, their goal was simply to survive. Then, as the years passed, some households (called *les millionaires*) succeeded where others failed. But all developed new expectations that not only were different from their original expectations but "did not always coincide with those envisioned by the project planners" (xxx).

For those who remained in Damesma, life also unfolded in ways that could not have been envisaged.

"My father was the *tenga naba* [village chief]," Ibrahim said. "Our family had always been in the village. We could not move as others did. There were times when I thought about it, but I knew my father's importance in that place and why we had to stay."

"Why did you want to move?" I asked. "Was it because of the drought, the famine?"

"Not really. From age seven, I wanted to go elsewhere. You feel it inside. You can't give words to it, but it's a strong feeling, to go to a big town, to move elsewhere. When visitors came, I always wanted to be present, to hear the stories about where they came from. I was always being chased away! When I saw people who lived in bigger villages or towns, I was curious to know what life was like in those places. There was no school in my village, so I was curious to know what school was like. I wanted to discover things on the other side, though I could also see that people in towns had more to eat than in the village."

I was surprised that Ibrahim would background climate change and hunger as the reasons why his thoughts turned to places beyond the horizon as offering the chance of a more fulfilling life. And I was intrigued that he should mention vague yearnings to explore the wider world in explaining his restiveness. When I was a boy, I had experienced the same allure of elsewhere, and I had encountered the same sentiments among other migrants—sentiments that echoed Salman Rushdie's meditation on *The Wizard of Oz*, in which the imagined world becomes the real world "as it does for us all, because the truth is that once we have left our childhood places and started out to make up our own lives, armed only with what we have and are, we understand that the real secret of the ruby slippers is not that 'there's no place like home' but rather that there is no longer any such as place *as* home: except, of course, for the home we make, or the homes that are made for us, in Oz, which is anywhere, and everywhere, except the place from which we began" (Rushdie 2012, 58).

"Where did you think of going?" I asked Ibrahim.

"I didn't think of going far. I thought mainly of going to Kaya, which was about ten kilometers from my village."[6]

"How old were you when you first went there?"

"I was twelve. Up to that time, my father was afraid to let us go to Kaya. He wanted us to know our traditions, to be strong in our customary way of life. Even now, I hear my father's voice saying, 'You must be a good example. You must honor the traditions.' But I did not want to spend all my life in Damesma. It was too limited [*limité*] for me."

"What were your first impressions of Kaya?"

"It was the first time in my life that I saw ice."

I instantly recalled Aureliano Buendia's last memory in Gabriel Garcia Marquez's *One Hundred Years of Solitude*—of a distant afternoon when his father took him to see a block of ice.

"I had never seen ice before," Ibrahim said. "I asked myself how it was possible. Was it magic, or what? It wasn't water. Water could not be solid. I could not believe it was real. But they were selling wooden sticks with ice formed around them. There was a long line to buy one. I asked what was going on. When they told me, I joined the line."

"When you returned to Damesma, what did you remember about Kaya?"

"I knew that my life would be better in a bigger place. I thought, 'Maybe one day I will go far,' but I had no way of doing this. I could not move without my family, and my family had to stay in Damesma, so I stayed too."

"How did you pass your days when you were a child in Damesma?"

"We had to go to the highlands to find firewood to give to our mother, and we also had to look after the horses, goats, and sheep. The animals were not penned. Everyone had a tether around its neck. You had to catch the tether as they were running all over the place, one going to the left, another going to the right. I remember all that very well."

"Did your father also farm?"

"Yes."

"What crops did he grow?"

"We had millet, which was widely cultivated. We grew some corn, rice, beans, cotton, potatoes, and sesame. But millet was the staple. That's what we cultivated most."

"When did you begin to have problems growing enough food to live on?"

"The problems started in the north and in the nearby highlands. In the lower-lying areas, the yields were all right, but the rocky soils in the highlands could not retain water, and there was not enough rain anyway. We would enrich the poorer, sandy soils by covering the ground with compost and manure, and we would leave a field fallow for ten years so it would become productive again. But as the drought got worse and the good land became more and more scarce, we had to cultivate the fields continually, and the yields fell off as the soils became exhausted."[7]

"When did you first experience hunger?"

"It was not only me. It was a whole generation. I grew up with hunger. It was only my older brother who knew what it was like to eat two or three times a day. By the time I was a child, we were already living with famine."

"How did you survive?"

"Honestly, it was painful. You're hungry, and there is no food. You are like a sick person because your stomach is constantly churning and making growling noises, and you feel very weak. Even when people say 'Let's go,' you can't move, you can't do anything, you don't have the physical strength."

"You must have eaten something."

"We ate leaves. Our mother collected leaves from the baobab tree to make a sauce. Sometimes she boiled the leaves; sometimes she dried them in the sun and kept them. If she had maize flour, she would mix the leaves with the flour and water and add a little salt. We ate leaves. No condiments. Nothing extra. We ate these leaves to fill our bellies."

"Only baobab leaves?"

"We gathered leaves from several trees—tueiga [baobab], kegelega, zilega, and two vines called lélungo and bulvaka."

"Did you kill livestock for food?"

"No. That would have been only a short-term solution. If you killed the animals, you would not be able to replace them. We drank the milk, but the only time we ate meat was when an animal was going to die, not when we were hungry."

"Were there times when you had real food?"

"Three months a year we would have real food—tomatoes, wild aubergines, okra, haricots, chickpeas, maize on the cob, and three kinds of millet: red, white, and small. For the other nine months, we would eat leaves. The adults could eat leaves, but the children could not always do so. They grew weak, they were sick for a while, and they died."

"As a child, you must have seen a lot of death."

"Yes, but you did not see the bodies. It is our custom, when someone dies, not to allow strangers to see the body. You will be told, 'So-and-so died'—that's all. The elders take care of that business. In their opinion, children don't have the mental strength to see a dead body. It would keep them from sleeping, and they would grow weak."

"Did you imagine that you might die of hunger?"

"Yes, of course. We didn't have anything to eat. I remember one year that was really, really bad. No one had anything. The animals were dying, people ate meat that was bad, and even the trees that produced those leaves were not there."

"You said before that many people were migrating south, but your family stayed in Damesma."

"Yes. Some people knew that now was the time to leave. Others knew this but did not have the means to move. Others stayed, thinking things would get better. There was an organization that helped villagers move, taking them in big trucks to better areas. It was when I was very young. I heard people talking about moving to Bitto or Bobo,[8] but I don't remember all the names of the places people moved to or the name of the organization that moved them."[9]

"But you stayed because your father was chief and was obliged to remain in the village?"

"Yes. His father and his father's father before him, going back hundreds of years . . . they had been *tenga naba* in Damesma. My father did think of sending some of the family away, but he would have to stay. If he left, the village would have to be abandoned. There would be no leadership, no government. Nothing would have been organized because he was the one who organized everything, who saw that things were working, that certain tasks were done. If he left, lawlessness would have followed. The strong would have exploited the weak. People would have been hurt. He had to protect everyone and keep the peace."

"But you did leave Damesma, didn't you, to go to school? Did your father consider this a risk, thinking you might lose touch with tradition if you got an education?"

"No, because I came home every day. Even though the school was in Delaga, eight kilometers away, we were still together. My father wanted it that way, the family close, the kids all in one place."

"Did your father value education?"

"Yes. My father was really an intellectual. He never went to school, but he had a sharp mind. His younger brother went to school. My father would take him every morning and bring him home every afternoon because in those days there were lions along the road, and lions sometimes attacked people. When he was a boy, my father didn't realize the importance of education, but later he would wonder why he had to walk his younger brother to and from school every day but not attend school himself. If he wanted to write a letter, he had to rely on his younger brother to write it. If he needed to read a letter, he would have to ask his younger brother to read it to him. So when he had his first son, he sent him to school. But my older brother didn't like it. It didn't work out. So my father sent his four younger sons, saying, 'Well, I am going to send you to school because I know it will help you in the future. It won't help me, but it will help you.' It was a complete joy for us to attend school, to learn how to read and write. People in the village would come to our father and say, 'I want your son to write a letter for me.' In the beginning, my father always said, 'Sure, it's not a problem,' but after a while, he began to say, 'No, you don't send your children to school, so why should my children write letters for you?' It was his way of encouraging other parents to send their kids to school. You know, in the village at that time, there was no telephone, no telegraph. You could only communicate by letter, so there was a problem with privacy. If you got someone from outside your family to write a letter for you, that person will know everything that is in the letter, and he could go and tell other people about your personal business. If it is your own son or you writing the letter, the contents remain a secret. But we also saw the advantages of being able to read and write for getting a job away from the village. We could escape."

Ibrahim completed elementary school, but secondary school was beyond his father's means.

"It was very sad," Ibrahim said. "I almost lost my mind. I had hoped to be like the others, to win a scholarship and continue with my education. Suddenly, it had to be abandoned. It was as though I had been abandoned. I lost hope completely because I saw that nothing would change. My one thought was that someone might offer to pay my school fees and that I could finish secondary school and get a job. My dream had been to become a doctor or to gain the technical skills to build a big house or start a business. Those were my dreams, but at that moment, without the means to pay for my schooling, I saw no future for me at all. The whole thing upset me so much that I let it go. It was something that simply befell me [*arrive à moi*]. I didn't have any more hope. I thought I was finished."

"What did you do?"

"I looked after my father's animals. I tended the crops."

"Did you see this as a worthwhile life?"

"No, because there is nothing you can learn from doing that."

When T. S. Eliot wrote in *Four Quartets* "What we call the beginning is often the end," he was probably not thinking of migrants and refugees. Yet this one line of poetry captures the bitter irony that every gain we make in life comes at the cost of something we must forfeit, forget, forsake, or leave behind. Ibrahim was not alone among the migrants I came to know in Europe who in beginning a new life lost touch with the old and came to regret it. "When I am here [Holland]," Ibrahim told me, "I am obliged to leave behind many things that I know, that I have seen, that I love, in order to participate in this society. Life is solitary here. People don't spend so much time *en famille*. Back home, when you have a problem, the whole family is involved. Here, when you have a problem, either you have to solve it alone or you expect the state to solve it. On the other hand, when I am in Burkina, I have to adapt to the rhythm of life there, which means I cannot do everything I want to do or become the person I dreamed of becoming."

If I have dwelled on Ibrahim's situation at some length it is because I have wanted to avoid reducing lived experience to categorical formulations such as structure versus agency or environmental determinism versus freewill. Self-alteration can be as adventitious as it is planned, and its repercussions can never be predicted. At any moment in a person's life, contrary moods, emotions, and imperatives will come to the fore or fade into the background, and it is often impossible to pin down the precise motives or purposes that inform these fluctuations in consciousness and behavior. Nevertheless, I have always assumed that the existential viability of any human life consists in a sense that one's own thoughts, feelings, words, and deeds matter to others and that this interplay of self and other is reciprocal rather than parasitic.

While collective existence depends on binding legal and moral laws (*nomos*), personal fulfillment in life (*phusis*) depends on more than slavish conformity to established norms, dutiful role-playing, or adherence to tradition. It involves going beyond the social world into which one is born and tapping into life itself, which knows no bounds.

For people everywhere, the process of leaving home, becoming responsible for oneself, and establishing a family or career of one's own is as necessary as it is arduous. We are born into a world that has been made by others at other times. Our conception and birth were not our choices. This is the burden of childhood: to be acted upon to such a degree that one's freedom to act on one's own initiative is continually curbed or compromised. To become an adult is not only to choose one's own path; it is to give birth to oneself and even create the kind of world in which one would like one's children to live. This hope may be illusory, but it is perhaps the most splendid illusion we ever entertain.

NOTES

1. Christopher Houston (2022). This phenomenological approach was also outlined and illustrated in a seminal paper by Paul Riesman (1986). Riesman's work was followed by Michael Jackson and Ivan Karp's edited 1990 volume, *The Experience of Self and Other in African Cultures*.
2. Ivan Karp calls this "the paradox of agency." In spirit possession, for instance, an individual voluntarily participates in a ritual process in which they will become possessed by a spirit. But unless they remain, albeit partially, in possession of themselves, they will be unable to return to their previous self-state. See Karp (1988, 36–52). See also Jackson and Karp's (1990, 20–21) *The Experience of Self and Other in African Cultures*.
3. This model of multiple selfhoods is not to be confused with multiple personality disorder, when, as Philip M. Bromberg (2006, 191) puts it, the normally "flexible multiplicity of relatively harmonious self-states... becomes a rigid multiplicity of adversarial self-states" (now known as dissociative identity disorder).
4. See W. B. Yeats's "An Acre of Grass": "Grant me an old man's frenzy / Myself must I remake" (1997, 308).
5. *No Direction Home*—Bob Dylan documentary, directed by Martin Scorsese (Dylan 2005). The title is from Dylan's song "Like a Rolling Stone" (*Highway 61 Revisited*).
6. Kaya is a provincial capital on the Mossi Plateau, a center for weaving and tanning. When Ibrahim first visited the city, it had a population of about thirty thousand.
7. Della E. McMillan provides details of the six major categories of arable land in and around Damesma, noting that "land types differ not only in natural soil fertility but in their vulnerability to flooding and drought, suitability for different crops, and ease of cultivation. Given the erratic rainfall, water retention is generally the most valued characteristic of a field" (1995, 177).
8. People in Damesma often referred to Bitto, a town near the Ghana border, and Bobo Dioulassa, a city inhabited by large numbers of Mossi migrants, as generic and general terms for the new settlements in the south-central and southwest areas, respectively (McMillan 1995, 21).
9. The organization was the Volta Valley Authority (Autorité des Aménagements des Vallées des Volta; AVV), and people were being moved from the densely populated Mossi Plateau and resettled in new villages in the sparsely settled river basins to the south.

REFERENCES

Arendt, Hannah. 1958. *The Human Condition*. Chicago: University of Chicago Press.
———. 2005. *On Revolution*. New York: Penguin.
Bromberg, Philip M. 1993. *Standing in the Spaces: Essays on Clinical Process, Trauma, and Dissociation*. Hillsdale, N.J.: Analytical Press.
———. 2006. *Awakening the Dreamer: Clinical Journeys*. Hillsdale, N.J.: Analytical Press.
Brontë, Charlotte. 1864. *Jane Eyre: An Autobiography*. New York: Harper.
Cardinal, Marie. 1984. *The Words to Say It: An Autobiographical Novel*. Translated by Pat Goodheart. Cambridge, Mass.: Van Vector & Goodheart.
Dylan, Bob, vocalist. 1965. "It's Alright, Ma (I'm Only Bleeding)." Track 10 on *Bringing It All Back Home*. Columbia Records.
———. 2005. *No Direction Home*. Directed by Martin Scorcese. Documentary film. American Masters. First aired September 27, 2005. Prime Video.
Horace. 1994. *Epistles*. Cambridge: Cambridge University Press.
Houston, Christopher. 2022. "Alternative Me? Anthropology and Self-Alteration." *HAU: Journal of Ethnographic Theory* 12 (2): 482–498. https://doi.org/10.1086/720356.
Jackson, Michael. 1995. *At Home in the World*. Durham, N.C.: Duke University Press.
———. 2021. *Coincidences*. Berkeley: University of California Press.
Jackson, Michael, and Ivan Karp. 1990. *The Experience of Self and Other in African Cultures*. Edited by Michael Jackson and Ivan Karp. Stockholm: Almqvist and Wiksell.
James, William. 1950. *Principles of Psychology*. Vol. 1. New York: Dover.
Karp, Ivan. 1988. "Laughter at Marriage: Subversion in Performance." *Journal of the Folklore Institute* 25 (1–2): 36–52.
McMillan, Della E. 1995. *Sahel Visions: Planned Settlement and River Blindness Control in Burkina Faso*. Tucson: University of Arizona Press.
Melville, Herman. 1990. *The Confidence Man: His Masquerade*. Harmondsworth: Penguin.
Miller, Henry. 1934. *Tropic of Cancer*. Paris: Obelisk Press.
Mitchell, Stephen A. 1993. *Hope and Dread in Psychoanalysis*. New York: Basic Books.
Montaigne, Michel de. 1993. *The Essays: A Selection*. Translated by M. A. Screech. Harmondsworth: Penguin.
Ngata, Sir Apirana T. 1972. *Rauru-nui-ā-Toi lectures and Ngati Kahungunu Origin*. Wellington: Victoria University Press.
Riesman, Paul. 1986. "The Person and the Life-Cycle in African Social Life and Thought." *African Studies Review* 29 (2): 71–198.
Rushdie, Salman. 2012. *The Wizard of Oz*. 2nd ed. London: Palgrave Macmillan.
Sreenivasan, Hari. 2022. *PBS Newshour*. S2022, E36. Aired February 5, 2022.
Yeats, W. B. 1997. "An Acre of Grass." In *The Poems*, 308. 2nd ed. New York: Scribner.

ACKNOWLEDGMENTS

It is a real pleasure to thank our students, our colleagues past and present, and our interlocutors for their contributions, implicit or explicit, to the generation of this book. Through you all, we encountered the privilege of becoming. We wish to name Professor Joel Kahn in particular, supervisor extraordinaire and intellectual mentor for us both.

J. P. & C.

NOTES ON CONTRIBUTORS

JEAN-PAUL BALDACCHINO is an associate professor of anthropology at the University of Malta. He is also a warranted practicing Lacanian psychoanalyst. He has published his research based on fieldwork in Korea, Malta, Italy, and Australia. His work appeared in the *Australian Journal of Anthropology, European Journal of Asian Studies, Korea Journal, British Journal of Psychotherapy, Social Compass, Critique of Anthropology,* and *Ethnicities,* among others. His latest publication is an edited volume with Professor Jon Mitchell: *Morality, Crisis and Capitalism: An Anthropology for Troubled Times,* published in 2022.

MAX HARWOOD is a sessional lecturer and adjunct fellow in the discipline of anthropology at Macquarie University and a senior associate with the New South Wales Government's Countering Violent Extremism program. His PhD dissertation comparatively studied Turkish and Israeli masculinity in the context of military conscription and historical nationalism. His current research is on modern White nationalism and far-right extremism—specifically the online subculture, politics, and phenomenology of Australian White nationalists—as well as the globalized phenomenon of replacement theory held by violent extremists. As an anthropologist, he specializes in ethnographic filmmaking.

GIL HIZI is a Humboldt Postdoctoral Fellow in Anthropology in the Global South Studies Center at the University of Cologne. He earned his PhD at the University of Sydney in 2018. His articles have been published in a number of journals, including *Ethos, Social Analysis, Asian Studies Review,* and *HAU.*

CHRISTOPHER HOUSTON is a professor of anthropology at Macquarie University, Sydney. He has carried out extensive fieldwork in Turkey on Islamic social movements, nationalism, urban processes in Istanbul, political activists, and the Kurdish issue. His recent books include *Istanbul, City of the Fearless: Urban Activism, Coup D'état, and Memory in Turkey* (2020) and *Theocracy, Secularism, and Islam in Turkey: Anthropocratic Republic* (2021).

MICHAEL JACKSON is an anthropologist and author with extensive fieldwork experience in Sierra Leone and Aboriginal Australia. He is a Senior Research Fellow in World Religions at Harvard Divinity School and is the author of numerous books of anthropology, poetry, and fiction.

MUHAMMAD A. KAVESH is an Australian Research Council DECRA Fellow at the Australian National University. He is the author of *Animal Enthusiasms* (2021) and coeditor of two journal special issues (*Anthropology Today* [February 2023] and the *Australian Journal of Anthropology* [2021]). He has also published with *American Ethnologist*, *Journal of Asian Studies*, *Oxford Journal of Development Studies*, *South Asia*, *Society & Animals*, and *Senses & Society*, among others. He is currently working on his second book project (on spy pigeons) and a coedited volume (*Nurturing Alternative Futures*).

GISELLA ORSINI is a senior lecturer in anthropology and a research associate at the Mediterranean Institute at the University of Malta. She is currently the head of the Department of Anthropological Sciences. Her research interests include gender and health, medical anthropology, body and culture, and eating disorders.

NIGEL RAPPORT is an emeritus professor of anthropological and philosophical studies at the University of St. Andrews and the founding director of the St. Andrews Centre for Cosmopolitan Studies. His most recent monograph is *Cosmopolitan Love and Individuality: Ethical Engagement beyond Culture* (2019).

KATHRYN ROUNTREE is an emeritus professor of anthropology at Massey University, New Zealand. She has published widely on contemporary Paganism and shamanism, pilgrimage and embodiment, the contestation of sacred sites, feminist spirituality and animism, and the relationship between religion and science. Her research fields include Malta, Turkey, Ireland, and New Zealand. Her recent edited books include *Cosmopolitanism, Nationalism, and Modern Paganism* (2017), *Contemporary Pagan and Native Faith Movements in Europe* (2015), and *Archaeology of Spiritualities* (coedited, 2012). Her monographs include *Crafting Contemporary Pagan Identities in a Catholic Society* (2010) and *Embracing the Witch and the Goddess* (2004).

BANU ŞENAY is a senior lecturer in the discipline of anthropology at Macquarie University, Sydney. Her current research on Islamic art pedagogies in Istanbul engages with debates in anthropology around skilled learning, ethics, and Islamic cultural politics. Her most recent book is *Musical Ethics and Islam: The Art of Playing the Ney* (2020).

JAAP TIMMER is an associate professor at Macquarie University and currently a Senior Fellow at the Aarhus Institute of Advanced Studies, Aarhus University, Denmark. His research focuses on historicity, religion, and sovereignty in Solomon Islands and Indonesian Papua.

INDEX

Page numbers in *italics* refer to figures.

ABC of Socialism, The (Huberman), 82
Academy of Fine Arts, Istanbul, 25
activism, 75; in Algeria, 85–86; apprentice, 88; in Istanbul, 73–74; self-change fostered through, 2; in Turkey, 85–86
actual, self-alteration as, 184
addicts (*nashai*), 172
Akerlund, Ebba, 105
Albitaiya (inselberg), 197
Albrecht of Urach, 96
Algeria, 73, 77–79, 85–87
Algerians, The (*Sociologie de l'Algerie*; Bourdieu), 73, 78
All Nations' Worldwide Watch (prayer network), 65
All Pacific Arise (APA), 57, 60–61, 65–66, 67
Al Noor Mosque, 92
Alter, Joseph S., 164–165
analysis: ethics of, 156–157; Jungian, 148; training, 148. *See also* psychoanalysis
analytical psychology, 148
Anarchism or Socialism? (Stalin), 82
Anderson, Benedict, 100
animists, Indigenous, 44
Annadorai, George, 66
Annual of Urdu Studies, at University of Wisconsin–Madison, 175n1
anorexia nervosa, 10–11, 116; distorted body image and, 121; morality motivating, 111–112; resistance to treatment of, 122
anthropologists, the "self" engaged by, 154
anthropology, 35; ethics and, 156–157; of psychoanalysis, 145–148; salvage, 93; as self-transformation, 158
Anthropology of Ethics (Faubion), 35
anti-colonial socialism, in Algeria, 77–79
apprentice activism, 88
aqal (intelligence), 170, 175
Arendt, Hannah, 194, 199
Argentina, 147
Arkadaş (Friend; film), 82

Armstrong, Herbert W., 58–59
art therapy, 122, *123*
Aryan symbols, 101
as if principle, 140
asmani tippler pigeon competition, 170
Atatürk, Kemal, 80
Atatürk Education Institute, 84
Atomea, Martha Safina, 63
Australian legal system, 4
autonomy, 8, 132–135
Autorité des Aménagements des Vallées des Volta (Volta Valley Authority), 201, 206n8
Azhar, Mirza Ali, 168

Babyn Yar, in Ukraine, 90
Bachelard, Gaston, 29
Bach-Zelewski, Erich von dem, 91
Badiou, Alain, 7, 154
Bakhtin, Mikhail, 19n4
Barker, John, 56
Bateson, Gregory, 180
"because motives," "in order to motives" contrasted with, 184
Beevor, Antony, 91
being, capacities of, 30–33
Belomor (Draskoczy), 76–77
bemari (disease), 172
Ben-Shahar, Tal, 140
Biehl, Joao, 8
Bilgin, Salih, 25, 27
Bird-David, Nurit, 44, 49
birth, 197–199
birth of a nation, death evoked in, 199
Bitto, in Burkina Faso, 206n8
Black Sabbath Ozzfest, 182, 185
Boas, Franz, 145
Bobo Dioulassa, Burkina Faso, 206n8
bodies: functional, 120–124; moral, 118–120, *123*; moral superiority compared through, 119

213

bodily symptoms, emotional distress discerning, 142n3
bodily techniques of self-alteration, 16
body, mind separated from, 117–118
bonheur (happiness; *xingfu*), 138–139, 152
Bourdieu, Pierre, 73, 77, 79, 85, 87
Bozarslan, Hamit, 87
breath (*nefes*), 30
Breivik, Anders, 92, 96–97, *103*; in "Knights Templar" uniform, 99, *100*; self-alteration by, 106–107; social life expunged by, 99; steroids abused by, 104; White nationalism epitomized by, 93
Britain, neoliberalism influencing, 1
Bromberg, Philip M., 206n3
Buber, Martin, 93
Buenos Aires, Argentina, 147, 158n1
Burkina Faso, 200–202, 205, 206nn7–8
Burt, Ben, 57
Bushido (samurai) code, 99

Cambodia, 199
capitalism, 142; neoliberal, 2, 4, 12, 34, 41; New Age spiritualities and, 46; self-improvement promoted by, 4, 128
Caputo, John D., 154
Cardinal, Marie, 197
care: harmony achieved through, 174; maternal, 171
Cassidy, Rebecca, 164
category of the self, sense of the self contrasted with, 5
Catholicism, 124n4, 158n2
causality of self-alteration, 3
Çayan, Mahir, 87
Cendrars, Blaise, 199
Champion Training (program), 130–131, 134–135, 138
chaxugeju (differential mode of association), 134
Cheney, Ann M., 117
chief, village, 201
China, 139, 141–142, 142n3; Jinan in, 130–132; positive psychology embraced in, 137–138; self-improvement in, 128–129; Shandong Province in, 130–132
Christchurch massacre, 92, 96
Christian Crusades, 102
Christianity, 52n2; Jungian analysis welcoming, 148; Malaita reviving, 58; Melanesia impacted by, 56; self-alteration and, 42; Solomon Islands influenced by, 12, 66–67
chronotope, 19n4
class, self-awareness of, 80
Clay, Henry, 42
cognitive-behavioral techniques, 142n4
cognitive behavior therapy (CBT), 147
Cohen, Anthony, 183
collective self, personal self contrasted with, 45
Collins, Randall, 140–141
colonialism, selfhood impacted by, 11
colonial literature, postcolonial resistance writings contrasted with, 168
Comaroff, Jean, 11
Comaroff, John L., 11
communication technologies, self-alteration enabled by, 17
Compendium, The (*2083*; Breivik), 94, 97–98, 103
complete human (*insan-ı kâmil*; perfect human), 29
"conceptual instrumentarium" for self-alteration, 3
consciousness, 184, 194; the individual attached to, 179; participatory, 51; Starhawk discussing, 47
Constance Hospital, 181–186
consulting rooms, 149
contexts of self-alteration, 3
conversation (*sohbet*), 31–32
cooking, gender associated with, 34
coop (*khokha*) competition, 163, 169–170, 175
cosmopolitan politesse, 188, 190–191
counselors, national exam licensing, 131–132
COVID-19 pandemic, rituals impacted by, 43, 48–49
craft (*techne*), 15
Crapanzano, Vincent, 145, 157, 158
crazy dancing (*kuangwu*), 131
criminals, political prisoners contrasted with, 76
Crisp, Arthur H., 121
cultural traditions of self-alteration, 10

Damesma, Burkina Faso, 200–202, 204, 206n7
dancing, crazy, 131
Dave, Naisargi, 87
death, 197; birth of a nation evoking, 199; fasting to, 15; living, 97; social, 198, 200

death squads, SS, 90
decision-events, 7, 59
declarations (*demeç*), 83–84
decolonizing movement, philosophy reevaluated by, 6–7
Deep Sea Canoe revelations, 65
Delaga, Burkina Faso, 204
demeç (declarations), 83–84
Denmark, 196–197
depression, 158n3
Descola, Philippe, 44
developmental stage of self-alteration, 183, 184
deviancy, normality transformed into, 120
Devrimci Yol (newspaper), 83–84
Dev Yol (Revolutionary Way; mass movement), 79
differential mode of association (*chaxugeju*), 134
Dikmen, Halil, 25
direction of travel of self-alteration, 183
disease (*bemari*), 172
distorted body image, anorexia nervosa and, 121
dividual, the individual contrasted with, 6, 19n1
"doctrine of emptiness," 98, 106
dönüştürücü (transformative), 28
Draskoczy, Julie, 76
Duranti, Alessandro, 26
Dylan, Bob, 198

Easterneuk, Scotland, 181
Eastern Highlands of New Guinea, 200
eating disorders, 119; contexts of care for, 113; female patients with, 124n2; illness narratives on, 112; residential center treating, 113, 115, 117, 120; self-alteration through, 111, 124; womanhood contextualizing, 117. *See also* anorexia nervosa; residential center, eating disorders treated at
ego (*nafs*), 37
8chan, 98
Einsatzgruppen (SS death squads), 90
Eliot, T. S., 205
embodied subjectivity, 182
Emerson, Ralph Waldo, 181, 187
emotional distress, bodily symptoms discerned through, 142n3
emulation of teacher, 36
enterprising self, 142n1

enthusiasm (*shauq*), 171, 172, 175
episteme, craft contrasted with, 15
Erdoğdular, Ömer, 35
Esterik, Penny Van, 116
ethical modifications, musical training influencing, 31
ethical subjectivity, 12
ethics, 35; of analysis, 156–157; anthropology and, 156–157; of self-alteration, 4; social, 187–190
ethnopsychology, Mauss impacting, 6
Europe, Burkina Faso contrasted with, 205
European ways (*sekgoa*), 11
Evangelical Fellowship of the South Pacific, 64
event, 7, 59, 153–154
existential power, individuality and, 179–183
extracurricular programs for self-improvement, 13
Eyre, Jane, 198

Facebook, 48
familial relationships, 138
famine, 203
Fanon, Frantz, 77, 87
fascism, "rugged virility" idealized by, 104–105
fasting, 62
fasting to death (*Sallekhana*), 15
Faubion, James, 35
female patients with eating disorders, 124n2
femininity, 116–117
Fernandez, James, 180
fieldwork, self-alteration engendered by, 19
Fire in the Islands! (book), 58
Fitzpatrick, Sheila, 79
flute, reed. *See* reed flute (*ney*)
flyers, pigeon. *See* pigeon flyers
folk songs (*türkü*), 81
Foucault, Michel, 150
Fouillé, Alfred, 44
4chan, 17, 98, 103, 107n1
Four Quartets (Eliot), 205
Four Winds School of Shamanic Healing, 42
Frank, Arthur W., 114
Frankl, Viktor, 137
French colonial system, 77
Freud, Sigmund, 13

García Márquez, Gabriel, 202
Gbenye, Christopher, 199
gecekondu (shantytowns), 81–82

Geertz, Clifford, 6
Gellner, Ernest, 191–192
gender, 10, 34, 83
genealogies, Ophir connected to, 60
gentle masculinity, 171
Glass-Coffin, Bonnie, 18
global, self-alteration and the, 191–192
God, Maeliau communing with, 61–63, 66
good society, 188–190
Gooldin, Sigal, 116
Gorky, Maxim, 73, 75, 85
Govindrajan, Radhika, 164
Great Replacement, The (*TGR*; Tarrant), 94, 105
Greek (*Unani*) medicine, 174
Greenwood, Susan, 48
Griffiths, Alison, 58
group identity, individual autonomy via, 132–135
Grubbs, Kathleen, 117
Guardian (newspaper), 1
Guevara, Che, 86
guidance (*Irsad*), 33
Gulag Archipelago (Solzhenitsyn), 75
Güney, Yilmaz, 82
gwa bi'u (shrine; tabu-sanctum), 65–66

Hagar Qim Neolithic temple, 43
hâl dili (language of disposition), 35
haphazard, self-alteration as, 184
happiness (*bonheur*; *xingfu*), 138–139, 152
Harding, Susan Friend, 3
harmony, care achieving, 174
hearing, capacities of, 30–33
Heart's Secret (program), 130–131, 133–134
Heelas, Paul, 41–46, 135
Heraclitus (philosopher), 195
Hermes' Dilemma (Crapanzano), 158
Hess, Tom, 65
Hezarfen (studio), 28
hierarchy of needs (Maslow), 137
Himmler, Heinrich, 90–91, 95
Hirschkind, Charles, 33
Hitler, Adolf, 96
hoca (master), 26
Hoca, Salih, 28, 32, 34
Honiara, Solomon Islands, 64
Horace (poet), 195
Houston, Christopher, 94, 194
Huberman, Leo, 82
human being (*insan*), 26

Human Potential movement, 45
humility (*tevazu*), 35–36
Humphrey, Caroline, 7, 9, 19n2, 59, 154, 157
Husserl, Edmund, 26, 75
"hyper"-masculinity, 171

Ibn Arabi, 29
identity: the individual creating, 180; individuality distinguished from, 134; pigeon flyers restructuring, 172–173
illness narratives, 112, 114–115
Illouz, Eva, 13
imaginary, self-alteration as, 184
imagination, Sufi poetry prompting, 29–30
Imperial Japanese Army (IJA), 95
inclination (*meyil*), 36
Indigenous animists, Western shamans compared with, 44
individual, the, 74; consciousness attaching to, 179; dividual contrasted with, 6, 19n1; Humphrey on, 19n2; identity created with, 180; self-alteration forced upon, 184; selfhood created by, 192; traditions influencing, 178
individual autonomy via group identity, 132–135
individual human self, 44, 51–52
individualism, 135–136
individuality, 187; existential power and, 179–183; identity distinguished from, 134; intimacy contrasted with, 188
individualization, 133–137
"in order to motives," "because motives" distinguished from, 184
insan (human being), 26
insan-ı kâmil (complete human; perfect human), 29
intelligence (*aqal*), 170, 175
interpersonal skills, positive psychology improving, 130
interpretative frameworks of self-alteration, 154–155
intersubjectivity, self-alteration engendered by, 8–9
intimacy, individuality contrasted with, 188
intoxication (*nasha*), 165
Irigaray, Luce, 190
Islam, 28, 33
Israel, 61–62, 178
Israelites, Malaita founded by, 59–60

Istanbul, 80, 88; activism in, 73–74; reed flute artists recontextualizing, 34–35; revolutionary politics in, 79
Istanbul Academy of Fine Arts, 25
Italian Ministry of Health, 113
Italy: Catholicism in, 124n4; Naples, 196–197; national health-care system of, 113; Rome, 196–197
I. V. Stalin White Sea–Baltic Sea Canal, 73, 75–76

Jainism, 15
James, William, 139, 195, 196
Japan, psychoanalysis in, 146–147
Japanese Psychoanalytical Association, 147
Japanese Zen. *See* Zen, Japanese
Jerusalem Council, 61
Jerusalem House of Prayer, 65
Jiao (teacher), 132–133
Jinan, in Shandong Province, China, 130–132
jingshen (spirit), 138
Judaism, 60–65
Jungian analysis, Christianity welcomed by, 148

Kabul Airport (Afghanistan), 197
Kafka, Franz, 5
Karaca, Kemal, 83–84
Karp, Ivan, 206n2
Kavesh, Muhammad A., 8
Kemalism, 80–81
Kenny, Katherine, 17
Kharkhordin, Oleg, 76
khokha (coop) competition, 163, 169–170, 175
King Wajid Ali Shah of Awadh (Azhar), 168
kinship terminology for nonhuman beings, 49
Kipnis, Andrew, 53n12
Kirkwood, William, 33
Kleinman, Arthur, 17, 142n3
"Knights Templar Log" (Breivik), 97
"Knights Templar" uniform, 99, *100*
Kohn, Eduardo, 44–45, 50–51, 53n14
kuangwu (crazy dancing), 131

Lacan, Jacques, 148, 152–153, 156–157, 158n1, 159n5
Laidlaw, James, 15
Lakoff, Andrew, 147, 158n1
Lambek, Michael, 157
Land of Ophir, The (Maeliau), 64, 68

language of disposition (*hâl dili*), 35
Lefebvre, Henri, 82
legal system, Australian, 4
Lester, Rebecca J., 116
Levinas, Emmanuel, 189
Li Chen, 131
life (*phusis*), 206
Lion of the Tribe of Judah, The (Maeliau), 68
listening, 30–33
Literature and Revolution (Trotsky), 74
living death, self-alteration completed in, 97
Locke, Peter, 8
lodges (*tekkes*), 27
London Olympics, 139
love (*pyar*), 49–50, 170, 173, 175
"loving speech" toward the Other, 190

maa ala pyar (maternal care), 171
maar (punishing), 173
Maasina Rule movement, 57
MacLaine, Shirley, 46, 52
Maeliau, Michael, 12, 17, 57; God communed with, 61–63, 66; Malaita changed by, 61; prophetic vision received by, 64–65; self-alteration by, 58, 60, 67–68
Magliocco, Sabina, 51
makam (musical mode), 30
Malaita, 57–58; Israelites founding, 59–60; Judaism and, 63–64, 65; Maeliau changing, 61; prophets in, 65–66; Remnant Church in, 63; SSEC influencing, 58
Malinowski, Bronislaw, 145
Malta, 10, 42, 53n15, 148
Malta Depth Psychology Association, 148
Mama Cocha (Incan goddess), 53n16
Maoism, 74–75, 134
Marvin, Garry, 164
masculinity, 103–104, 171
Maslow, Abraham H., 137
mass murder, moral relativism justifying, 105
master (*hoca*), 26
Masud, Naiyer, 11–12, 166–169, 172, 175n1
material transformation, 99–103
maternal care (*maa ala pyar*), 171
Matiabe, Aruru, 63
Matthew, Gareth, 15
Mauss, Marcel, 5, 6, 173
McMadden, Roy, 185, 186
McMillan, Della E., 200–201
Melanesia, 56, 63–65

Melville, Herman, 196
Mendaña y Neira, Álvaro de, 59
mental strength, thinness demonstrating, 119
Mesnevi-ya Ma'navi (Doublets of meaning; Rumi), 29
Messick, Brinkley, 33
Metamorphosis (Kafka), 5
metaphors, 32
methods of self-alteration, 3, 14–18
meyil (inclination), 36
migrants, social death experienced by, 198, 200
Mill, John Stuart, 178
Miller, Henry, 199
mind, body separated from, 117–118
Ministry of Health, Italian, 113
mirror therapy, 120–122
modification, 26
"Moment That Changed Me, A" (column), 1
Money-Kyrle, Roger, 151
Montaigne, Michel de, 196
morality, anorexia nervosa motivated by, 111–112
moral laws (*nomos*), 206
moral relativism, mass murder justified through, 105
moral superiority, bodies compared through, 119
Moran, Dermot, 38
more-than-human self-alteration, 166–169
Mosse, George L., 98, 103, 104
motives, "because" contrasted with "in order to," 184
mourning genres, 84
multiple personality disorder, 206n3
multiple selfhoods, 206n3
Murdoch, Iris, 188
Muse, John, 169
musical mode (*makam*), 30
musical training, ethical modification influenced by, 31
mutualistic relationship, 164, 175
myna (bird), 166–167
Myna from Peacock Garden, The (*Taos Chaman ki Myna*; Masud), 11–12, 166–169

nafs (ego), 37
Naples, Italy, 196–197
narratives: of illness, 112; of self-alteration, 17–18; the self reconceptualized through, 113–115

nasha (intoxication), 165
nashai (addicts), 172
national exam, counselors licensed through, 131–132
national health-care system of Italy, 113
National Liberation Front (FLN), 77
National Movement Party (Turkey), 84
nature of the self, 4
Nazis, 90, 95
nefes (breath), 30
nefs. *See* self (*nefs*)
neoliberal capitalism, 2, 4, 12, 34, 41
neoliberalism, 1, 13
neoliberalization, 12
neoshamanism. *See* Western shamans
New Age spiritualities, 41, 45–47
New Guinea, 200
New Year's Eve, new beginnings celebrated during, 196–197
New Zealand government, 96
ney. *See* reed flute (*ney*)
neyzens. *See* reed flute artists (*neyzens*)
Nietzsche, Friedrich, 178, 179, 182
nomos (moral laws), 206
nonhuman beings, kinship terminology for, 49
normality, deviancy transforming into, 120
norms: self-alteration and, 140; thinness not motivated by, 11; workshops and, 134, 138
Nussbaum, Martha, 191
nutritional therapy, 121

Obadia, Julienne, 135
obituaries, declarations contrasted with, 83–84
O'Connor, Richard A., 116
Ohlendorf, Otto, 90–91
Ohnuki-Tierney, Emiko, 147
Olympics, in London, 139
One Hundred Years of Solitude (García Márquez), 202
One New Man in Christ, The (Annadorai), 66
One of Us (nonfiction), 90
"On the Inconstancy of Our Actions" (Montaigne), 196
Operation Barbarossa, 90
Ophir, genealogies connected to, 60–61
organizational mode of association (*tuanti geju*), 134
Oslo terrorist attack, 90, 92, 96
Other, "loving speech" toward the, 190

Ouedraego, Ibrahim, in Burkina Faso, 200
Overman (*Übermensch*), 183
Özbek, Bülent, 32, 81
Özçimi, Sadrettin, 32
Ozzfest, Black Sabbath, 182, 185

Pagans, modern, 42, 47–48, 52n3
Pakistan, 164, 169–170, 175
Pakistani men, mutualistic relationship influencing, 164
pandemic, COVID-19, 43, 48–49
Papua New Guinea, 63
Parekh, Bhikhu, 191
participation in self-alteration, 18, 85
participatory consciousness, 51
Pentecostal Principle, The (Wariboko), 67
People's Liberation Army (THKO), 82
People's Republic of China, 138
perekova (reforging), 76
perfect human (*insan-ı kâmil*; complete human), 29
perpetual modification, self-alteration as, 25–30
personal change, self-alteration as about, 37
personal self, collective self contrasted with, 45
phenomenology, 94
philosophy, decolonizing movement reevaluating, 6–7
phusis (life), 206
physical labor, redemptive path of, 76
physical withdrawal, 97
pigeon flyers: in coop competition, 163; enthusiasm motivating, 172, 175; identity restructured in, 172–173; knowledge advantaging, 171–172; pigeons as interdependent with, 174; the self recontextualized by, 165
play, process of, 170
poetic imagination, reed flute and, 27–30
poetic speech, 32–33
political prisoners, criminals contrasted with, 76
porous individualization, 135–137
porous self, 136
positive energy (*zheng nengliang*), 139–140
positive psychology, 129; China embracing, 137–138; interpersonal skills improved through, 130; self-improvement via, 141
postcolonial resistance writings, colonial literature contrasted with, 168
posthumanism, 53n12

power (*shakti*), 164
prophets, in Malaita, 65–66
psychoanalysis, 146–153, 158n2; anthropology of, 145–148; in Buenos Aires, 147, 158n1; event in, 153–154; as inquisitorial confession, 150; in Japan, 146–147; reflexivity led to by, 155; as talking cure, 149; transformation in, 153–154
psychology: analytical, 148; positive, 129 (*see also* positive psychology)
psychotherapy, 148
Psychotherapy Profession Act, 148
punishing (*maar*), 173
pyar (love), 49–50, 170, 173, 175

Ram, Kalpana, 94
Rapport, Nigel, 6, 140–141
Read, Kenneth, 200
rebirth, 197–198
reed flute (*ney*), 8, 11; poetic imagination and, 27–30; Sufism bonded to, 27; symbolic discourse on, 29; transformative powers of, 28, 30
reed flute artists (*neyzens*): apprenticeship of, 25–27, 33–34, 37, 39; Istanbul recontextualized in, 34–35; self-alteration of, 18, 26
reflexivity, psychoanalysis leading to, 155
reforging (*perekova*), 76
relationship, mutualistic, 164, 175
religion, 42, 46. *See also* self-religion
religious cultures for self-alteration, 2
Remnant Church in Malaita, 63
replacement theory (terrorist subculture), 93, 96, 100
Report of the Royal Commission of Inquiry into the Terrorist Attack on Christchurch Masjidain (report), 107n1
residential center, eating disorders treated at, 113, 115, 117, 120
Revelation of the Glory of the Lord, The (Maeliau), 68
revolutionary political projects, self-alteration as imagined by, 73
revolutionary violence, 86
Revolutionary Way (*Dev Yol*; mass movement), 79
Revolution in the Revolution? (Guevara), 86
Revolution within the Revolution, The (Bourdieu), 78
Rhodes, Richard, 90

Ricoeur, Paul, 146
Riesman, Paul, 206n1
Rip It Up (Wiseman), 139
rituals, 43, 48–49, 53n9, 141
Rogers, Carl, 137–139
Rome (Italy), 196–197
Rose, Nikolas, 142n1
Rossmanith, Kate, 4
Rountree, Kathryn, 7, 9, 10–11, 17, 18
"rugged virility," fascism idealizing, 104–105
Rumi, Celaleddin, 29
Rushdie, Salman, 201
Russia, Stalinist, 16

Sallekhana (fasting to death), 15
salvage anthropology, replacement theory examined by, 93
Samhain (festival), 51
samurai (Bushido) code, 99
Sauser, Frédéric-Louis, 198–199
Saving the Modern Soul (Illouz), 13
Sayin, Niyazi, 25, 27, 32, 34–36, 38
scale of self-alteration, 183
Schütz, Alfred, 184
Schutzstaffel (SS), 90–92
Scotland, 178, 181
"Searching for a Melanesian Way of Worship" (Maeliau), 63
secret, self-alteration as, 184
Seierstad, Asne, 105
sekgoa (European ways), 11
self (*nefs*), 30; enterprising, 142n1; individual human, 44, 51–52; porous, 136
self, the, 10–14, 36; anthropologists engaging with, 154; apprenticeship changing, 37; changing conception of, 5–9; Crapanzano on, 145; cultural composition of, 7; enterprising, 142n1; individual human self contrasted with, 52; mutability of, 195; narratives reconceptualizing, 113–115; personal contrasted with collective, 37; pigeon flyers recontextualizing, 165; porous, 136; preconceiving of, 43–45; sense of contrasted with category of, 5; within social life, 183
self-acceptance, self-improvement balanced with, 46
self-alteration. *See specific topics*
Self and Self-Transformation in the History of Religions (Shulman and Stroumsa), 19n3

self-awareness of class, 80
self-change, activism fostering, 2
self-help culture, neoliberalism and, 13
selfhood: colonialism impacting, 11; the individual creating, 192; as multiple, 206n3
self-improvement: capitalism promoting, 4, 128; in China, 128–129; extracurricular programs for, 13; self-acceptance balanced with, 46; via positive psychology, 141
self-made man (trope), 41–42
self-perception as outsider, 115
self-religion, 42; Heelas coining, 41; individual human self focused on by, 51–52; New Age spiritualities as, 46–47
self-states, 195, 200
self-transformation, anthropology as, 158
Seligman, Martin E. P., 128–129, 137–139
Sengupta, Sagaree, 168
sense of the self, category of the self contrasted with, 5
Sermon on the Mount (Bible), 65
shakti (power), 164
shamans. *See* Western shamans
Shandong Province, China, 130–132
shantytowns (*gecekondu*), 81–82
"shape-shifting," internal, 9
shauq (enthusiasm), 171, 172, 175
shrine (*gwa bi'u*; tabu-sanctum), 65–66
Shulman, David, 19n3
Sierra Leone, 197
Silverstein, Brian, 36
Simmel, Georg, 187
Sisimia, Zebulon, 63
sistren (women), 10, 48–50
Smith, Karl, 136
social death, migrants experiencing, 198, 200
social ethics, self-alteration and, 187–191
socialism, 73, 77–79
social life, 187; Breivik expunging, 99; Emerson on, 181; the self within, 183
socially derived, self-alteration as, 184
society, good, 188–190
Sociologie de l'Algérie (*The Algerians*; Bourdieu), 73, 78
sohbet (conversation), 31–32
Solomon Islands, 12, 57, 64, 66–67. *See also* Malaita
Solzhenitsyn, Aleksandr, 75
Somers, Margaret R., 114
Sonnenrad (symbol), 101

Sorensen, Birgitte Refslund, 198
South Punjab, Pakistan, 169–170
South Sea Evangelical Church (SSEC), 57, 58, 63, 64
Soviet Union, 73, 78–79
spirit (*jingshen*), 138
spiritual practices for self-alteration, 2
sport, self-alteration through, 164–165
Sreenivasan, Hari, 197–198
Stalin, Joseph, 82
Stalinist Russia, 16
Stalin's White Sea (Gorky), 75
St. Andrews, Scotland, 178
St. Anthony's Day, Naples celebrating, 196–197
Starhawk and M. Macha NightMare, 53n14
steroids, anabolic, 104
Stroumsa, Guy G., 19n3
students, shantytowns worked in by, 81–82
subjective rectification, 153
subjectivity, embodied, 182
Sufi music pedagogy, self-alteration through, 38
Sufi poetry, imagination prompted by, 29–30
Sufism, 27, 37
Sufi tales, Islam constructed through, 28
Sullivan, Steve, 117
Susuro (boy), 200
Susuroka, New Guinea, 200
Suzuki, D. T., 91, 95, 104
Sviri, Sara, 37

tabu-sanctum (shrine; *gwa bi'u*), 65–66
tabu-speakers (*wane ni fo'a*), 65
Taigo, Furukawa, 98
Taos Chaman ki Myna (*The Myna from Peacock Garden*; Masud), 11–12, 166–169
Tarrant, Brenton, 91, 96–97, 101, 102, 103; *Compendium* inspiring, 98; self-alteration by, 106–107; steroids abused by, 104; White nationalism epitomizing, 93
teacher (*mürebbi*), 36
techne (craft), 15
techniques of self-alteration, 14–18
tekkes (lodges), 27
teleological, self-alteration as, 184
temporal dimension of self-alteration, 183
temporality of self-alteration, 3
temporary, self-alteration as, 129
tenga naba (village chief), 201

tevazu (humility), 35–36
theology of the event, 154
Theosophical Society, 52n1
therapy, 151; art, 122, 123; familial relationships prioritized in, 138; mirror, 120–122; nutritional, 121
thinness, 124n5; mental strength demonstrated through, 119; moral value associated with, 114; norms not motivating, 11; self-alteration signaled through, 120
Third Reich, 95, 103–104
Toren, Christina, 19
traditions, the individual influenced by, 178
training analysis, 148
transformative (*dönüştürücü*), 28
transformative experience, pedagogical mechanisms of, 32–33
Trompf, Garry W., 57
Trotsky, Leon, 74
Tsing, Anna, 169
tuanti geju (organizational mode of association), 134
Turkey, 73–74, 80, 82, 85–86. *See also* Istanbul
Turkish Republic (Young Turks), 80
Turkish Revolutionary Path (TDY), 82
türkü (folk songs), 81
2083 (*The Compendium*; Breivik), 94, 97–98, 103

Übermensch (Overman), 183
Ukraine, Nazis occupying, 90
Unani (Greek) medicine, 174
Unfinished (Biehl and Locke), 8
University of Wisconsin–Madison, 175n1
Utøya terrorist attack, 90, 92, 96

Vick, Michael, 165
Victoria, Brian, 92
village chief (*tenga naba*), 201
Villoldo, Alberto, 42
violence, revolutionary, 86
visible, self-alteration as, 184
visualizations, 50
Volta Valley Authority (*Autorité des Aménagements des Vallées des Volta*; AVV), 201, 206n8

Wacquant, Loïc J., 165, 175
Wajid Ali Shah (sultan), 167–168

Wane'efo, Erustus, 63
wane ni fo'a (tabu-speakers), 65
Ward, Graham, 46
Wariboko, Nimi, 67
Weber, Max, 136
Weir, Roger, 181–186
Western shamans, 42–44, 48, 52n5
WhatsApp, 17, 48
White, Geoffrey M., 66
White nationalism, 93, 100–101, 105
White Sea Canal. *See* I. V. Stalin White Sea–Baltic Sea Canal
Wiredu, Kwazi, 7
Wiseman, Richard, 139–140
withdrawal, physical, 97
Wizard of Oz, The (film), 201
Wolff, Karl, 91
womanhood, cultural ideas of, 117

women (*sistren*), 10, 48–50
workshops on self-alteration, 132–134, 138, 140–141
Wretched of the Earth, The (Fanon), 87

xingfu (happiness; *bonheur*), 138–139, 152

Young Turks (Turkish Republic), 80
Yunxiang, Yan, 136

Zagzebski, Linda, 36
Zaman, Abdul Qader, 197–198
Zen, Japanese, 99; "doctrine of emptiness" from, 98; Nazis and, 95; SS weaponizing, 92
Zen and Japanese Culture (Suzuki), 95, 105
Zhang Li, 135, 138
zheng nengliang (positive energy), 139–140
Zoom, 42, 48